Praise for *A Rising Tide*

"Oh, how I loved this visual and culinary walk through my favourite corner of the world. This is so much more than just an excellent cookbook, it offers a glimpse into our past, present, and future here in Atlantic Canada."

ALAN DOYLE, *musician, actor, and author of*
All Together Now, A Newfoundlander in Canada, *and* Where I Belong

"Atlantic Canada holds a special place in my heart. The spirit and energy of the people and places are incredible. They share a true love of local food and genuinely celebrate their passionate farmers, fishermen, and culinary artisans. This is why I am excited about *A Rising Tide*. Just flipping through the pages brings back great memories of my East Coast travels. I can't wait to cook some of these delicious dishes for my family and create new memories around the dinner table."

LYNN CRAWFORD, *chef*

A Rising Tide

A Rising Tide

A Cookbook of Recipes & Stories from Canada's Atlantic Coast

DL Acken & Emily Lycopolus

appetite
by RANDOM HOUSE

Appetite by Random House® and colophon are registered trademarks of Penguin Random House LLC.

Library and Archives Canada Cataloguing in Publication is available upon request.
ISBN: 978-0-525-61067-0
eBook ISBN: 978-0-525-61068-7

Photography by DL Acken
Food Styling by Aurelia Louvet
Printed and bound in China

Published in Canada by Appetite by Random House®,
a division of Penguin Random House Canada Limited.

www.penguinrandomhouse.ca

10 9 8 7 6 5 4 3 2 1

appetite
by RANDOM HOUSE | Penguin
Random House
Canada

For Felicity, who calls it as she sees it.
Thank you for your truth and for experiences to last a lifetime.

—Danielle

For Beth, who truly embodies every characteristic of East Coast hospitality,
has walked alongside, and made me feel like family from the day we met.

—Emily

For Bill and Myrna—for all the laughs, hot tub dips, and endless bottles
of wine. Thank you.

—Danielle and Emily

Contents

Preface

When I close my eyes, I can still feel the fading heat of the afternoon sun on my face in the forests of the Annapolis Valley in Nova Scotia. I remember smelling the wind-fallen apples and being in awe that the wild lands around us were teeming with fruit-bearing trees. That was the moment I fell in love with the foods of Atlantic Canada. Sure, I've had my fill of straight-from-the-sea lobster dinners, eaten more than my share of Prince Edward Island oysters, and indulged in many a decadent Digby scallop dish, but those apples, baking on the warmed, uncultivated earth hit me in a way I had never expected. They were at once enticing and familiar yet somehow exotic, and tied to something older, deeper, more instinctual.

I suppose in a way this connection is not surprising. My people have been coming to these lands for generations, the last being my father, who arrived in Halifax Harbour from London in 1967. Long before him, my husband's Scottish ancestors had sailed across the sea to claim their place in the New World. This landscape, its people and foods, has always been a familiar comfort to me; traditional dishes like beer-battered cod,

toad-in-the hole, and a delicious fool or steamed pudding for dessert have long been staples in my home. But I was moved that day as the simple scent of apples drove my desire to explore the larger culinary world of Atlantic Canada. Even today, while I call Canada's West Coast home, I find myself continuously yearning for the Atlantic shores. In writing this book, I wanted to understand more thoroughly this place, the people, and the foods and producers that define the culinary scene here, to truly discover the heart of this place. "Let's go find it!" Emily said, and so we did.

—DL Acken

I have spent many a winter afternoon curled up on the couch with a little cup of tea and a freshly baked scone, listening to my mom read *Anne of Green Gables*. Even before I could read, those stories of Atlantic Canada fuelled my imagination and stole my heart. "Anne" days were commonplace when I was a child. We would bake plum pudding like Marilla and talk as if Mrs. Lynde were our neighbour. These activities, along with my father, who spent his working life in the agricultural sector, always coming home with stories of the farmers of Atlantic Canada, made the region very real to me. So, as a young teen, setting foot for the first time in Atlantic Canada, visiting the red sand cliffs of Prince Edward Island, witnessing the Fundy Tides of New Brunswick, and experiencing the orchards of the Annapolis Valley, I felt entirely at home, my heart content.

Years later, I moved to Halifax for work and was introduced to a budding culinary scene and a group of people whose ingenuity is second to none. A hearty, resilient community that can weather any storm. I loved how history, combined with the natural terroir and human innovation, created a new culinary identity based on some of the world's best seafood, fertile soil, and wildness being incorporated into familiar homegrown dishes. It was here that my palate expanded. My appreciation for quality ingredients grew as I enjoyed my first community supported agriculture (CSA) box from TapRoot Farms in Port Williams, Nova Scotia, and the trajectory of my future pivoted to one focused on connecting people and food around the kitchen table.

Of all the places I've lived, the Atlantic shores continue to call me back, again and again. This book is for me the culmination of so many loves: sharing the culinary stories of the region, growing a deeper understanding of the culture, and celebrating the innovation and creativity of small businesses and producers. When I feel the red sand squish between my toes as the Atlantic waves lap along the shore, I close my eyes and feel like a little girl again, and my heart knows it's home.

—*Emily Lycopolus*

Introduction

The time has never been better for a cookbook that focuses on the unique foods of Canada's Atlantic terroir. Steeped in culinary tradition, yet bursting with contemporary cuisine, these provinces offer a wealth of locally grown and artisanally produced foods common across the region. For years, these were provinces of industry, but times have changed: the coal mines have closed and the Grand Banks of Newfoundland no longer teem with cod. Today agri-tourism and grassroots food production, led by young creatives, have become the new face of the region's culinary scene, and the region is undergoing an edible renaissance while still managing to stay tethered to tradition. Young innovative chefs and food purveyors are choosing to call these provinces home, build businesses here, and create a renewed food industry that stands firm in its unique culinary heritage while looking forward to a local, sustainable, and very modern spot on Canada's burgeoning food scene.

Today people like chef Peter Tompkins and his wife Jennie Wilson of 11th Mile in Fredericton are choosing to leave the anonymity of Toronto and open restaurants in their home provinces, while resorts such as Newfoundland's Fogo Island Inn are attracting international acclaim for their unique and innovative reimagining of Atlantic Canada's local cuisine. Community farming initiatives like Heart Beet Organics in Prince Edward Island and TapRoot Farms in Nova Scotia have become the produce source of choice for chefs and home cooks alike. Likewise, wild foods are being given starring roles in restaurants all across New Brunswick, Newfoundland, and beyond. And this is just the beginning. With chefs like Jeremy Charles, Jonathan Gushue, Jane Crawford, Bryan Picard, and Dave Smart at the helm, Atlantic Canada is set to become not just the pinnacle of Canadian cuisine but also an example of culinary cultural innovation to be reckoned with on the international stage. All the dishes served by these chefs, whether they are meals in critically acclaimed restaurants or bar snacks in local craft breweries, have the same starting point: they are based on traditional ingredients and time-honoured recipes that have been shared daily in home kitchens across the Atlantic region for centuries.

This book is the culmination of an incredible journey through the Atlantic Coast's terroir and its culinary renaissance.

The question of why two West Coasters would write a book focused on Atlantic Canada is one that we considered deeply while dreaming up this project. The answer is quite simple: we have a love for the place, the people who live there, and the producers and foods that define the culinary scene.

This book is the culmination of an incredible journey through the Atlantic Coast's terroir and its culinary renaissance, ultimately bringing Atlantic food traditions to your home, and introducing you to some of the people who make it all possible. And what a journey it was: over half a year on the road, countless interviews, hours of research, introductions to people we now count as friends, and innumerable meals that will forever live in our memories. We foraged for mushrooms, berries, and wild herbs in Newfoundland, watched the sun rise over oyster beds in Prince Edward Island, explored Nova Scotia from the Annapolis Valley to the top of the Cabot Trail, and fished for sturgeon on the great Saint John River in New Brunswick. We travelled for over forty-eight hours from our homes in Vancouver to the Fogo Island Inn—off the northwest coast of Newfoundland—by planes, trains, automobile, and ferry—and it was worth every minute! It was in their PEI bed and breakfast that we met Ang and Mo, who fed us and shared their incredible hospitality as well as their love for their adopted province. We laughed for hours over pints of local PEI ales with chef Jane Crawford in Charlottetown, and drank beers with Jerry Hussey in Bonavista, who gave us an insider's view of the cod industry in Newfoundland. After sampling spirits and cocktails with Steinhart Distillery owner Thomas Steinhart, we sat down with him at one of the finest views afforded anywhere in Nova Scotia and, to our delight, were presented with plates heaped with German schnitzel and spätzle and warming mugs that were more vodka than coffee. Local Newfoundland lichenologist Felicity Roberts patiently answered every question we threw at her, showed us every fabulous restaurant in St. John's, got us up to our knees in a bakeapple bog, and joined us on a five-hour road trip up to the gorgeous Bonavista peninsula, putting up with our new-found Mary Brown's obsession along the way. Old friends Bill and Myrna in the Annapolis Valley, Cathy and Danny in Parrsboro, and Beth and Gary in Halifax opened their doors and welcomed us as if we were family returning from a journey away. In every corner of the great Atlantic coast, our hearts filled to overflowing with an even deeper love and respect for the place, the people, and, of course, the food.

A Rising Tide begins with an overview of Atlantic Canada's culinary influences and current trends (page 5). We've provided a list of items (page 15) that make it easy to bring the tastes of the East Coast into your kitchen, but since some of these recipes involve hyper-local and incredibly seasonal ingredients—from sweet gale and lovage to primrose and Jonah crab—we've offered you substitution ideas so you can make these recipes regardless of where you are. While we recommend using as many of the local foods listed in the recipes as you can, we have also recommended ingredient substitutions to ensure the results are tasty no matter what is available to you.

Each province has its own chapter with recipes for every meal of the day, and most also have drink pairings. They are a mix of our own recipes, inspired by our travels, and recipes contributed by local chefs. You'll also find stories and essays featuring ingredients fairly common across the entire region and known to define the province. Finally, at the end of the book (page 311), there are menus for every season, just in case you're craving a beachside picnic or a winter warm-up brunch. Our desire for this book is that you'll come to know the individual provinces as well as understand the collective cultural experiences they share.

This book is a testament to the chefs and home cooks of the region. It is for those who call this place home and for the visitors who love the people, the place, and, most notably, the foods. We invite you to ride along with us as we set sail to the wilds of Newfoundland, drive slowly through the pastoral beauty of Prince Edward Island, hit the burgeoning craft restaurant scene in New Brunswick, and stand silently in Nova Scotia's Annapolis Valley to marvel at the simple scent of apples baking on the earth. We hope this book will live in your kitchen and be covered in handwritten notes and coffee rings, all while you travel along with us through scenic Atlantic Canada.

—*Danielle and Emily*

The Foods &
Flavours of Atlantic Canada

"A rising tide floats all boats" is a saying common to all four of the Atlantic provinces. It's a reflection of individuals coming together to form a community, the whole being stronger than the sum of its parts. Here—in this land that produces uniquely Atlantic flavours, where provincially rooted chefs marry creativity to tradition—we see the power of individuals working together to strengthen and redefine the East Coast culinary identity.

The Maritime provinces—New Brunswick, Nova Scotia, and Prince Edward Island—along with Newfoundland and Labrador offer a unique culinary cultural region within Canada. Cut off from the rest of the country by the Gulf of St. Lawrence and perched on the edge of the Atlantic Ocean, they have their own blended mosaic of cultures: Scottish, Irish, English, French Acadian, and African Nova Scotian along with the aboriginal Mi'kmaq, Maliseet, and Métis influences. The early European settlers brought industry to these fertile lands and waters; coal and cod quickly became the backbone of the local economy, influencing the pattern of life people lived. The fruits of these labours, combined with long-born traditions brought from respective homelands, determined the dishes that were shared around tables. Foods were simple and homegrown: people fished and worked their farms, eating what the sea and land provided, creating a sense of cultural familiarity in kitchens across the region. Even in the twentieth century, as people left their farms for city life, the energy and fishery industries evolved due to the changing natural resources and governmental regulation, and mass production of ready-made foods in grocery stores increased, the East Coast food identity remained strong. These days you can still find the Irish staples of corned beef and cabbage in Newfoundland's

Jiggs' dinner and Scottish oatcakes in Nova Scotia; African, Caribbean, and American Southern influences prevail throughout the African Nova Scotian communities, while Acadian Rapûre, or Rappie Pie, is still a common dish in New Brunswick. Forged through years of immigration layered over the native flora and fauna, East Coast kitchens are as unique as the delicious foods they create.

Where the Wild Things Are

Look to the sides of the roads throughout the Atlantic provinces and wherever you see cars or trucks stopped, you'll find folks fishing, hunting, or combing the undergrowth for wild foods. From the mushrooms that flourish on the dark forest floors to the plump rosehips that grow unchecked along the sides of riverbanks and the huge schools of capelin rolling onto the beaches of Newfoundland, the natural abundance of the region is highly evident and always truly remarkable. If you don't fancy fishing or foraging, though, most wild ingredients can be easily sourced at local farmers' markets when they're in season.

Of course, sustainability of wild stocks as well as the environmental impact of harvesting them is always an issue, and responsible practices should be adhered to. This includes abiding by fishing and hunting regulations. When in doubt, follow the foragers' creed: Take only what you need, leave enough for others as well as for natural replenishment, and always treat the lands and waters with the respect they deserve.

Wild fruits are perhaps one of the most beloved of the foraged harvests, and once preserved they are also a great source of vitamins throughout the winter months. During berry season you literally can't walk across parts of Newfoundland without feeling and hearing the fresh, juicy pop beneath your feet. It's no wonder you find families deep in the bogs, bent at the knees with buckets by their side. Generations of fruits like wild currants, crabapples, and tart sour cherries—left behind by early homesteaders—are coveted by chefs across Prince Edward Island and New Brunswick, while in Nova Scotia, the apples that grow wild in the forests of the Annapolis Valley are worth their weight in gold. No matter which province you find yourself in, you are never far from freshness during the warmer months.

Indigenous edible plants grow in abundance in the plains, marshes, tundra, and forests. The wild versions of leeks, garlic, and carrots are delicious and offer an interesting variation on their cultivated cousins. Fiddleheads, samphire (sea asparagus), beach pea, sea rocket (part of the mustard family), and goose tongue (a marsh grass brought to the early Acadians' attention by the Mi'kmaq First Nations) can be found throughout homes and commercial kitchens alike, while botanicals such as wild caraway, sweet gale, wild rosemary, currant leaf, Labrador tea, caribou moss, lavender, and juniper appear everywhere from top menus to country preserves to the artisanal beers, ciders, and liquors crafted across the provinces.

Fresh fruits and vegetables abound in backyard gardens throughout the region, while farmers' markets, brimming with bounties of wild and cultivated produce, fill the menus of chefs and home cooks. Dishes like Peas, Carrots & Potatoes (also known as Hodge Podge) (page 50), Fiddlehead Fritters (page 188), and Sorrel & Lovage Salad (page 261) highlight the early spoils of spring, while warming bowls of Buttermilk Turnip Soup (page 259) and slices of Apple Crumble Cream Pie (page 77) honour the autumnal harvest. The First Nations Peoples taught the early settlers the joys of native berries and goose tongue marsh grasses, and these foraged finds still hold a prominent place in the Atlantic kitchen today.

Meat, both wild and domestic, has always been an important staple in the Atlantic diet. Venison, moose, rabbit, duck, grouse, and other migratory birds make up the mainstay of wild meats. Although less common, bear, seal, and whale do appear on the tables of both home cooks and cutting-edge restauranteurs. Hunting seasons vary, and licences allocated by provincial lottery can be hard won, but in a place where communities are tight, there always seems to be someone who knows someone who has a bit of game to share. Preserved meats are a staple for many, and you're apt to find potted, salted, dried, and cured varieties in any hunter's pantry.

Hearty bowls of Rabbit Ragù (page 280), platters filled with Moose Balls (page 286), and elegant plates of perfectly seared Cranberry Hoisin Duck Breast (page 213) are a testament to the deliciousness that can be created by those holding provincial hunting licences. Heritage livestock, descendants of the animals brought across the sea by their human European counterparts, are also popular, and you'll find many of the smaller artisanal farms include these breeds as part of their larger permaculture systems. Today you'll still find traditional dishes such as Beef Wellington (page 137), Saltwater Lamb (page 291), and Beef Short Ribs (page 144) are commonly eaten and enjoyed alongside modern offerings such as Turkey Roulade (page 72), Cider-Braised Pork Tacos (page 131), and Crispy Fried Chicken with Pad Thai Fries (page 135).

As the most famous of the wild foods from the area, seafood almost needs no mention here. The fresh fish, shellfish, and mollusks of the waters of the Bay of Fundy; Northumberland, Cabot, and Belle Isle Straits; and the mighty Atlantic are legendary. Add to these the fresh-water fish that fill the many rivers, lakes, and ponds across the provinces and you can begin to understand why the East Coast is considered a seafood lover's paradise.

If you're already a seafood devotee, you'll know there is nothing like cracking open an icy cold ale and diving into a platter of Freshly Shucked Oysters (page 115). Whether it's a One-Pot Lobster Dinner (page 65) shared on the beach among friends, a bowl of Seafood Chowder (page 52) sipped slowly in the comfort of your own home, or an indulgent breakfast of Scrambled Eggs & Lobster (page 171), the Atlantic Ocean always provides the perfect dish for any occasion. We suggest trying Cider-Seared Scallops (page 59), a classic East Coast Lobster Roll (page 31), or the quintessential Fish Cakes (page 107) to dip your culinary toes in the water. You can feel good about using these marine delights too, as the fishermen here are passionate about following sustainable practices and take pride in harvesting top-quality Atlantic seafoods.

Inside the Atlantic Pantry

Open almost any pantry door across Atlantic Canada and you'll find a unique combination of spices, herbs, canned foods, dried goods, and cellar-stored roots—ingredients that weave together the culinary stories of these provinces and form the backbone of flavours common to the region.

For seasoning, savory leaf and sea salt reign supreme here, and you'll find both sold in large quantities in almost every grocery store. Alongside these are the indigenous flavours of dried mushrooms foraged from the forest floor; dulse grown in sandy seabeds; and juniper, spruce tips, wild rosemary, lavender, and sweet gale gathered from shrubs across the region. Spices such as ground ginger, cinnamon, and mustard add a welcome warmth to many a winter's dish, while vinegars bring an acidic note to counter the richness of traditional East Coast cooking. For sweetness, look to honey, molasses, maple syrup, and maple sugar as common replacements for white and brown sugar.

Of course, to these classic notes has come a new, contemporary set of flavours. A new wave of immigrants are choosing to call the Atlantic shores home, and with them they are bringing the spices and tastes of their native countries. Falafels (page 251) and shawarma are popular snacks for many modern-day East Coasters, and we've been inspired to add turmeric, sumac, and other adopted seasonings to otherwise traditional dishes.

In the pantry you'll also find the tastes of Atlantic Canada preserved. In an area where the growing season is short but sweet, the tradition of preserving with acid, sugar, and fat in order to enjoy fresh flavours throughout the year is an inherited art form. The jarring of jams and jellies is an annual summertime activity, as folks harvest fruits and vegetables at their sweetest and plumpest to enjoy through the long winter months. Likewise, the potting and drying of meats and fish during the licensed hunting and fishing periods ensures that bellies are full when game, fish, and other seafood are off-season. For generations, the people of Atlantic Canada have been lining their pantry shelves with dried salt cod, salt beef, fish, and potted meats, such as moose, venison, rabbit, and duck. For those with limited time or access to the agricultural or woodland regions, there is no shortage of artisanal, crafted goods in the shops and farmers' markets that abound.

Apples, carrots, parsnips, turnips, and, of course, potatoes keep perfectly in the dry climates afforded by root cellars, supplying much-needed vitamins throughout the year. It's no surprise that many of these are the foundation upon which traditionally inspired nouveau dishes are created. Chef Jonathan Gushue's Turnip & Mustard Seed (page 256) is a perfect example of this.

Acid, Sugar, & Fat

When you sit down to dine at an East Coast table, you'll find the table is weighed down by side dishes, sauces, jars, and bottles, not to mention your own plate. There's a reason for this: Atlantic Canadians love a heaviness to their food that comes from a liberal use of fabulous butters, creams, and sweet lard. To cut through this richness, they serve up a plethora of condiments, jellies, jams, and pickles that offer a sweet or acidic counterpoint to balance the meal. Most people are familiar with the malt vinegar and tartar sauce—a well-known "pickle" with acidic notes—traditionally served with Haddock & Fries (page 66), but the list of other accompaniments common across the region is as vast as the variety of dishes they're offered with.

With the short growing season on the East Coast, preserves have always held a special place within the Atlantic diet. Acid, sugar, and fat are the primary methods of preservation for keeping the freshness of the season, both for fruits and vegetables as well as meats. They also offer a balance to the inherited richness of the food. Quick Pickles (page 179) are the perfect complement to Dulse Salt–Seared Pork Chops with Roasted Garlic Mornay (page 210), and chef Jesse Vergen's Bottled Quahogs (page 185) add a delightful punch of acidity to a creamy Seafood Chowder (page 52).

Acid abounds in both sweet and salty pickled fruits and vegetables picked at the peak of their plumpness for enjoyment throughout the year. If you haven't tried pickled wild blueberries yet, we highly recommend making a batch when fresh berries are in season! Other common brined pickles are cucumber, carrots, beets, green beans, and onions. Try swapping out the traditional white vinegar for malted to further deepen the natural zing in some of the more savoury options.

Many of the more complex pickles found their place in the Atlantic diet by way of immigration. Mustard Pickle (page 110), a cousin of the English piccalilli, is found throughout the four provinces and is perfect as an accompaniment to a salt-cured ham or Moose Roast (page 290), or mixed with a drop of mayonnaise to bring a fabulous pop to any sandwich. Likewise, Chow Chow (page 179), brought to the region through its Acadian roots and now a staple in both Atlantic Canada and Cajun communities across the Southern United States, marries perfectly with most potted meats and is a lovely addition to any fried fish or chicken dish.

Sweet and savoury jellies hold their own special place on Atlantic tables, and there are a few companies now making artisanal varieties with flavours to die for. We highly recommend exploring Newfoundland's The Dark Tickle Company and Beverly McClare's

Tangled Garden preserves from Nova Scotia—her Hot Spiced Dill Jelly is truly out of this world! In our own kitchens, we love the spicy Sea Buckthorn Hot Pepper Jelly (page 180) as an accompaniment to any charcuterie board.

Of course, Atlantic Canada is famous for its deliciously rich foods—and in this case fat equals flavour. Compound butters are an easy way to punch up the flavour profile of any dish. Try the Black Garlic Butter served on our Heirloom Tomato Sandwich (page 116) or Whipped Molasses Butter to top Newfoundland's traditional Toutons (page 242), both of which make kicking up the flavour profile of a dish as easy as turning on a food mixer.

We hope that in discovering the flavours of Canada's East Coast, you'll get a taste of what it means to truly eat Atlantic. The people, and culture, and food of this place are bound together in a beautifully woven network that has shaped the region's unique culinary identity. In Nova Scotia, winemakers have come together to create Tidal Bay, a new appellation white wine specific to the Fundy shores, and in Newfoundland, traditional wildcrafting ways of life now make up the bulk of culinary tourism. In PEI, chefs raise heritage breed livestock, buy direct from farmers, and forage in abandoned overgrowth to deliver the most authentically provincial flavours possible, while in New Brunswick, the grower-processor-kitchen circles are so tight everyone is on a first-name basis. Today's Atlantic kitchen is the backbone of East Coast hospitality: come for a meal and leave as a part of a much larger family. When the community works together, everyone grows together, and sharing food around the table is the chosen way to celebrate the spoils of that effort. As a rising tide floats all boats, so the Atlantic Canadian community is coming together to create a thriving food industry, and in doing so has launched a unique and unified culinary identity.

Sea Buckthorn Hot Pepper Jelly, Chow Chow, & Quick Pickles
Charcuterie Board recipe (right) pictured on page 179.

Spice | Caraway | Cardamon | Cassia | Ca

min | Curry | Dill | Ginger

nder | Marjoram

Ingredient Notes

When choosing your ingredients, select the freshest possible. Starting with quality ingredients is always the best recipe for making delicious food, and the simpler the dish the more this applies. Try shopping at farmers' markets or market stands or, better yet, get to know your local farmer or artisanal producer, as this ensures you'll always have access to top-quality ingredients.

We'll be the first to admit this is an extremely regional book. We talk about sweet gale and make lovage creams, mention primrose sorbet and use Jonah crab. These are hyper-local ingredients and incredibly seasonal. However, our hearts' desire is for this book to live in your kitchens, and not on your shelves, so we want to make it as accessible as possible for you to cook from, wherever you are. With that in mind, on page 16 you'll find a list of the general ingredients you should have on hand when cooking from this book, and then a list of substitutions for the specifically East Coast ingredients that can be harder to find if Atlantic Canada isn't where you call home.

General Ingredients

Unless otherwise indicated, please note:

- Black pepper is freshly cracked black pepper
- Butter is unsalted
- Citrus juice is freshly squeezed
- Cream cheese is full-fat
- Eggs are Large
- Flour is all-purpose

- Fruits and vegetables are medium-sized
- Heavy cream is 18%
- Herbs are fresh
- Milk is 2%
- Molasses is fancy molasses
- Neutral oil is canola or grapeseed
- Oats are rolled

- Olive oil is extra virgin
- Onions are yellow cooking onions
- Parsley is curly leaf
- Sea salt is coarse
- Sugar is white, granulated
- Whipping cream is 35%
- Whole milk is homogenized, 3.25%

East Coast Ingredient Substitutions

Substitution explanations, where necessary, are in parenthesis:

Fresh Meat

- Denver steak: substitute with ribeye or top sirloin
- Moose: substitute with bison or lean beef
- Rabbit: substitute with chicken thighs or any dark chicken or turkey meat
- Saltwater lamb: substitute with lamb

Fish and Seafood

- Arctic char: substitute with sockeye or other salmon
- Atlantic cod: substitute with haddock, hake, halibut, or any meaty white fish
- Capelin: substitute with sardines, herring, or any smelt
- Jonah crabs: substitute with Dungeness or rock crab, or canned fresh crab packed in water

Berries

- Bakeapples: substitute with raspberries (1 cup bakeapples = 1 cup golden raspberries plus 2 tablespoons Meyer lemon juice; or ¾ cup fresh raspberries and 1 tablespoon lemon juice)
- Crowberries: substitute with blackberries
- Damson plums: substitute with Italian prune plums
- Haskap berries: substitute with blackberries and blueberries (1 cup haskap berries = ½ cup blackberries and ½ cup blueberries plus 1 teaspoon fresh rosemary leaves)
- Partridgeberries: substitute with cranberries
- Sea buckthorn berries: substitute with mango (1 cup sea buckthorn berries = ⅓ cup fresh mango pulp and ⅔ cup lemon juice plus 2 tablespoons olive oil)
- Wild blueberries: substitute with highbush blueberries (page 27)

Seasonings

- Dried dulse: substitute with ground nori or nori flakes
- Labrador tea: substitute with bay leaves and/or rosemary (1 tablespoon Labrador tea = 1 bay leaf (fresh or dried) plus 1 teaspoon fresh rosemary or 2 teaspoons dried rosemary; discard bay leaf before serving)
- Spruce tips: substitute with bay leaves and/or rosemary (½ cup spruce tips = 1 large sprig fresh rosemary plus 1 whole bay leaf (dried or fresh); if using in stock, soup, or braise, discard herbs before serving)
- Sweet gale: substitute with thyme (for a soup, stock, or braise, use an equal volume of thyme leaves plus 1 bay leaf, discard bay leaf before serving; for a dry rub, substitute with an equal volume of crushed dried thyme and crushed dried bay leaves)

Nova Scotia

Recipes

Nova Scotia may be famous for its delicious Digby scallops, traditional seafood chowder, and ever-present lobster rolls, but these days it's also a hotbed of culinary innovation and hyper-local fare. From the seafaring South Shore to the abundantly fertile farms of the Annapolis Valley and all the way up to the wilds of Cape Breton Island, Nova Scotians are embracing their regional roots and crafting foods that taste of the land and sea.

The French arrived to the Atlantic shores in the early seventeenth century and, developing strong ties with the Mi'kmaq people, quickly learned what indigenous foods the region offered. Today the Acadian contribution to both the culture and cuisine is still alive and thriving across the entire province. The first African Nova Scotians arrived at approximately the same time; their collective culinary identity parallels the Acadian experience and is at once wholly Atlantic while still being layered with African, Caribbean, and American Southern influences. Waves of European settlers followed: the Scots, English, Irish, Flemish, and Portuguese—each bringing recipes from their homelands that can still be found on Nova Scotian tables today.

Given the province's maritime history—where for generations fishermen have lived in harmony with the waters, hauling their fruits of the sea to their kitchen tables—it's only natural that seafood is the backbone of the culinary scene. With Nova Scotia stretching from the Bay of Fundy in the west and jutting into the great Atlantic Ocean in the east, it's easy to see why lobsters, scallops, oysters, mussels, and crabs appear on menus everywhere.

Of course, there is much more than seafood to celebrate here. The Annapolis Valley, with a microclimate created by two mountainous ridges, fertile glacier deposits, and the Bay of Fundy's extraordinary high tides, produces most of the Atlantic region's stone fruit along with local apples, berries, and, of course, award-winning wines. There are long-held homesteads with deep roots here, owned and maintained by families who are constantly adapting how they work the land in order to meet the changing demands brought on by the province's burgeoning culinary agri-tourism industry.

The Annapolis Valley is where you'll find Noggins Corner Farm, whose orchard-tending tradition stretches back ten generations. Their farm store is now a must-see for tourists and locals looking to pick up produce as well as taste the delicious house-crafted cider. Another must-see comes in the form of the beautiful vineyards and restaurant of Lightfoot & Wolfville, which seamlessly marry hundred-year-old family traditions with trendsetting luxury. The increase of industry doesn't seem to be slowing either. Domaine de Grand Pré has defined the Valley as a world-class viticulture region by producing award-winning wines and adding European elegance into the mix, while innovative farmers like Josh Oulton of TapRoot Farms share the valley's produce with Haligonian city dwellers through the practice of community shared agriculture.

Yet not all fruits are classically cultivated within the province. When it comes to self-propagating foods, wild blueberries (page 27) are the largest fruit crop and reign supreme. Oxford, Nova Scotia, is the wild blueberry capital of the world, with over one thousand producers working 40,000-plus acres for an annual average yield of 40 million pounds—that's a lot of blueberries! You'll find these tiny berries in sweet and savoury restaurant dishes as well as taking top shelf in some of the best cocktail bars throughout the province; and if you ever see a simple sign for BLUEBERRY PIE on the side of a Nova Scotian road, pull over immediately, as it will be the best slice you'll ever eat—we promise!

Given the plethora of local ingredients on hand, it's no surprise that Nova Scotia is drawing waves of chefs and culinary artisans to its shores. Top mixologists craft cocktails featuring haskap and rhubarb gins, maple liqueur, and even lobster-infused vodka. While ten to fifteen new restaurants open in the province every year, most of them become neighbourhood favourites in short order due in no small part to serving local foods. The Canteen, Edna, 2 Doors Down, Bar Kismet, and The Press Gang are of particular note at time of writing. Outside of Halifax, Sarah Griebel and Andrew Aitken of Wild Caraway (page 33) in Advocate Harbour serve up foods that people will drive literally hours to lunch upon. Meanwhile, chefs like Bryan Picard of The Bite House (page 83) and Dave Smart of Bessie North House (page 50) are reinventing the dining experience with tasting menus served in uniquely intimate settings. Reservations are a must, as they can be fully booked up to a year in advance, but trust us when we say they are well worth the wait.

No matter where you eat in Nova Scotia, you're sure to be fed well by friendly folk with a passion for all that their beautiful province provides.

Wild Blueberry Pancakes & Syrup

SERVES 4

*Red Barn's Sparkling Blueberry
as a base for mimosas*

Blueberry Syrup:

1½ cups fresh or frozen wild
  blueberries

½ cup maple syrup

2 Tbsp lemon juice

1 Tbsp cornstarch

Pancakes:

3 cups flour

⅓ cup sugar

3 tsp baking powder

1½ tsp baking soda

1 tsp sea salt

½ tsp ground nutmeg

⅔ cup melted butter

3 cups whole milk

1 tsp vanilla extract

3 eggs

Heat-tolerant oil, for greasing

Butter, for serving

STORAGE: The pancakes are best enjoyed the day they are made. The syrup will keep in an airtight container in the fridge for up to 3 weeks.

Wild blueberries are one of the true gems in Atlantic Canada. They are much smaller than their larger, highbush cousins commonly found in grocery stores, and being a wild, uncultivated crop, they have a complexity of flavours that makes these pancakes one of our favourite pancake recipes ever. Topped with wild blueberry syrup, this breakfast is a blueberry lover's dream come true.

To Make the Syrup: In a small pot, mash the blueberries gently with a wooden spoon or spatula. Stir in the maple syrup. In a small bowl or glass, whisk together the lemon juice and cornstarch until no lumps remain. Add the lemon mixture to the blueberry mixture. Place the pot over medium heat and simmer until the mixture is warm and the berries are soft, 3 to 5 minutes if cooking fresh and up to 7 minutes if cooking from frozen. Increase the heat to medium-high and bring the mixture to a boil. Stirring constantly, boil the syrup for 1 minute. Remove from the heat and allow to cool slightly before transferring to a serving jug. Keep the syrup in the fridge until ready to use. Just be sure to warm it up in the microwave before serving.

To Make the Pancakes: Preheat the oven to 325°F and place a large ovenproof serving dish in the oven.

In a large mixing bowl, whisk together the flour, sugar, baking powder, baking soda, salt, and nutmeg until light and fluffy and no lumps remain. Make a well in the centre of the dry ingredients. Pour the butter, milk, vanilla, and eggs into the well and, using a fork, begin mixing them together. As the wet mixture combines, begin to whisk in the dry ingredients until fully combined.

Preheat a griddle or skillet over medium heat and add a little oil to grease the pan. Pour ⅓ cup of batter into the pan, allowing it to flow into an even circle. Cook for 45 seconds to 1 minute, just until bubbles start to form evenly across the top. Flip the pancake, and cook for 30 to 45 seconds, until golden and cooked through.

Transfer to the serving plate in the oven to keep warm and repeat with the remaining batter.

When you're ready to serve, remove the pancakes from the oven and serve with extra butter and the syrup.

HARVESTING WILD BLUEBERRIES

The rolling hills of wild blueberry bushes that cover much of Atlantic Canada are easy to miss as you're buzzing down the highways . . . in any season except autumn, when the plants turn a vibrant red, covering the ground with what looks like streaks of fire. On this late summer day in Parrsboro, Nova Scotia, the bushes are a deep chartreuse, covered by the crop of tiny berries spread throughout the underbrush like an indigo carpet. Emily Davison bends down and picks a few berries off a bush. "It's almost harvest. We'll start picking any day now," she says as we walk up the brush-strewn hill.

Wild blueberries like those at Davison's Farm are a staple crop in Nova Scotia. They are much smaller than the commercial high-bush variety and are a natural by-product of the logging industry. "The bushes grow as a natural ground cover after deforestation," Emily explains, "but it can take a hundred years for them to naturally spread enough to fully cover a field." She is home on summer break and can't wait to get back to school. Ironically, she finds school work easier than her duties on the farm, although you can tell she loves the work. Her great-grandfather built this homestead on the shores of the Bay of Fundy, and after the fields were logged, the blueberries appeared. They have been growing in abundance ever since.

Emily's brother and father are working on a harvester sitting beside the barn, getting it ready for the six-week picking season. Mechanical harvesting is essential, as hand-harvesting involves combing the berries off the bush with a contraption somewhere between a rake and a dustpan. It's back-breaking work, and even someone with years of experience can only pick a few hundred pounds a day. Once the berries have been harvested, the fields will be mowed completely and the two-year growing cycle will begin again with a whole new generation of plants being born from the underlying expanding root matrix.

Wild blueberries are unique, as they are one of the few plants where the berries not only vary from crop to crop, but those growing side by side on the same bush can also look and taste completely different from each other. This diversity is about much more than just natural fluctuation due to terroir; it's genetic. The plants are regenerant, or clonal. As they spread, they pass on the same genome, but how the clone chooses to express itself in each plant can differ wildly. The cloning process also acts as a protective mechanism: if disease hits one plant, its neighbour may be immune, ensuring survival for the field as a whole. This means that in addition to the natural fluctuations in characteristics due to terroir, the plants vary from bush to bush, propagating in a multitude of colours from light pink to deep indigo and ranging in taste from extremely sweet to tart and tannic.

Of course, any crop, wild or otherwise, needs pollinators, and wild blueberries in and of themselves don't contain enough protein and nutrients in their pollen to keep a bee population healthy throughout the growing season. Ensuring the bushes have healthy, natural propagation is a challenge, so the Davisons plant red clover and other wildflowers along the field's edge to encourage bee health and create a sustainable ecosystem. As stewards of the land, they also see the value of being involved in scientific groundwork to protect the environment, and so they share their farm with researchers from the agricultural school at Dalhousie University. These scientists are learning that the Fundy shores have unique mineral deposits and other substances, all of which are absorbed by the plants, creating extremely high antioxidant profiles that differentiate them from wild blueberries that grow elsewhere in the province.

Such innovation and creativity define the Davison farm philosophy, and by leveraging their combined engineering backgrounds to develop harvesters for this unique crop, the family has moved the farm into a class of its own. Modernization and forward thinking, along with the passion they display for their crops, have become a part of daily life, and they are committed to supporting other farmers and the industry as a whole. As harvest approaches and the berries begin to roll in, the energy around the farm is palpable. Emily and her family are excited to discover the flavours that the current year's crop has delivered, and as the pies start to come out of the oven, the love of wild blueberries is celebrated here in the fields and around kitchen tables across the province.

East Coast Lobster Roll

SERVES 4

Saltbox Brewing Company's
Holy Mackerel! Pale Ale

1 Tbsp olive oil

¼ cup chopped celery

1½ tsp smoked paprika, divided

½ cup mayonnaise

¼ cup chopped green onions

1 Tbsp lemon juice

1 tsp sea salt

½ tsp black pepper

2 lb cooked lobster meat,
chopped into ½-inch pieces

4 top-split sandwich buns or buns
of your choice

2 Tbsp melted butter

1 clove garlic

4 lemon wedges, for serving

Fresh Whipped Tartar Sauce
(page 109) or dipping sauce of
choice, for serving

Ask any number of East Coasters how to make a lobster roll and you'll
get just as many recipe variations in response. Everyone seems to have
a special ingredient that makes theirs the best, and we've figured ours
out too: fresh Atlantic lobster!

In a large skillet over high heat, place the oil, celery, and the ½ teaspoon of
paprika. Sauté for 2 to 3 minutes, until the celery begins to wilt and becomes
translucent. Set aside to cool in the skillet.

Transfer the cooled celery mixture to a large bowl and add the remaining
1 teaspoon paprika, the mayonnaise, green onions, lemon juice, salt, and
pepper. Add the lobster and, using a wooden spoon, stir to combine. Chill,
uncovered, in the fridge for 5 to 10 minutes.

Meanwhile, preheat the broiler to low. Slice the buns along the top seam
and spread open. Lightly brush the inside of each bun with the melted
butter and place the buns butter side up under the broiler until the edges
and insides start to crisp and turn golden, about 1 minute. Remove from
the oven. Slice the garlic clove in half and rub the cut side of the clove on
the inside of each warm bun.

Fill each bun with one-quarter of the chilled lobster mixture. Garnish
each plate with a lemon wedge and serve immediately with your choice
of dipping sauce on the side.

STORAGE: The filling is best enjoyed the day it's made, but will keep in an
airtight container in the fridge overnight.

Jonah Crab Spring Rolls

SERVES 6

Lightfoot & Wolfville's Bubbly Rosé

It was the sea, and its incredibly fresh and varied seafood, that brought Sarah Griebel and Andrew Aitken to Advocate Harbour. As Andrew explains, "You can grow a garden anywhere but you can't move the ocean." Together they created Wild Caraway, a beautiful home they converted into a restaurant across from the Bay of Fundy. Hospitality is key here: they pride themselves on serving delicious meals filled with food made from scratch that honours the ingredients and ensures customers leave feeling satisfied. These spring rolls are just one example of how they do just that. Jonah crab is an Atlantic species closely related to the Dungeness crab of the Pacific. They are known to get tangled in lobster traps, causing a bit of a nuisance for the lobster industry, but dishes like this one prevent them from going to waste. Wild Caraway pairs these spring rolls with Sweet Cicely Vinaigrette (pictured and see recipe on page 34), but they go nicely with Fresh Cranberry Relish (page 214), Chow Chow (page 179), or Fresh Whipped Tartar Sauce (page 109) too. (Note that you need to make the vinaigrette a week before you plan to cook this dish.)

---

2 cups shredded green cabbage

¼ cup (2- to 3-inch knob) julienned fresh ginger

½ lb Jonah crab meat

1 large carrot, julienned

½ cup finely sliced red onion

6 cloves garlic, crushed

½ cup chopped cilantro

¾ cup mayonnaise

½ tsp sea salt

½ tsp black pepper

¼ tsp chili flakes

½ cup breadcrumbs

1 egg

12 (8-inch) spring roll wrappers

Neutral oil, for frying

Dipping sauce, for serving

Bring a large pot of salted water to a rolling boil and prepare an ice bath in a mixing bowl. Place the cabbage and ginger in the boiling water and boil for 30 seconds. Using a slotted spoon, remove them from the water and transfer to the ice water to stop them cooking. Once cooled, drain, place on a clean tea towel, and squeeze dry.

Drain the crab meat through a fine-mesh strainer or double layer of cheesecloth, pressing or squeezing to drain off any excess water.

In a large mixing bowl, combine the blanched cabbage and ginger with the carrots, onions, garlic, cilantro, mayonnaise, salt, pepper, and chili flakes. Gently fold in the crab. Sprinkle with the breadcrumbs and, using your hands, gently mix in until fully combined. The mixture should be firm to the touch.

In a small bowl, beat the egg with 1 tablespoon of water and set aside.

(continued)

To make the spring rolls, place ½ cup of the filling on the centre third of a spring roll wrapper and shape it to form a small log, leaving about 1 inch of space on either side of it. Fold the short edge of the wrapper over top of the filling and fold in each of the sides onto itself. Roll up the spring roll tightly and use a pastry brush or the back of a spoon to seal it with the egg wash. Set aside and repeat with the remaining filling and spring roll wrappers.

When you're ready to serve, pour 2 inches of the oil into a heavy-bottomed pot or skillet and bring it to 350°F over medium-high heat, using a candy thermometer to monitor the temperature. Deep-fry two to three spring rolls at a time for 1 to 2 minutes, until deeply golden and crisp, using tongs to turn them once. Give the oil 1 to 2 minutes to return to temperature between batches. Repeat for the remaining spring rolls.

Serve with the Sweet Cicely Vinaigrette below or your dipping sauce of choice.

STORAGE: The cooked spring rolls will keep in an airtight container in the fridge for up to 2 days or in the freezer for up to 3 months. To reheat, bring to room temperature and bake for 10 minutes at 350°F or until warmed through.

Sweet Cicely Vinaigrette

MAKES 2 CUPS

Sweet Cicely Vinegar:

2 cups green sweet cicely seed pods

1⅓ cups white wine vinegar

Sweet Cicely Vinaigrette:

⅔ cup Sweet Cicely Vinegar

1 Tbsp sugar

½ tsp salt

⅛ tsp xanthan gum

3 drops green food colouring

1⅓ cups neutral oil

The recipe is in two parts and takes a minimum of 1 week to make, unless you have sweet cicely vinegar kicking around!

For the Sweet Cicely Vinegar: Using a knife, crush the seed pods and transfer to a sterilized 4-cup Mason jar. Fill with the vinegar, ensuring the pods are submerged. Cover tightly with a lid and let sit for 1 week, minimum, and no more than 3 weeks. Strain and reserve the vinegar.

For the Sweet Cicely Vinaigrette: In a large bowl, combine ⅔ cup of the Sweet Cicely Vinegar with the sugar, salt, xanthan gum, and food colouring. Using an immersion blender, gradually mix in the oil in a slow, steady stream until well combined.

STORAGE: The vinaigrette will keep in an airtight container in the fridge for up to 3 weeks.

Recipes contributed by Andrew Aitken, Wild Caraway

Crab Dip & Crackers

SERVES 4
(MAKES 2½ CUPS OF DIP)

Gaspereau Vineyards' Tidal Bay

Walking into The Canteen in Dartmouth, we can't decide if it's the light and airy feeling of the space or the two kids sitting at the bar that's making us smile. Chef Renée Lavallée greets us, and we begin chatting. "My kids are growing up in our restaurants. We eat here now as a family at least once a week. The staff are our family too," she says. After cooking all over the world, she and her husband Doug opened The Canteen in 2017. "We wanted it to feel like home, like walking into our house," she says smiling. "There is just so much happening here: the camaraderie among the chefs, producers growing incredible ingredients, which in turn inspires creativity in the kitchen." The food is, as a result, playful, fun, and approachable. Renée's crab dip and handmade crackers are no exception. The crackers are plentiful, and we never mind having leftovers—they are delicious with Josey's Lobster Dip (page 39) too!

Crackers:

1½ cups flour

1 tsp baking powder

1 tsp sea salt

1 Tbsp sugar

¼ cup cold salted butter, cubed

½ cup sour cream

1 egg

½ cup Everything Bagel Seasoning mixture (see note on page 36)

For the Crackers: In a food processor or large mixing bowl, mix the flour, baking powder, and salt with the sugar until fully combined and no lumps remain. Add the butter. If using a food processor, pulse or combine until the dough has the consistency of fine gravel. If using a mixing bowl, mix in the butter with a pastry blender or two knives until the dough has the consistency of fine gravel. In a small bowl, whisk together the sour cream and egg and then gently mix or pulse into the flour mixture. The dough will be quite sticky.

Turn the dough out onto a lightly floured surface and knead in the Everything Bagel Seasoning mixture. Wrap the dough in plastic wrap and chill in the fridge for at least 1 hour, or up to 8 hours, to allow it to firm up and set.

Preheat the oven to 350°F. Line two half baking sheets with parchment paper.

Divide the dough into four pieces. If using a pasta roller, on a lightly floured surface, use a rolling pin to roll a piece of dough into a rectangle 3 to 4 inches wide and long enough that it will roll easily through the pasta maker. Roll the dough through the pasta roller, or continue to roll by hand, until it is ¼ inch thick. Repeat with the remaining pieces of dough. Cut the dough into strips or triangles, you'll get 5 to 6 dozen depending on the shape.

Place the crackers on the prepared baking sheet about ½ inch apart. Bake for 9 to 12 minutes, until golden and crisp. Remove from the oven, transfer to a wire rack, and allow to cool completely.

(continued)

Crab Dip:

4 oz cream cheese, softened

½ cup sour cream

½ cup mayonnaise

3 lemons

2 tsp garlic powder

1 cup minced crab meat

¼ cup chopped dill, plus extra
  for garnish

Sea salt

For the Crab Dip: Using a stand mixer fitted with the paddle attachment, beat the cream cheese for about 2 minutes, until it is soft and fluffy and has almost doubled in volume. Add the sour cream and mayonnaise and beat for 1 minute to fully combine, scraping down the sides of the bowl to ensure all the ingredients are mixed.

Zest the lemons, reserving some for the garnish, and add the zest to the cream cheese mixture along with the garlic powder. Juice two of the lemons and add the juice to the mixture. Scrape down the sides of the bowl and beat for 30 seconds to 1 minute, just to combine everything.

Drain the crab meat through a fine-mesh strainer or a double layer of cheesecloth, pressing or squeezing to drain off any excess water. Add the crab to the cream cheese mixture, mix on the lowest speed to combine, and then scrape down the sides of the bowl again. Add the dill and continue to mix until all the ingredients are evenly incorporated. Taste the dip and season with salt to taste.

Using a spatula, transfer the dip to a serving bowl and chill, covered, in the fridge for 30 minutes to allow the flavours to develop.

Serve the dip with the crackers and garnish with additional dill and lemon zest if desired.

STORAGE: The dip will keep in the fridge overnight but is best enjoyed the day it's made. The crackers will keep in an airtight container at room temperature for up to 1 week.

NOTE: Everything Bagel Seasoning is available at your local grocery store. It is equal parts dried garlic flakes, dried onion flakes, sesame seeds, poppy seeds, and sea salt.

Recipe contributed by Renée Lavallée, The Canteen

Josey's Lobster Dip

MAKES 2 CUPS

Luckett Vineyards' Tidal Bay

If you're ever looking for a good lobster recipe, look no further than your local lobsterman. While we were chatting with lobsterman Jim Fraelic and his family in Brooklyn, Nova Scotia, they began to share all the unique ways they like to enjoy these tasty crustaceans. It didn't take long for Jim's wife Liz to pull her recipe box to find this recipe, which of course was handwritten and without measurements. "Jim's father Josey created it years ago," she told us, "wanting to make a lobster dip that didn't taste like everyone else's." He succeeded! The spiciness of the mustard and cumin and the freshness of the lemon pair with the sweetness of the fresh lobster meat to create a delicious and unique dynamic.

1 stalk celery

2 green onions

½ cup mayonnaise

1 Tbsp grainy Dijon mustard

2 tsp lemon juice

2 tsp minced parsley

1 tsp minced oregano

1 tsp paprika

½ tsp ground cumin

½ tsp sea salt

1 cup shredded lobster meat

Crackers or crostini, for serving

Finely dice the celery and green onions and set aside.

In a mixing bowl, whisk together the mayonnaise, mustard, and lemon juice until fully combined. Add the parsley, oregano, paprika, cumin, and salt, and mix until fully combined. Fold in the celery, green onions, and lobster meat until well coated with spiced mayonnaise mixture.

Using a spatula, transfer the dip to a serving bowl and chill, covered, in the fridge for 30 minutes to allow the flavours to develop.

Serve chilled with crackers or crostini.

STORAGE: The dip is best enjoyed the day it's made, but will keep in an airtight container in the fridge overnight.

Pickled Garlic Scapes

MAKES 2 PINTS

While we both love fresh garlic scapes fried with a bit of olive oil when spring rolls around, their season is always too short. Pickling them has become our favourite way to enjoy their fresh flavour throughout the year. Try these pickled garlic scapes as an accompaniment on your next charcuterie or cheese board (page 179).

1 lb garlic scapes, trimmed

2 tsp black peppercorns, divided

2 tsp mustard seeds, divided

1 tsp fennel seeds, divided

1 tsp coriander seeds, divided

1 tsp chili flakes, divided

3 cups white wine vinegar

1 cup water

¼ cup sea salt

6 Tbsp sugar

Sterilize two pint-size Mason jars, lids, and rings by washing them in the dishwasher or boiling them in water for 5 minutes. Set aside to air-dry. This will only take a few minutes.

Coil the garlic scapes tightly and insert them into the jars. Continue adding scapes until the jar is tightly packed and only ¼ inch of headspace remains at the top. Stuff the space in the centre of the jars with straight scape ends until they are full. Add 1 teaspoon each of the peppercorns and mustard seeds to each jar. Then add ½ teaspoon each of the fennel, coriander, and chili flakes to each jar. Set aside.

To make the pickling liquid, in a large pot, bring the vinegar, 1 cup of water, salt, and sugar to a rolling boil, stirring until the salt and sugar dissolve. Carefully pour this brine over the garlic scapes. If the scapes start to pop up, use a sterile knife to push them back into the jar so that they are fully submerged, leaving at least ⅛ inch headspace to ensure the jar will seal. Wipe the jar rims with a sterile cloth or paper towel, place the lids on the jars and tighten the rings down. Let sit at room temperature for 24 hours to cool. The lids will seal and pop. If a jar doesn't seal, keep it in the fridge.

STORAGE: Store the sealed jars in a cool, dark place for 6 weeks before opening. After opening, store in the fridge and enjoy within 1 week.

NOTE: If using a pint jar instead of a 500ml mason jar, you will have leftover brine, as a pint is only 473ml. Ensuring the scapes are covered with brine is essential.

GROWING GARLIC SCAPES

For those unfamiliar, scapes are the first 12 inches that sprout in the early days of spring from garlic bulbs planted in the early autumn, a precursor to the deeply pungent crop to come. They are deep green and have a soft, sweet garlicky flavour. Scapes are delicious pickled, fried, made into pesto, or grilled simply on the barbecue with a splash of olive oil—they also curl in every direction and are hard to control at the best of times. Harvesting is not an easy chore, but Shannon Jones of Broadfork Farm in River Hebert, Nova Scotia, happily snaps off the scapes from the larger stocks and, smiling, swats away a mosquito. "I like mosquitos," she says. "They remind us that we're not at the top of the food chain!" A true farmer at heart, she and her partner Bryan Dyck moved to this deeply rural corner of the province, leased a few acres of land, and decided to start a produce farm. It's not an exercise for the faint of heart, but as we walk around the property, we can see that for Shannon and Bryan, this has been an adventure fuelled by their passion for working the land and growing beautiful food. The pair's goal is a "plant to order" farm model that produces the vegetables local chefs and home cooks want to work with. Everyone can buy carrots, broccoli, or cabbage at the store, but through this unique collaboration with the culinary community, you will find, in addition to scapes, varietals like patty pan squash, broccolini, purple potatoes, and red Russian garlic. This not only fills holes in the market, but also allows Shannon and Bryan to grow what they love.

Of course, it's not just interesting crops such as garlic scapes that have brought Broadfork Farm success: seeding based on what is best for their customers as well as the land also reduces the financial risk faced by many more traditional farms. "Here," as Bryan explains, "if one crop isn't thriving, another probably is." They're also practical seed savers, allowing their crops to go to flower in order to contribute to the seed bank. Shannon tells us that raising the plants to maturity is also healthier for both the soil and the farm as a whole. The flowers provide for the bees, ensuring pollination, and after the seeds are saved, the plants are then put down into the earth under black tarps to naturally compost, allowing for carbon, nitrogen, and other essential nutrients to land back into the soil, creating a more fertile ground for future crops.

Across the Bay of Fundy at TapRoot Farms, Josh Oulton and Patricia Bishop run a larger enterprise but share much of the philosophy employed at Broadfork. For these generational family farmers working 300+ acres of land in the Annapolis Valley, biodiversity is their primary mandate. Seeing a large variety of crops in the fields is Josh's favourite part of what they do: "It's the key to successful organic farming," he says. "There needs to be good, healthy food in the fields," and this can only happen through crop rotation and giving the earth a chance to breathe, rest, and replenish its energy. As we walk by a patch of overgrown land, a drift of happy pigs trots out of the bushes to say hello. "They'll turn this field over in no time," Josh explains, "fertilizing and aerating as they go."

TapRoot Farms was one of the first in the area to start sharing garlic scapes in their community supported agriculture (CSA) boxes, mostly because they wanted to reduce waste. Instead of turning the early blooms into compost, they saw an opportunity to both focus the growth of the garlic bulb crop and introduce Nova Scotians to the versatility and depth that cooking with scapes can offer. That's what it's all about here. To grow the very best ingredients you have to be a conscious farmer: bee health, soil health, bugs, weeds, and worms are all incredibly important, as is the connection between crop and kitchen. TapRoot has some beautifully innovative ways in which they allow these natural processes to play out—it's what established them as a forerunner in the CSA movement, and what keeps their produce in high demand.

Today there is a lot more competition for farmers thanks to the popularity of the local food movement, but neither farm sees this as detrimental. In fact, it allows for more sales, more markets, and increased awareness of how good produce should look and taste. More and more people are seeking out healthy, organically grown vegetables from farmers who work ethically with sustainability in mind. Garlic scapes might be a small component of this larger reality, but they're a perfect microcosm of the philosophy that drives the farmers in this region, whether they're working 5 acres or 300: this delectable vegetable isn't left to waste while the bulbs continue to grow, but is instead incorporated into community supported agriculture boxes to be celebrated as a sign that the growing season has begun.

Honey Whisky Roasted Parsnips

SERVES 4 AS A SIDE

Glenora Distillery's Glen Breton

8 small to medium parsnips (see note)

¼ cup honey

2 Tbsp olive oil

2 Tbsp whisky (such as Glen Breton)

1 tsp sea salt

2 tsp fennel seedz

Naturally sweet and uniquely flavourful, parsnips are one of our favourite root vegetables to enjoy when the colder months of their growing season set in. Decadently tossed and roasted in both honey and whisky, these sweet tubers are a perfect side for Saltwater Brined Beef (page 143), Beef Wellington (page 137), or Saltwater Lamb (page 291).

Preheat the oven to 375°F. Line a rimmed baking sheet with parchment paper.

Peel the parsnips, leaving them whole and the stems attached if possible, and lay them on the prepared baking sheet.

In a small bowl, whisk together the honey, oil, whisky, and salt. Using a pastry brush, evenly coat the parsnips with the mixture. Drizzle any remaining mixture over top.

In a small skillet over medium-low heat, gently toast the fennel seeds until they are aromatic and evenly toasted. Keep a close eye on them so they don't burn. Sprinkle the seeds over the parsnips.

Bake in the centre of the oven for 35 to 40 minutes, until golden brown and fork-tender. Serve immediately.

STORAGE: The parsnips will keep in an airtight container for up to 1 week in the fridge.

NOTE: If you can only find large parsnips or ones that are very tapered, only use four, slice them in half or quarters lengthwise, and follow the recipe as directed.

Dorothy's Cast Iron Skillet Cornbread

SERVES 4

Propeller Brewing Companies
Ginger Beer

African Nova Scotians have been residing in Nova Scotia since the early 1600's. Wendie L. Wilson is a journalist and an educator who is at the fore-front of defining their culinary traditions and sharing the collection of recipes passed down by her ancestors. In explaining the connection between history and food throughout the black communities across the region, Wendie says:

"'Scotian' food is hearty, delicious, and made with soul. As the earliest black settlers to Nova Scotia, our ancestors overcame unmeasurable hardships to survive and thrive. African Nova Scotian cuisine is a collection of recipes spanning Africa, the Caribbean, and the southern US, infused with cooking methods borrowed from these various cultures using what the land and water had to offer in Nova Scotia. There is also overlap with traditional Atlantic Canadian-inspired recipes, spices, and cooking style; these traditional dishes are part of our history, culture, and stories told through food.

Many of our dishes are heavily influenced by what our relatives would have been accustomed to eating before the waves of immigration that lead to "freedom" in Canada.

---

1 Tbsp shortening

1 cup cornmeal

1 cup flour

1 tsp salt

½ tsp baking soda

3 Tbsp white sugar

2 eggs

⅓ cup melted butter

1 cup buttermilk

Butter, for serving

Preheat the oven to 400°F and place a cast iron skillet in the oven for at least 15 minutes.

In a small mixing bowl, whisk together the together the cornmeal, flour, salt, baking soda and sugar. In a separate small bowl, whisk the eggs until combined, and then beat in the melted butter and buttermilk. Fold the wet ingredients into the dry ingredients until just combined. Do not over mix.

Remove skillet from the oven and add the shortening. Place back in the oven to allow it to melt and season the pan, about 1 to 2 minutes. Remove the skillet from the oven again and swirl the pan to evenly coat. Add the batter, spreading it evenly in the pan.

Bake until the cornbread is golden and a toothpick inserted comes out clean, about 20 to 25 minutes. Serve hot with a smear of butter.

STORAGE: Cornbread will keep in an airtight container at room temperature for up to 3 days.

Recipe contributed by Wendie L. Wilson

Peas, Carrots & Potatoes

SERVES 4

Jost Vineyards' Tidal Bay

"When I'm thinking of Nova Scotian cuisine, hodge podge, fresh spring vegetables boiled in plain cream, is at the top of the list," says chef Dave Smart of Bessie North House, a gem of a restaurant tucked away in Canning, Nova Scotia. "It's not something I grew up with in Scotland," claims the engineer turned culinary mastermind, "but it's a classic around these parts."

Armed with fresh seasonal baby vegetables from the garden, a curious mind, and some outlandish ideas, he started with the basics: "I took to blanching each of the vegetables separately, preserving their colour and nutritional value." From there, he thought it would be fun to brighten up what is traditionally an unflavoured cream sauce with fresh chive and mint herbal notes. Much tinkering in the kitchen resulted in a beautiful herbaceous cream sauce that gently warms up the blanched vegetables, creating a delicate, yet uncomplicated spring dish. This is just one example of the incredible innovation at work in the kitchen of Bessie North House.

50

Blanched Vegetables:

2 Tbsp sea salt, divided

1 cup baby carrots

1 cup mixed green and yellow beans

1 cup peas

2 cups quartered new potatoes

1 bay leaf

Chive and Mint Cream Sauce:

2 Tbsp butter

1 tsp vegetable oil

½ cup finely diced celery root

¼ cup finely diced shallot

½ tsp sea salt, plus more to taste

½ cup dry white wine

2 cups vegetable stock

2 cups whipping cream

¼ cup chopped chives

1 Tbsp chopped mint

½ tsp white pepper, plus more to taste

Small handful of pea shoots,
  for garnish

Small handful of microgreens,
  for garnish

For the Blanched Vegetables: Bring a large pot of water with 1 tablespoon of salt to a rolling boil and prepare an ice bath in a large pot or mixing bowl. Boil the carrots just until tender, 4 to 5 minutes. Using a slotted spoon, immediately transfer the carrots to the ice water to stop them from cooking. Once they've cooled, remove from the ice water and set aside. In the same pot, boil the green and yellow beans until brightly coloured and just tender, 1 to 2 minutes, and transfer to the ice water immediately. Once they've cooled, removed from the ice water and set aside. Refill the ice bath as needed to keep the water cold. In the same pot again, boil the peas until tender, 30 seconds to 1 minute, and transfer to the ice bath. Once they've cooled, remove from the ice water and set aside.

In the same pot, cover the new potatoes with cold water and 1 tablespoon of salt. Add the bay leaf and bring to a boil. Turn the heat down to a simmer and cook until the new potatoes are just fork-tender, 5 to 7 minutes. Drain, discarding the bay leaf, and transfer to an ice bath.

When all the vegetables are fully cooled, blot them dry. They can be stored in an airtight container in the fridge for up to 2 days if you want to prepare them ahead of time.

For the Chive and Mint Cream Sauce: In a large saucepan over medium heat, melt the butter with the oil. Add the celery root and shallots, and sweat with ½ teaspoon of salt until the celery root starts to soften and the shallots are translucent, 3 to 4 minutes. Mix in the wine and reduce the sauce by three-quarters. The pan will be almost dry. Add the stock and cream, increase the heat to high, and bring to a boil. Turn down the heat to low and gently simmer, covered, until the celery root is very soft, 7 to 9 minutes. Remove from the heat and stir in the chives and mint. Transfer the cream mixture to a blender in batches and purée until completely smooth. Strain the cream mixture through a fine-mesh strainer to remove any lumps. Add the white pepper, and season to taste with salt and more white pepper (if required). The mixture should coat the back of your spoon, but you can add additional stock if you desire a thinner consistency.

When you're ready to serve, place the vegetables in a large pot, cover with the chive cream, and place over medium heat just to heat the vegetables through, 3 to 5 minutes. Taste and adjust the seasoning if required. Spoon into serving bowls and garnish with pea shoots and microgreens.

STORAGE: The vegetables and cream will keep in separate airtight containers in the fridge for up to 2 days. Once you've combined them, they are best enjoyed the day they are made.

Recipe contributed by Dave Smart, Bessie North House

Atlantic Seafood Chowder

SERVES 4–6

Luckett Vineyards' Phone Box White

Seafood chowder is taken seriously on the East Coast. So much so that competitions abound between chefs, and travellers can enjoy official Chowder Trails to sample the myriad variations across the province. Inspired by a delicious meal at Founders House in Annapolis Royal, Nova Scotia, we like to keep it simple with the very freshest of ingredients cooked in a lightly spiced cream broth so that the seafood can really shine.

½ lb halibut

½ lb haddock

2 fresh lobster tails

12 fresh scallops, shelled (see page 51)

1 Tbsp vegetable oil

1 large onion, diced

½ cup diced celery

1 Tbsp flour

4 cups vegetable or fish stock

½ lb new potatoes, halved

¼ lb carrots, diced

1 cup frozen or fresh peas

1 cup whipping cream

2 Tbsp thyme leaves

Pinch of cayenne pepper

Pinch of paprika

1 tsp sea salt, plus more to taste

Black pepper

2 sprigs thyme, for garnish

Chop all of the fish and lobster meat into 1-inch pieces. If the scallops are larger than 1 inch, cut them into 1-inch pieces as well. Place in the fridge until ready to use.

Warm the oil in a large saucepan over medium heat, add the onion and celery and cook for 8 to 10 minutes, until soft and slightly translucent. Stir in the flour and cook for another 2 minutes. Whisking constantly, slowly add the stock and simmer for 3 to 4 minutes. Add the potatoes and carrots and cook for 12 to 15 minutes, until the vegetables are cooked through.

Add the peas, cream, thyme leaves, cayenne pepper, and paprika. Stir until well combined.

Gently fold in the fish and simmer for 7 minutes. Add the lobster meat and scallops and continue to simmer for another 3 minutes. Add the salt, and then season to taste with more salt (if required) and pepper. Garnish with thyme sprigs and serve immediately.

Fire-Grilled Brown Butter Scallops

SERVES 4

Lightfoot & Wolfville's Ancienne Chardonnay

16–20 fresh Digby scallops

Sea salt and black pepper

1 cup butter

This is our favourite way to enjoy sweet, succulent, and meaty Digby scallops: freshly shucked and poached in its shell in a delicious nutty browned butter over an open fire on the beach. Simplicity at its best. Enjoy these with Sorrel & Lovage Salad (page 261) for a light and delicious meal.

To clean and prepare the fresh scallops, using a sharp knife, carefully run the blade along the edge of the scallop parallel to the shell's rim to pop it open. Slide the knife back up to detach the adductor muscle, the scallop, from the top of the shell. Remove the roe from the shell and discard, and detach the muscle from the base.

Prepare a charcoal or wood fire or preheat a grill to high heat.

Pat the scallops dry with a paper towel, lightly season with salt and pepper, and place back in the scallop shells.

Working quickly, in a skillet over medium heat, melt the butter, then cook it for 2 to 3 minutes, stirring constantly. As the butter starts to turn golden, remove from heat and continue to stir. When the butter smells nutty and caramelized, set aside in the skillet.

To cook on a grill over a fire, place the scallop shells directly on the grill and gently pour 1 tablespoon of brown butter over each one. Cook for 2 to 3 minutes. Using tongs, carefully remove one shell from the grill and, using a small knife, gently slice the scallop open to ensure it is opaque all the way through. The butter will be bubbling. Carefully remove the scallops from the heat and serve immediately.

To cook on the stovetop, brown the butter over medium heat, turn down the heat to medium-low, and add three or four scallops to the pan. Sear for 1 to 2 minutes in the butter, spooning some butter over top. Flip the scallops carefully and repeat on the other side. When cooked, they should be deeply golden brown on both sides and opaque all the way through. They will continue to cook for a few minutes once removed from the heat, so be sure not to overcook them. Transfer to a plate and serve immediately. Repeat with the remaining scallops.

STORAGE: Scallops are best enjoyed as fresh as possible, and the day they are cooked, but can be stored in an airtight container in the fridge for up to 1 day.

CATCHING SCALLOPS

Walking down the docks during the Digby Scallop Days festival, we find scallops grilled, poached, fried, seared, added to a hot dog–style bun, and classically wrapped in bacon. There is also a shucking demonstration to enjoy them raw, a unique treat, as most scallops are shucked at sea, flash-frozen, and stored in bags set on ice in the boat's hold.

One of the true delicacies from the Bay of Fundy, this sweet and succulent bivalve is not only incredibly delicious but is also packed with protein and high amounts of omega-3 fatty acid. Compared to the more common Bay variety found along the Atlantic and Pacific coasts of North America, Digby scallops are larger (1½ to 2 inches in diameter) and live in the cold North Atlantic waters that run from the Bay of Fundy up to Labrador. The extreme tides in this region create perfect beds for these strong, beautiful scallops to grow in. Bay scallops are also farmed, while Digby scallops are only wild-harvested.

At the festival, we watch as a fisherman grabs a large pink and white shell from its glistening bed of melting ice and slides his shucking knife carefully into the scallop. With a smooth twist of his wrist, he pops it open. He then detaches the adductor, the piece we know as a scallop, from the top of the shell. Once open, the muscle and roe—or coral—is exposed. The roe is edible, but, although stronger in flavour than the scallop, is typically not saved. Using the knife, he pulls the roe out of the shell and, with another swipe, detaches the muscle from the base, leaving a perfect, fresh scallop in his hand.

Digby, Nova Scotia, after which the Digby scallops are named, is the heart of the scallop fishery in Atlantic Canada. In 1920, three Digby fishermen, J. W. Hayden, Roland Wormell, and Arch Amero, pioneered commercial scallop fishing, and today almost everyone who lives in Digby is connected to the industry. During the festival, the streets are teeming with locals and tourists excited to celebrate this treasured ingredient. For some it's also the end of the season and time for a well-deserved rest. This is not easy work: the hours are long, and the boats are at sea for days at a time in order to access the large deep-water beds. Now, with sustainability quotas in place for scallops, many of the larger boats in the harbour are there to stay until mid-October, when the annual quotas renew. There are also smaller boats, which take less in a catch and are thus able to fish all year round. The boats themselves are different in shape and size from lobster boats and other traditional fishing vessels, as they hold the heavy weight of the equipment at their stern and have cabins and work areas close to the bow—this ensures stability and safety for fishermen during the days and weeks at sea.

It's evident from talking to the scallopman that he and his fellow fishermen love what they do, and take great pride in not only providing a superior product but also keeping our oceans healthy and the industry sustainable. While the scallops we find at the fish counter may seem a common Atlantic ingredient, the labour of love it takes to harvest and bring them to shore is definitely worth a festival of celebration!

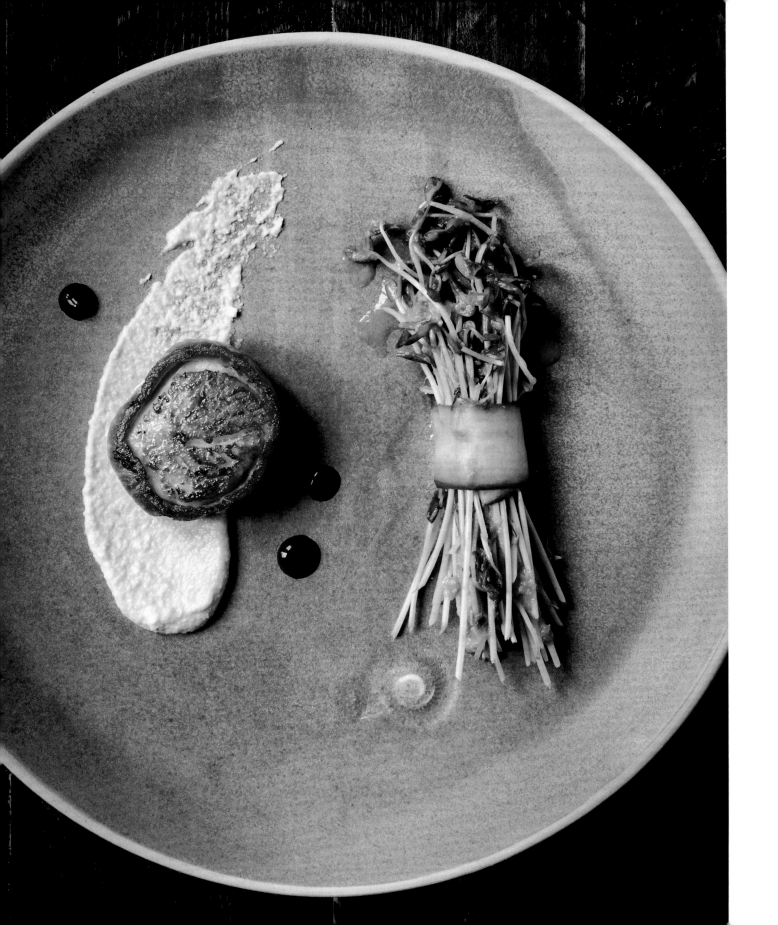

Smoked Salmon-Wrapped Scallops

SERVES 4

Benjamin Bridge's Nova 7

The Press Gang in downtown Halifax is a memory-packed place for us. We've both enjoyed significant moments here, including weddings and anniversaries, and the food served is truly worthy of such special occasions. We sit down at the table by the window, where the cool afternoon sun is shining in, and are joined by chef Bryan Corkery, who shares with us his passion for fresh, local ingredients. Determined to source and share the best of what this province has to offer, he explains that all of the fish he uses come in straight off the boat and are butchered on-site. He offers us a peek in the kitchen, where a huge tuna, the length of the counter, is in the midst of being processed, and the freshness makes us instantly hungry for the exceptional meal we know lies ahead.

We're grateful to chef Bryan for sharing his recipe for seared scallops wrapped in smoked Atlantic salmon, paired with microgreens tossed in a smoked tomato vinaigrette and elegantly wrapped in a cucumber ribbon. Finished with edamame bean and red beet purées, they're the perfect dish for any celebration.

Edamame Bean Purée:

½ cup edamame beans

1 tsp sea salt

½ cup whipping cream

2 Tbsp butter

Red Beet Purée:

1 large sugar beet

2 tsp olive oil

2 tsp cornstarch

¼ cup cold water

For the Edamame Bean Purée: In a small saucepan over high heat, bring the edamame to a boil in ¼ cup of water. Turn down the heat to medium and stir in the salt, cream, and butter. Simmer until the edamame are tender, 25 to 30 minutes. Using an immersion blender, blend the mixture to form a thick purée. Strain through a fine-mesh strainer to remove any lumps. Transfer to a small bowl, and chill, covered, in the fridge for 30 minutes to set.

For the Red Beet Purée: Preheat the oven to 400°F. Trim the ends of the beet and cut it into 1-inch pieces. Place on a sheet of aluminum foil and drizzle the oil over top. Wrap tightly and roast until the beets are extremely soft and tender, about 30 to 45 minutes. Remove the beets from the oven, open the foil to allow the beets to cool slightly, and then purée in a food processor fitted with the steel blade until no lumps remain. Place the puréed beet in a small saucepan. In a small glass or measuring cup, whisk the cornstarch into the cold water to form a slurry and add to the puréed beet. Place the pot over medium heat and bring to a boil, stirring constantly. Boil for 1 minute, then remove from the heat. Using an immersion blender or food processor, purée the beet mixture again and this time strain it through a fine-mesh strainer to remove any lumps. Transfer to a small bowl and chill, covered, in the fridge for about 1 hour to set.

(continued)

Smoked Tomato Vinaigrette:

2 Roma tomatoes

2 cloves garlic

2 tsp sugar

1 tsp sea salt, plus more to taste

¼ cup tomato juice

2 Tbsp apple cider vinegar

½ tsp liquid smoke

¼ cup olive oil

To Serve:

1 English cucumber, skin on

2 cups microgreens

8 large Digby scallops, shelled

8 pieces smoked Atlantic salmon or lox

2 Tbsp butter

For the Smoked Tomato Vinaigrette: Roughly chop the tomatoes and discard the seeds. In a blender, purée the tomatoes, garlic, sugar, salt, tomato juice, vinegar, and liquid smoke until completely smooth. With the blender running on low speed, slowly pour in the oil through the feed tube in a steady stream to emulsify into the dressing. Transfer to a small bowl and season to taste with salt, if needed. Cover and chill in the fridge until you're ready to use it, up to 1 week.

To Serve: When you're ready to serve, use a vegetable peeler to slice the cucumber into long strips. Toss the microgreens in half of the vinaigrette. Take approximately ½ cup of the greens, shake off any extra vinaigrette, wrap the greens in one strip of cucumber, and place on a serving plate. Spoon a dollop of edamame bean purée on the plate, opposite the microgreens, and spread it to form a smear on the plate. Repeat with the remaining three serving plates.

Rinse the scallops and pat them dry with a paper towel. Line a plate with paper towel and set aside. Wrap the circumference of each scallop in a piece of smoked salmon and secure with a toothpick. In a small skillet, melt the butter over medium-high heat. Working in batches, sear the scallops for 1 minute per side to cook through and create a beautiful golden crust. Transfer the scallops to the lined plate to drain. Place two scallops on the edamame bean purée smear on each serving plate. Using an eyedropper or a skewer, decorate each plate with a few drops of the beet purée. Drizzle a little of the remaining salad dressing over the microgreens and serve immediately.

STORAGE: The scallops and microgreens are best enjoyed the day they are made. The purées and vinaigrette will keep in separate airtight containers in the fridge for up to 1 week.

Recipe contributed by Bryan Corkery, The Press Gang

Cider-Seared Scallops *with* Sugar Beet Risotto

SERVES 4

No Boats On Sunday's Cranberry Rose Cider

4 small red beets

8½ cups chicken stock

2 large shallots

2 cloves garlic

1 small fennel bulb

2 Tbsp olive oil

4 Tbsp butter, divided

1 tsp sea salt, plus more to taste

1 tsp black pepper, plus more to taste

2 cups Arborio rice

2 cups dry cider, divided

12–16 fresh Digby scallops, shelled

1 cup grated Parmesan cheese

Scallop season starts in October, when the root vegetables are just coming out of the garden. This risotto is a brilliant marriage of the two. Vibrant in colour and flavour, the earthy, deep-red beets perfectly enhance the juicy sweetness of the scallops seared in a crisp, dry cider. If you're feeling adventurous, try cooking this with the Cranberry Rose Cider from No Boats On Sunday. The subtle flavours of the berries and rose infuse into the scallops and pair perfectly with the beet and fennel. Just make sure you save a glass to enjoy while you're stirring!

Preheat the oven to 400°F.

Trim the ends of the beets and slice them in half. Wrap the beets tightly in a sheet of aluminum foil and roast until extremely soft and tender, 30 to 45 minutes. Remove the beets from the foil and allow to cool to room temperature. Peel off the skin and, using a box grater, finely grate the beets. It's best to do this with gloves on as the beets will stain your fingers for days!

In a large pot over medium-low heat, warm the stock.

Finely mince the shallots and garlic (see page 60). Dice the fennel, reserving the tops for garnish.

In a large skillet over medium heat, place the oil and 2 tablespoons of the butter. Add the shallots and fennel and sauté for about 2 minutes until just translucent. Stir in the salt and pepper, allowing the shallots and fennel to sweat. Add the rice and, stirring constantly, allow the rice to absorb the butter and oil until it turns translucent and quite glossy. This will take about 2 minutes. Add the beets and garlic, stirring to combine. Slowly add 1 cup of the cider, stirring continuously. It will bubble up. Once the rice has fully absorbed the cider, add 1 ladleful of stock, stirring constantly until the rice has fully absorbed the liquid and the pan is dry. Repeat until there are two to three ladlefuls of stock left, the rice is tender and soft yet still textured, the beets have almost dissolved, and the mixture is magenta. If the risotto is too goopy, let the liquid boil off and keep stirring; if it's too crunchy, add some more stock and keep cooking until the rice is tender. Remove from the heat and set aside.

(continued)

59

In a separate pot over medium heat, pour in the remaining 1 cup of cider, bring to a boil and reduce for 2 minutes, then turn down the heat to medium-low, and whisk in the remaining 2 tablespoons of butter, creating a rich glaze.

Pat the scallops dry. Being careful not to overcrowd the pan, add three or four scallops at a time, and sear for 1 to 2 minutes per side, spooning the glaze over top while they cook. They should be well browned and crisp on the outside and no longer translucent on the inside when cut. Transfer to a side plate. Repeat with the remaining scallops.

Place the risotto back on the stovetop over medium heat, pour in one ladleful of warm stock, and stir the risotto until combined. The risotto will have congealed a bit while you were preparing the scallops.

After the risotto has loosened, add half a ladle of stock and the cheese. Stir well to combine, and cook until the cheese melts. Remove from the heat and immediately transfer to a serving platter. Top with the scallops and reserved fennel tops, drizzle with any remaining cider glaze, and sprinkle with salt, pepper, and extra Parmesan if desired.

STORAGE: The risotto will keep in the fridge for up to 3 days and can be reheated with a little stock. The scallops are best enjoyed the day they are made.

On Finely Mincing

When finely mincing aromatics—such as onions, shallots, or garlic—the goal is to cut them smaller than a grain of rice. For shallots or onions, the trick is to slice them in half horizontally and place the flat cut side on the cutting board. Make three or four small slices parallel to the cutting board, but only slice three-quarters of the way through. Now slice downward on the onion, perpendicular to those slices, leaving one end intact to hold the onion together. Finally, slice downward on the onion again, this time perpendicular to the last set of cuts. The small bits will fall off easily and be the perfect size. Discard the ends or add to the dish for more flavour, but remove this large piece before serving. Repeat with the garlic, or use a garlic press.

LANDING LOBSTER

It's hard to believe that in the not-so-distant past lobster was considered a poor man's food—tossed into dishes for added protein, not necessarily flavour—and definitely not the delicacy we know it as today. But oh how times have changed! From family boils on the beach to bibbed dinners at village community halls, and with culinary innovators favouring this king crustacean above all others, the love of lobster now runs deep across the Atlantic provinces.

The industry has taken a while to gain prominence as well. Lobstering used to be an off-season job for many, but after the cod moratorium in 1992 it became a main source of income, and today employs close to thirty thousand people across the Atlantic region. Jim Fraelic, who started lobstering in 1979, has seen the industry grow, and he describes the current situation as a "gold rush." He explains that cod and pollock feed on crustaceans and that when he was a child fishing with his father, they would often find market-size lobsters in the guts of their catch. Today, due to the significant decrease in fish stocks throughout the Atlantic and thus a lack of predators, lobster numbers are increasing.

Lobster is now Nova Scotia's number one seafood export and Atlantic Canada's most valuable fishery. Thousands of pounds of live Nova Scotia lobsters take off from the Halifax Stanfield International Airport every day, shipped in bulk across the globe. There is no real limit to the amount of lobsters that can be caught. Instead, conservation is imposed through coveted licences and designated trap numbers. Each licence denotes the number of traps a lobsterman is allowed to set, and the Lobster Fishing Area—LFA—they can fish within.

Essentially, lobstermen can catch and haul as many lobsters as their boats can handle during the season.

These restrictions were introduced about fifty years ago and were based on what Jim calls "effort control"—the amount of work it takes for a lobsterman to maintain the gear and the time it takes to check the traps. It's a challenging and time-consuming process that imposes a natural limitation on the amount of work that can physically be done by a crew. Once the traps are set, they fall under the fixed gear category in the Fisheries Act, which means they need to be checked every seventy-two hours. Thus, the amount of lobster that can realistically be caught under these efforts creates a natural quota.

Of course, the work doesn't end with the season: much of the off-season is spent overhauling gear, repairing traps, and looking after the boats. Yet it's a good living and one that many aspire to—that is, if they can obtain a permit. Today the prized lobster licences have reached their max and there won't be any more allotted or created, so anyone wanting to enter the industry must purchase one from someone wanting to sell theirs. The mantle is passing from the mostly over-fifty demographic to a younger generation primed to buy up licences from retiring lobstermen and keep the Atlantic lobstering life alive. "It's a good life," Jim tells us, and from what we can tell, a very delicious one as well! The work is hard and the hours long, yet for Jim, the freedom of working for himself as well as the ability to spend time with family and friends during the off-season is worth it—as is bringing this favourite delicacy to the table for all to enjoy.

One-Pot Lobster Dinner

SERVES 4

No Boats On Sunday's 100% NS Cider

Seafood Seasoning:

3 cloves garlic, smashed

2 bay leaves

5 whole cloves

1 Tbsp celery seeds

2 Tbsp sea salt

1 Tbsp black pepper

1 Tbsp chili flakes

2 tsp smoked paprika

2 tsp mustard powder

Pinch of grated nutmeg

Pinch of ground cinnamon

Boil:

1 lb new potatoes

2 (about 2 lb each) live lobsters
  (see note)

½ lb garlic sausage, cut into 1-inch
  rounds

2 onions, quartered, skins attached

4 ears of fresh corn, husks and silks
  removed, cut into thirds

2 lb fresh bearded mussels

Melted butter, for serving

You haven't really lived the Atlantic life unless you've had a proper lobster dinner. Available in almost every small coastal town, this one-pot dinner is just as easy to make at home as it is at the beach, which is always our preferred place to lay out a table laden with foods from the sea. If you do find yourself having a beachside boil-up, try omitting the sea salt and using fresh sea water instead for an extra kick of flavour. There is no ceremony here—this feast is traditionally drained and then dumped from the pot onto a clean table for everyone to tuck right in.

Bring a large pot of water to a boil on an outdoor cooker or the stovetop on medium-high heat. Cover a table with fresh butcher paper or a clean plastic picnic-style tablecloth.

In a small bowl, mix together all the seasoning ingredients.

Cut a cheesecloth into two (9-inch) squares and overlap them. Place the seafood seasoning ingredients in the centre of the cheesecloth. Gather the edges of the cheesecloth to form a loose sack and tie it securely with kitchen twine.

Add the seafood seasoning package to the boiling water. Add the potatoes and cook for about 10 minutes, just until fork-tender. Add the lobsters, sausages, and onions and cook for 10 minutes, until the onions are soft and lobster shells are bright red. Add the corn and mussels and boil for 5 minutes, just until the mussel shells open.

Drain off the water and pour the contents of the pot out onto the prepared table.

Serve immediately with melted butter and wash down with plenty of cold cider.

NOTE: If using larger lobsters, add 5 minutes boil time per ½ pound before adding the corn and mussels.

Tall Ship Ale *&* Fries

SERVES 2

*Garrison Brewing Company's Tall
Ship Ale*

Beer-battered haddock and fries are a must-have whenever visiting the
Atlantic provinces, and we've found the secret to success lies in the ale! Our
go-to beer for this recipe is the Tall Ship Ale from the Garrison Brewing
Company, located directly across from the famous Seaport Farmers' Market
on the Halifax boardwalk. A true malted ale, it lends a nuttiness and depth
to the batter that enhances the bright, buttery haddock flesh. Be sure to
pour a pint for yourself—a perfect pairing served alongside the fish and our
home-cut oven-roasted fries. Now you're talking a perfect summer meal.

3–4 starchy yellow potatoes, peeled
and cut into ½-inch-thick wedges

¼ cup olive oil

2 tsp sea salt

1 tsp black pepper

1½ cups flour

½ cup cornstarch

1 Tbsp baking powder

1 tsp white pepper

1 (341 ml) bottle of Garrison Brewing
Tall Ship Ale (or other favourite
strong ale)

4 cups neutral oil

2 (each 4–6 oz) haddock fillets

Sea salt

Fresh Whipped Tartar Sauce
(page 109), for serving

Beer or malt vinegar, for serving

To make the fries, preheat the oven to 425°F. Line a large rimmed baking
sheet with parchment paper.

In a large bowl, toss the potato wedges with the oil, salt, and black pepper,
and place on the prepared baking sheet, being sure not to overlap the slices.
Bake for 15 minutes, flip the wedges over, and bake for another 10 minutes,
until the wedges are golden brown and crisped on the edges. Turn off the
oven without opening the door and keep the chips warm in there until you're
ready to serve.

In a large mixing bowl, combine the flour, cornstarch, baking powder, and
white pepper. Reserve ½ cup of the dry ingredients and set aside. Whisking
constantly, slowly add the beer to the main bowl of dry ingredients and mix
until the batter is smooth.

In a deep Dutch oven, preheat the oil to 350°F, using a candy thermometer to
monitor the temperature. Line a plate with paper towel.

Drop a small amount of batter into the oil. It should sizzle and crisp up
quickly. Place the haddock on a paper towel. Dry and pat away any excess
moisture. Working with one piece at a time, coat each fish in the reserved
dry ingredients, then dip into the beer batter, and carefully submerge the
fish into the oil. Deep-fry until the fish is crispy and golden, flipping halfway
through to cook both sides evenly, 3 to 5 minutes in total. Using a large
slotted spoon, lift out each fillet, drain on the prepared plate, and sprinkle
with salt. Serve immediately with tartar sauce and beer or malt vinegar.

Creamy Carbonara Scape Gnocchi

SERVES 4

Lightfoot & Wolfville's Tidal Bay

Gnocchi:

2 baking potatoes (russet or other
  starchy variety)

12–15 large garlic scapes

1 cup ricotta cheese

2 eggs

1 tsp sea salt

2½ cups flour, plus more for dusting

Creamy Carbonara:

4 egg yolks

2 Tbsp olive oil

½ cup whipping cream

1 cup grated Parmesan cheese,
  plus extra for garnish

Sea salt and black pepper

In the early summer months, when scapes are in season, we use them in everything. Finding inventive ways to eat them is a challenge we look forward to every year! Fresh scapes, leftover potatoes in the fridge, and a craving for gnocchi is how this recipe was born.

For the Gnocchi: Preheat the oven to 375°F.

Wash and scrub the potatoes and pierce them several times all over with a knife. Place directly on the bottom rack of the oven and bake for 45 to 50 minutes, turning once or twice to ensure they bake evenly. Remove from the oven and allow to cool.

While the potatoes are baking, bring a large pot of salted water to a boil. To blanch the garlic scapes, boil until they are bright green and slightly soft in texture, yet still a bit firm, 2 to 3 minutes. Using tongs, remove the scapes from the water, shaking off any excess, and transfer to a cutting board. Set the pot aside, and reserve the water for cooking the gnocchi later. Roughly chop the scapes and transfer to a food processor fitted with the steel blade or a high-powered blender. Purée the scapes. Add the ricotta and blend until the mixture is completely smooth and uniformly light green. Set aside.

Slice the potatoes in half, scoop out the flesh, and finely rice the potatoes to ensure they are as lump-free as possible. If you don't have a ricer, mash the potatoes slightly and press them through a fine-mesh strainer. This should yield about 3 cups of riced potatoes.

Place the potatoes in a large bowl, make a small well in the centre of them, and add the eggs and salt. Using a fork, whisk the eggs together and then gently fold them into the potatoes to make a paste-like mixture. Add the scape ricotta purée, and use a fork to mix and combine them. Mixing gently, add about 1 cup of flour at a time to make a soft dough. It will be quite sticky to begin with. Form the dough into a ball, dust it generously with flour, and then wrap in plastic wrap and chill in the fridge for 15 to 20 minutes to allow it to firm up. On a well-floured surface, divide the dough into four pieces and roll each piece into a log about 18 inches long and 1 inch in diameter. Cut the logs into ½-inch rounds. Dust each piece with flour.

(continued)

If you would like to fork the gnocchi (which is technically not necessary, although Emily's nana always reminds her that taking the time to fork the gnocchi allows it to hold the sauce better), use your thumb to gently press the fork into the gnocchi lengthwise, folding the two outer sides in toward the centre, and rolling the back of your fork over top to create those classic gnocchi lines. You can, of course, use a gnocchi paddle for this if you have one. Dust the gnocchi with flour and set aside.

For the Creamy Carbonara: In a mixing bowl, whisk together the egg yolks and oil until creamy and slightly frothy, then add the cream and continue to whisk until fully combined, about 30 seconds. Add the Parmesan cheese, and salt and pepper to taste, and whisk until combined.

Pour the carbonara mixture into a large saucepan and place over medium-low heat. Stirring constantly, pour in the reserved gnocchi cooking liquid and allow the egg mixture to warm slowly for 1 to 2 minutes. Add the gnocchi and continue to stir until the egg has started to thicken and the gnocchi are well coated in the sauce.

Transfer to serving plates, garnish with some Parmesan.

STORAGE: Once cooked and prepared, the gnocchi and carbonara are best enjoyed the day they're made. Uncooked gnocchi can be frozen on a baking sheet to prevent them from sticking, then transferred to an airtight container and kept in the freezer for up to 6 months. Cook from frozen and boil until the gnocchi start to float on the surface of the water.

Denver Steaks *with* Dragon's Breath Béarnaise

SERVES 4

Domaine de Grand Pré's Castello

4 Denver or top sirloin steaks

Sea salt and black pepper

1 small shallot

2 Tbsp dried summer savory

½ cup dry white wine

½ tsp black pepper

4 egg yolks

1 cup salted butter, melted

¼ cup crumbled and pressed Dragon's Breath Blue cheese or blue cheese of choice, plus extra for garnish

Sprig of rosemary, for garnish (optional)

Tristan Jennings and Chris Cobb, the masters behind the Butcher Shop at the famous Masstown Crossroads in Nova Scotia, are some of the most creative carnivores we've met. They have a passion for animals, ensuring they are raised and slaughtered humanely. Between them they have learned fifty ways to break down a cow, and the creativity with which they do this is impressive. The Denver steak featured in this recipe is a long-lost cut, similar to a boneless short rib. The exquisite quality of this thick, tender, succulent piece of meat is only made better by adding a rich béarnaise. Here the sauce is flavoured with Dragon's Breath Blue from That Dutchman's Cheese Farm, a favourite Nova Scotian blue ensconced in black wax that's a spoonable soft cheese similar to Gorgonzola. This meal will put the best of Nova Scotia on your plate.

Sprinkle the steaks liberally with salt and pepper and allow to rest in the fridge for up to 12 hours (just be sure to bring them to room temperature before cooking) or at room temperature for 1 hour.

Mince the shallot (see page 60) and place it in a small saucepan with the savory and wine. Bring to a slow boil over medium-low heat and reduce until only 2 tablespoons of liquid are left. Mix in the ½ teaspoon of pepper and set aside for 10 minutes to cool.

In a small blender, pulse the egg yolks until liquefied and starting to absorb the fat. Add the wine reduction and blend on low speed. With the blender still running on low speed, slowly add 4 or 5 teaspoons of the melted butter through the feed tube, 1 teaspoon at a time. In a slow and steady stream, add the remaining butter, ensuring it is emulsifying into the egg yolk mixture. If the mixture looks like it's starting to separate, stop adding the butter and allow the blender to run for a few moments before you begin to add it again, very slowly. Stop the blender once the butter has been absorbed. Add the cheese and pulse a few times to combine.

To keep this béarnaise warm until you're ready to serve, pour it into a gravy boat or small jug. Place the boat or jug in a bowl. Boil some water and fill the bowl with the hot water until it is at least halfway up the sides of the jug. Ideally it should reach the top of the sauce, but you must ensure the water doesn't spill into the sauce. Set aside.

(continued)

Preheat the grill to high heat and brush with a little heat-tolerant oil. Place the steaks on the grill and cook to the desired doneness (see sidebar, below). Remove the steaks from the grill and rest, covered, for 5 minutes to allow the juices absorb and the meat to finish cooking.

Remove the béarnaise from the bowl of water. Place the steaks on individual serving plates and drizzle some béarnaise on top of each one, with more on the side as needed. If desired, serve with any leftover Dragon's Breath Blue and garnish with fresh rosemary.

STORAGE: The steak will keep in an airtight container in the fridge for up to 3 days. The béarnaise will keep in an airtight container in the fridge for up to 2 days and can be reheated in a double boiler, although it is best served the day it's made.

On Doneness

The following information is for a ¾-inch steak. If needed, increase the cooking time by 30 seconds per side for every ¼ inch of added thickness.

For a rare steak: Sear 2 minutes per side, until it has an internal temperature of 120°F.

For a medium-rare steak: Sear 2 minutes and 30 seconds per side, until it has an internal temperature of 130°F.

For a medium steak: Sear 3 minutes per side, until it has an internal temperature of 140°F.

For a medium-well done steak: Sear 3 minutes and 30 seconds per side, until it has an internal temperature of 150°F.

For a well-done steak: Sear 4 minutes per side, until it has an internal temperature of 160°F.

Turkey Roulade *with* Blood Sausage Stuffing

SERVES 6

Lightfoot & Wolfville's Pinot Noir

We firmly believe that turkey should be served more than once or twice a year. This recipe makes it easy to scale down from a huge holiday celebration to an elegant dinner party while still enjoying the most delicious of birds. As blood sausage is readily available at butcher counters across the Atlantic region, we've added it to our stuffing to give a deep punch of flavour and spice to a traditional pork sausage recipe. The apple brandy gravy rounds it out and is, of course, perfect for a whole bird as well.

Blood Sausage Stuffing:

¼ cup butter

2 Tbsp olive oil

2 stalks celery, diced

1 small fennel bulb, diced

1 medium onion, diced

4 oz pork sausage, casing removed

4 oz blood sausage, casing removed

3 Tbsp chopped flat-leaf parsley

1 Tbsp dried savory

1½ cups apple brandy, divided

1 tsp sea salt

1 tsp black pepper

1 cup chicken stock

1 cup dried breadcrumbs

Turkey Roulade:

1 (about 5 lb) boneless, skin-on, whole turkey breast, butterflied and flattened

Sea salt and black pepper

2 Tbsp butter, softened

For the Blood Sausage Stuffing: In a large skillet over medium heat, melt the butter with the oil. Add the celery, fennel, and onions and cook for about 5 minutes, until softened. Add both sausages and cook, stirring often, until the sausages are browned through, 7 to 10 minutes. Stir in the parsley and savory and cook for another minute. Deglaze the skillet with 1 cup of the brandy, scraping up any brown bits from the bottom, and cook until most of the liquid has been absorbed. Season with the salt and pepper. Add the stock and breadcrumbs and stir to combine.

For the Turkey Roulade: Lay the turkey breast flat on a plastic wrap–lined cutting board, skin side up, and season with salt and pepper. Turn the turkey over and spread the stuffing mixture in an even layer across the meat, being sure to leave 1 inch free along one of the long edges. Using the plastic wrap to help you pull the meat, tightly roll the turkey breast into a log shape. Tie the roll with kitchen twine in five or six places. Wrap tightly in the plastic wrap and chill in the fridge for at least 30 minutes so it holds its shape.

When you're ready to roast, preheat the oven to 425°F.

Remove the turkey from the fridge, discard the plastic wrap, and let the turkey rest at room temperature for 10 to 15 minutes. Rub the turkey with the butter and sprinkle with salt and pepper. Place a wire rack in a roasting pan and set the roulade on top. Roast for 30 minutes, then lower the oven temperature to 350°F and continue roasting for approximately 1 hour, or until the skin is golden brown and crispy and a meat thermometer inserted into the centre reads 155°F. Remove from the oven and let rest for at least 10 minutes before slicing into rounds. Keep the drippings.

Apple Brandy Gravy:

Pan drippings from Turkey Roulade

¼ cup flour

1 cup chicken stock

1 cup apple brandy

2 Tbsp butter

For the Apple Brandy Gravy: Place the roasting pan with the turkey drippings on the stovetop and add the flour. Cook over medium heat, stirring constantly, until the drippings are thick and the flour turns a darker brown, about 10 minutes. Add the stock, brandy, and then the butter. Stir the gravy until well combined. Serve hot alongside the turkey roulade.

STORAGE: The turkey roulade will keep in an airtight container in the fridge for up to 4 days. The gravy will keep in the fridge, covered, for up to 1 week.

CULTIVATING APPLES

When you're driving through the Annapolis Valley, it's hard to miss the apple orchards. Whether you're cruising along Highway 102 or bumping down a road off the beaten track, the vistas are dominated by pops of green, red, and yellow orbs strung like brightly coloured lights in perfect rows, each with a sign at the end displaying the varietal name. This is apple country.

We're sitting on the back deck at Suprima Farms Ltd. with Richard Hennigar, who's sharing his stories and passion for apples with us. He's spent his whole life in the Annapolis Valley, moving to his current small town outside of Wolfville in 1953. To say apples are in his blood is an understatement: his grandfather moved from the South Shore of Nova Scotia over 115 years ago and planted the family's first apple trees in 1905. After witnessing the challenges his father and grandfather faced with the conventional apple industry, Richard followed his instincts and decided to leave big business behind, selling directly to the consumer instead. In 1992, he cut out the middlemen in order to maximize his margins and profitability without compromising on quality, and he got started on doing what he loves: growing apples on his own terms. "If you're a cog in a giant wheel, you don't control your own destiny," he explains.

With the evening sun shining across the patio, glasses filled with fresh apple juice, Richard smiles and tells us, "Being a farmer is just a combination of moments, most of sheer joy and others of terror. If you're trying something and it doesn't work, then try something new." The goals for his 10 acres remain the same as they were twenty years ago, although it has taken this many years to create the orchard of his dreams. Today he's growing varieties that were developed at the Atlantic Food and Horticulture Research Centre in Kentville, Nova Scotia—including Novamac, Novaspy, and Prima—all of which have impressive pedigrees that include crabapple, making them less prone to scabbing and reducing the need for spray or any other intervention. The orchard has been cultivated without a drop of fossil fuel for over twenty years now, and all of the trees are hand-pruned. The grass is allowed to grow unimpeded, then flattened once it becomes brittle in July with a technique Richard invented called "grass bending." This involves humans (usually Richard himself) crawling over every inch of the 10 acres and manually weaving the grass into a flat mat with his body. This may sound eccentric, but Richard noticed that when he stopped mowing, the ant hills returned. The ants increase the sulphur content of the soil, naturally allowing nitrogen fixation to occur and eliminating the need for artificial fertilizers. "The ants and worms are both happy now," he explains. "They're the under-story of this land." The grass bending also allows him to keep the orchard floor free of ground fall, which harbours incubating apple maggots. Once harvest rolls around, the apples are hand-picked. If motorized vehicles are ever needed, electric golf carts are employed. Selling fresh apples in season and juice year round at local farmers' markets allows Richard to stay and work at the orchard he loves.

Down the road, at Noggins Corner Farm, another successful model is at play. Ten generations have been farming this property, stretching back to 1760, and they now hold over 1,400 acres of land, growing forty-two varieties of apples, fifteen varieties of pears, and plenty of stone fruits and berries. Their market store, a favourite stop when heading out of Wolfville, sells not only fruit but also jams, jellies, fruit leathers, apple chips, and even sugar-free purées created in their own food lab as well as cider from their in-house cidery. Some of their produce is shipped out of province, selling mostly to Ontario and the USA. This is vertical integration at its strongest: from cultivation and recipe development to agri-tourism and an educational outreach program, Noggins Corner Farm is dedicated to teaching people where their food comes from, how it's grown, and the care and attention that goes into every piece of fruit that they sell.

Come to the Annapolis Valley in the spring and kick off the growing season with the much anticipated Apple Blossom Festival, or stop by in the autumn, when chefs and home cooks alike honour the harvest with both sweet and savoury recipes alongside glasses of cider, brandy, and liqueur. Whenever you arrive here in apple country, we're sure you'll agree that there's cause to celebrate this most delicious fruit.

Apple Crumble Cream Pie

SERVES 8

Domaine de Grand Pré's Pomme d'Or
   Ice Cider or 45 Fortified White Wine

Packed with warm spices, caramel, and so many apples, this pie piles all the autumnal flavours into each and every bite. The Pomme d'Or Apple Cream Liqueur, a mix of iced cider and cream—the Baileys of the apple world and not to be trifled with—made at Grand Pré Wines in the Annapolis Valley, adds incredible character to the caramel.

Pastry:

1½ cups flour

1 tsp fine sea salt

1 tsp baking powder

½ cup butter, chilled but not solid, cubed

1 egg

2 tsp lemon juice

¼ cup cold water

Filling:

¾ cup sugar

½ cup whipping cream

½ cup Pomme d'Or Apple Cream Liqueur or 2 Tbsp of brandy + ⅓ cup whipping cream

2 tsp ground cinnamon

1 tsp ground nutmeg

1 tsp ground allspice

½ tsp ground cloves

6 large apples (such as Granny Smith, Spy, or Cortland)

4 Tbsp cornstarch, divided

2 Tbsp lemon juice, divided

For the Pastry: In a large bowl, whisk together the flour, salt, and baking powder. Add the butter. Using two knives or a pastry blender, cut in the butter until the mixture resembles coarse oatmeal. Whisk together the egg and lemon juice in a ½-cup measure, fill the measure with the cold water, and pour into the pastry. Fold the wet ingredients into the dry ingredients. Be careful not to overwork the pastry. It just needs to pull together to form one large ball. Wrap with plastic wrap and chill in the fridge for 30 minutes, or up to 12 hours.

For the Filling: In a large, heavy-bottomed pot, place the sugar and 2 tablespoons of water. Mix together until the sugar is completely wet and then place the pot over medium heat. Allow the sugar to dissolve and begin to caramelize. Don't stir while this is happening. It will begin to bubble and then turn a light golden brown. Continue to cook, swirling the pan once or twice to ensure it's browning evenly. When it reaches a rich deep-brown colour and smells heavenly, remove from the heat. Gently pour in the cream, whisking constantly to incorporate it into the caramel. It will bubble up vigorously, but continue to whisk and it will settle. Whisk in the liqueur, mix in the spices, and set aside.

Remove the pastry from the fridge.

Peel, core, and thinly slice the apples. In a large bowl, toss the apples with 2 tablespoons of the cornstarch and sprinkle with 1 tablespoon of the lemon juice.

(continued)

Crumble:

1 cup packed brown sugar

¾ cup flour

¾ cup butter, cubed

1 tsp ground cinnamon

½ tsp ground nutmeg

Ice cream, for serving

Lightly dust your surface and, using a rolling pin, roll out the pastry until it's just under ¼ inch thick. Roll the pastry around the rolling pin to transfer it easily to a 9-inch pie plate. Lay the pastry evenly over the plate, ensuring there is an inch or so of pastry draped over the sides. Sprinkle the pastry in the bottom of the pie plate with the remaining 2 tablespoons of cornstarch, add the apples, spreading evenly and mounding in the centre, and drizzle with the remaining lemon juice.

For the Crumble: In the bowl used for the apples, use your fingers to combine all the crumble ingredients to create a soft, buttery crumble.

To Assemble: Preheat the oven to 425°F. Line a rimmed baking sheet with parchment paper.

Trim the pastry so you have a 1-inch border around the pie plate. Fold the pastry over the lip of the plate and then inward onto to itself to create a thick rim crust. Flute the pie by pressing the pastry border into the rim of the plate, using a fork to seal it. Sprinkle the crumble over the apples and pat it down a little to ensure it stays in place. This is a generous amount of crumble and piling it on top makes for a very tasty pie!

Slowly and carefully drizzle the spiced caramel evenly over the pie, over and around the crumble, allowing it to soak into all the crevices.

Place the pie on the prepared baking sheet to catch any drips while it's cooking. Bake for 15 minutes, then turn down the heat to 350°F without opening the oven door and bake for an additional 45 minutes. The pie will be bubbling, with a golden-brown crust.

Remove from the oven and allow to cool completely before slicing. Serve with a scoop of ice cream to complete the cream pie experience!

STORAGE: The pie will keep in an airtight container in the fridge for up to 1 week.

Gingerbread *with* Single Malt Hard Sauce

MAKES 1 (9-INCH) CAKE

Big Spruce Brewing's Cereal Killer

The Red Shoe Pub in Mabou, Nova Scotia, is home to the famous Rankin Family and is a hub of traditional music and foods for those travelling around Cape Breton. It also happens to have the best gingerbread cake in the world. This is our variation, inspired by too many pieces consumed while listening to spectacular fiddle music. It pairs perfectly with our hard sauce, which features single malt Scotch whisky. We recommend using the traditionally crafted Glen Breton Single Malt Whisky, made just up the road at the Glenora Distillery from the pure waters of the Cape Breton Highlands. Be sure to serve the cake warm so the sauce can soak right into each and every bite.

Hard Sauce:

1 cup butter, softened

2½ cups icing sugar

¼ cup good single malt Scotch whisky

Cake:

½ cup butter, softened

2½ cups flour, divided

½ cup sugar

1 egg

1 cup molasses

½ cup unsweetened applesauce

1½ tsp baking soda

1 Tbsp ground ginger

2 tsp ground cinnamon

1 tsp ground cloves

½ tsp fine sea salt

1 cup hot water

For the Hard Sauce: Using a stand mixer fitted with the paddle attachment, beat the butter to a fluffy consistency. Add the icing sugar and whisky and continue to beat until all the ingredients are thoroughly combined. Set aside until ready to serve.

For the Cake: Preheat the oven to 350°F. Grease and flour a 9-inch square pan. Set aside.

Using a stand mixer fitted with the paddle attachment, beat the butter and the sugar until light and fluffy. Beat in the egg and then add the molasses and applesauce. Switch to a wooden spoon and stir well to combine without overmixing.

In a separate bowl, sift together the flour, baking soda, spices, and salt. Add the dry mixture to the wet ingredients and fold until just combined. Add the hot water and stir lightly until the batter is uniformly mixed. Pour into the prepared pan and bake in the centre of the oven for 1 hour, or until a toothpick inserted in the centre of the cake comes out clean. Let rest in the pan for at least 5 minutes before serving.

Serve the cake straight from the pan while it's still warm, with a generous dollop of sauce on top.

STORAGE: Once warmed and combined the cake with the sauce should be enjoyed the day they are made. Separately, the cake will keep in an airtight container in the fridge for up to 3 days. The sauce will keep in an airtight container in the fridge for up to 1 week.

Ice Wine Panna Cotta *with* Dried Fruit Compote

SERVES 6

🍷 *Domaine de Grand Pré's Vidal Icewine*
or Haskap Sparkling Wine

When it comes to creating menus dedicated to the local terroir, chef Jason Lynch of Le Caveau restaurant, which is part of the Domaine de Grand Pré vineyard, has long been at the forefront of Annapolis Valley cuisine. Sitting at a table on the patio overlooking the grapevines, he explains his philosophy on steadfastly adhering to a farm-to-table approach: "It just makes sense, really. I want the farmer to get paid, instead of the big corporations." Pulling together local produce and connecting it with the land and the wine is what he does best, and this panna cotta of his is no exception. It's the perfect late-harvest dessert and an elegant finish for any special occasion.

2 Tbsp cold water

1¾ tsp unflavoured powdered gelatin

2 cups heavy cream

4 Tbsp sugar, divided

Fine sea salt

2 whole vanilla beans or 2 tsp vanilla
   paste

1 cup + 2 Tbsp Vidal Icewine, divided,
   plus more for drizzling

1 cup chopped dried fruit (such as
   raisins, apricots, cranberries)

Coat six (5-ounce) ramekins generously with butter and chill in the fridge for
10 to 15 minutes to allow the butter to set.

In a small bowl, place the 2 tablespoons of cold water and sprinkle the gelatin
over top. Set aside to bloom and soften, about 5 minutes.

In a large saucepan, mix together the cream, 3 tablespoons of the sugar, and
a pinch of salt, and place the pan over medium heat. While the cream
mixture is starting to warm, use a small knife to cut each vanilla bean
lengthwise. Scrape the seeds into the cream. Add the pods as well. (Or simply
stir in the vanilla paste.)

Increase the heat to high, stirring gently once or twice, and bring the mixture
to a boil. As soon as the cream is boiling, turn down the heat to medium and
let the cream continue to boil for 1 minute, stirring constantly. Watch closely
so it doesn't boil over.

Remove the pan from the heat and whisk in the gelatin, the remaining
1 tablespoon of sugar, and the 2 tablespoons of ice wine until the gelatin
is dissolved, about 30 seconds. Strain the cream through a fine-mesh sieve
into a bowl or liquid measuring cup and discard the vanilla seeds and beans
(if using).

Cover the bowl with plastic wrap, pressing it directly on the surface of the
warm cream to prevent a skin from forming. Chill in the fridge for 25 to
30 minutes, until cool and slightly thicker than heavy cream but not set.
Divide the mixture between the prepared ramekins and chill, uncovered,
in the fridge for at least 3 hours, or up to overnight.

While the panna cotta is setting, place the dried fruit in a bowl, pour the
remaining 1 cup of ice wine over top, and cover. Let sit at room temperature
for at least 3 hours, allowing the fruit to plump up and absorb the wine.

Once the panna cotta is set, use a small knife to cut around the outside of
each ramekin and turn the panna cotta out onto a dessert plate. Place a
spoonful of fruit mixture on top of each panna cotta, drizzle some more ice
wine around the custard, and serve.

STORAGE: The panna cotta in the ramekins will keep wrapped in plastic
wrap in the fridge for up to 5 days. The turned-out panna cottas will keep
wrapped in oiled plastic wrap, so they don't stick, for up to 5 days. The
plumped dried fruit will keep in an airtight container in the fridge for up
to 1 month.

Recipe contributed by Jason Lynch, Le Caveau

Sage & Flax Shortbread

MAKES 2 DOZEN

Along the quiet, winding roads of Cape Breton, it's hard to believe that tucked down a hidden laneway is The Bite House, one of Canada's finest restaurants. Situated in a small white house, it is as inviting as they come. Serving no more than twelve people only a few nights a week, the space makes you feel more like you're at a private dinner party at a friend's home than a restaurant. Most ingredients are foraged or grown on the neighbouring biodynamic farm and, with short seasonal availability, Bryan makes the most of what he has. These shortbreads are just one delicious example of his creativity. At The Bite House, they serve these as a dessert along with a honey-flavoured ice cream, or with fried apples and dried black currants.

1 cup flax seeds

1 cup salted butter, softened

¾ cup sugar

¼ cup finely chopped sage

¼ cup honey

2 egg yolks

2 cups whole white flour (see note) or 1½ cups all-purpose flour + ½ cup wheat germ

STORAGE: The shortbread will keep in an airtight container at room temperature for up to 1 week or in the freezer for up to 3 months.

NOTE: Whole white flour from Speerville Flour Mill is a stone-ground unbleached white flour that has 85% of the wheat kernel and all the wheat germ, creating a rich yet light flour perfect for baking.

Preheat the oven to 350°F. Line a baking sheet with parchment paper.

In a small skillet over medium heat, toast the flax seeds, shaking the pan gently to ensure the seeds brown evenly and don't burn. Set aside to cool at room temperature.

Using a stand mixer fitted with the paddle attachment, combine the butter, sugar, sage, and honey on medium-high speed for 2 to 3 minutes, until creamy. Lower the speed and add the egg yolks. Turn the mixer back up to medium speed and continue to mix for an additional 1 to 2 minutes, until fully combined.

Turn the speed back down to low and, with the mixer running, add the flour about ¼ cup at a time until just mixed, then add the flax seeds and mix to combine. Stop the mixer, scrape down the sides of the bowl, and mix again for 1 minute to form a soft dough and ensure everything is evenly combined.

Turn the dough onto a lightly floured surface and, using a floured rolling pin, roll it out to between ½ and ¼ inch thick. Cut out small rounds, about 2 inches in diameter, and place them ½ inch apart on the prepared baking sheet. Bake for 10 to 12 minutes, until just golden and starting to brown around the edges. Transfer to a wire rack and let cool completely.

Recipe contributed by Bryan Picard, The Bite House

Hot Milk Cake *with* Black Currant Buttercream

MAKES I (8-INCH) TWO-
LAYER CAKE OR I (9- BY
13-INCH) SHEET CAKE
OR I (10-INCH) BUNDT

Benjamin Bridge's NV Rosé

Cake:

¾ cup whole milk

4 eggs

1 cup sugar

2½ cups flour

2 tsp baking powder

½ tsp fine sea salt

¾ cup cold butter, cubed

1 tsp vanilla extract

Buttercream:

1 cup butter

5 cups icing sugar

½ cup black currant purée or jam

This traditional cake—perfect for birthdays, special events, or afternoon tea with friends—is a staple in many Nova Scotian households. Soft and delicate, it's versatile enough to work as a two-layer, a Bundt, or sheet cake, and the buttercream frosting made with black currants adds both a bright flavour and a fun colour. The trick to this cake is to lower the temperature of the scalded milk by adding cold butter before combining it with the egg-filled batter.

For the Cake: Preheat the oven to 350°F. Prepare two (8-inch) round cake pans or one (9- by 13-inch) sheet pan or one (10-inch) Bundt pan by greasing with a pat of butter and dusting with flour.

In a small saucepan over medium heat, heat the milk, stirring gently until scalding and just starting to froth naturally. Set aside for 2 minutes to cool slightly.

While the milk is heating, in a stand mixer fitted with the whisk attachment, whisk together the eggs and sugar on medium-high speed for about 3 minutes, until the mixture is very light in colour and soft, creamy ribbons form. Sift the flour, baking powder, and salt together. Add the cold butter to the milk, whisking until it has fully melted and incorporated. Stir in the vanilla. With the mixer running on low speed, add one-third of the flour, then half of the hot milk, ensuring each addition is incorporated. Repeat until all of the flour and milk have been incorporated. Whisk on medium speed for 1 minute. The batter will be quite stiff yet extremely creamy.

Pour the batter into the prepared cake pan(s), dividing evenly if using two, and use, using an offset spatula to spread it in an even layer. Bake in the centre of the oven for 30 minutes for two round cakes, 40 to 45 minutes for a sheet cake, or 50 to 55 minutes for a Bundt cake, until evenly golden and risen and a toothpick inserted in the centre comes out clean. Run a knife around the outside of the cake as soon as it comes out of the oven. Let the cake cool for 2 to 3 minutes, then invert it onto a tea towel and remove the cake pan. Place a wire rack on the cake and invert so it's upright on the wire rack to cool completely.

For the Buttercream: Using a stand mixer fitted with the paddle attachment, beat the butter for 1 minute, until light, fluffy, and creamed. Sift 2½ cups of the icing sugar and add to the butter 1 cup at a time, scraping down the sides of the bowl after each addition. Add the black currant purée, then add the remaining icing sugar and beat until fully incorporated, no lumps remain, and the frosting is stiff yet fluffy-looking.

To Assemble: If you've baked two round cakes, place one on a stand or platter and spread with one-third of the buttercream, making sure to get right to the edges. Place the second cake upside down on top and spread half of the remaining buttercream on top of the cake and down the sides to cover both layers completely. Spread the remaining frosting on top of the cake to cover. If you've baked a sheet cake or Bundt, cover the top and sides with the buttercream. Let rest, uncovered, in the fridge for 20 minutes to set before serving.

STORAGE: Once the cakes have cooled, they can be wrapped in plastic and stored in the fridge for up to 3 days before frosting or kept in the freezer for up to 3 months. The frosted cake will keep in an airtight container in the fridge for up to 5 days. The frosting will keep in an airtight container in the fridge for up to 2 weeks. Just bring the frosting to room temperature and beat for 1 to 2 minutes before using.

Upside-Down Blueberry Grunt

SERVES 4

Annapolis Cider Company's Earl Blue

If there was ever a "provincial dessert" for Nova Scotia, blueberry grunt would definitely be in the running. It has even been celebrated on a Canadian postage stamp! This simple, sweet dish of light, fluffy biscuits and stewed blueberries is a hearty and welcome ending to any meal. The biscuit texture is traditionally crispy on top and very soft on the bottom from the blueberries. This upside-down version creates a lovely fluffy finish throughout and even more blueberries to enjoy! It is perfect for a cool early-autumn evening, when the blueberries are at their best and the teapot is still buried in the cupboard.

Blueberries:

4 cups fresh or frozen wild blueberries

2 lemons, zested and juiced, divided

⅓ cup sugar

2 Tbsp cornstarch

Pinch of ground nutmeg

Biscuits:

1¼ cups flour

2 Tbsp sugar

1½ tsp baking powder

½ tsp fine sea salt

2 Tbsp butter, cold, cubed

½ cup milk

1 egg

2 tsp white wine vinegar

Ice cream, for serving

For the Blueberries: Place all the blueberries in a large saucepan, drizzle with the lemon juice, and scatter half the zest over top. Cover the pan with its lid, place over medium-low heat, and cook for 3 to 5 minutes, just to soften the berries.

In a small bowl or measuring cup, combine the sugar, cornstarch, and nutmeg. Sprinkle over the berries and stir to combine. Increase the temperature to medium-high and bring the berries to a boil, stirring well. Stir for 1 minute and then remove from the heat. Set aside.

For the Biscuits: Preheat the oven to 375°F. Grease a 9-inch square baking pan or 2-quart baking dish with butter.

In a mixing bowl, whisk together the flour, sugar, baking powder, and salt. Using a pastry blender or two knives, cut the butter into the flour mixture until it has a coarse oatmeal texture. In a liquid measure or small bowl, whisk together the milk, egg, and vinegar. Pour this mixture into the flour mixture. Using a fork, mix gently to form a soft ball.

Divide the dough into four rounds, form each portion into a disc shape, and place in the prepared pan. Pour the blueberry sauce over the biscuit dough and sprinkle with the remaining lemon zest.

Bake for 20 minutes, until the blueberries are bubbling and the biscuits have risen.

Enjoy this warm with a scoop of ice cream.

STORAGE: The grunt will keep in an airtight container in the fridge for up to 3 days.

Haskap Sorbet

MAKES 3 CUPS

Steinhart Distillery's Haskap Cassis

The Lahave River Berry Farm has been growing and propagating certified organic haskaps on Nova Scotia's South Shore since 2013. Farm owners Melissa Mersey and Chris Berry currently have three main varieties of these prolific berries growing (each bush averages 1½ to 2 pounds of fruit per season), although as a research-focused operation for Atlantic-grown haskap, they're always testing many more varieties in their nursery. For those unfamiliar, haskap is a delicious berry that looks like an elongated blueberry and tastes like a lovely mix of sweet blueberry, tart raspberry, and rich blackberry with deeply herbaceous notes—or a bumbleberry pie in one morsel! The double skin creates a very inky purple dye, so the berries stain easily when handled. Packed full of antioxidants and healthful properties, they are lovely in everything from juice to liqueurs, jams, pies, and crumbles. This tasty and beautiful sorbet is just one of the ways we love to showcase this incredible fruit. (You'll need an ice cream maker for this recipe.)

4 cups frozen haskap berries

1 cup sugar

2 Tbsp lemon juice

Place the frozen berries in a saucepan and thaw at room temperature, letting all the juice collect in the pan.

Mash the berries gently and bring to a simmer over medium heat. Add the sugar, stir a few times, and allow it to dissolve fully. This takes about 5 minutes. Pour the berry mixture into a blender or food processor and pulse two to three times to break up the skin and flesh of the berries. Pour the mixture through a fine-mesh strainer set over a bowl. Using a spoon, press the mixture against the sides of the strainer to extract all the juice, leaving the skins and seeds behind. Discard these.

Add the lemon juice to the berry juice mixture. You should have approximately 3 cups of juice mixture. Cover with plastic wrap, making sure it touches the surface of the juice to prevent a skin from forming, and chill in the fridge for at least 3 hours, or up to 8 hours.

Prepare your ice cream maker according to the manufacturer's instructions. Pour the cooled juice into the ice cream maker and churn according to manufacturer's directions. Using a spatula, transfer to a 5- by 9-inch loaf tin or container and chill in the freezer, uncovered, for 6 hours or until very firm.

STORAGE: Once frozen, the ice cream will keep, covered, in the freezer for up to 6 months.

Drunken Plums

MAKES 1 (4-CUP) JAR

Ironworks Distillery's Vodka

½ cup sugar

1 tsp vanilla bean paste or 1 whole
  vanilla bean

½ lemon

½-inch knob fresh ginger

4 cups halved and pitted plums

2 sticks cinnamon

4 whole star anise

1 cup vodka (40% alcohol)

Ice cream, for serving (optional)

Preserving fruit in alcohol is a long-standing tradition that is still enjoyed across the Atlantic region today. It's the perfect method for saving the glut of fruits that abound at harvest time up and down the Annapolis Valley. The Bishop family of Noggins Corner Farm in Wolfville know a thing or two about fruit and its preservation. They've been growing their extensive orchards of plums, peaches, nectarines, and apricots, as well as fifteen varietals of pears and forty-two types of apples, for ten generations. The farm also has an educational centre where they host school groups and tours, enabling visitors to really understand where their food comes from. If you're lucky enough to grab a bushel or two of stone fruit from Noggins Corner Farm and can't quite eat it all fresh, use this recipe to savour the flavours of summer when the winter months descend.

Sterilize a 4-cup Mason jar, lid, and ring by washing them in the dishwasher or boiling them in water for 5 minutes. Set aside to air-dry. This will only take a few minutes.

In a small saucepan, bring the sugar and ¼ cup of water to a boil over medium-high heat. Turn down the heat to low, add the vanilla, and simmer for 1 minute. Remove from the heat.

Slice the lemon into ¼-inch rounds. Peel the ginger and cut it into thin slices.

Arrange the plums in the jar along with the lemons, ginger, cinnamon sticks, and star anise. Tap the jar on the counter to allow the plums and spice to settle. If using the vanilla bean, remove it from the syrup, slice it lengthwise, and scrape the seeds into the syrup.

Bring the syrup back to a boil over medium-high heat, add the vodka, turn down the heat, and simmer for 1 minute, just to warm the vodka. Slowly pour the syrup over the fruit and spices, leaving ¼ inch of headspace below the rim of the jar. Tap the jar gently on the counter to help release any air bubbles and ensure the fruit is submerged. Clean the rim, place the lid on the jar and tighten the ring down. Let sit at room temperature to cool for 24 hours. The lid will seal and pop. If the seal doesn't set, that's okay, as the alcohol will preserve the fruit as long as it is fully submerged. Place in a cool, dark spot to rest for 3 months to infuse the fruit and allow the spices to mingle, creating a delicious concoction.

Serve the plums on their own, or over a scoop of ice cream.

Prince Edward Island

Recipes

Prince Edward Island (PEI) is the kind of place that you want to get lost in, to wander the red dirt roads and immerse yourself in the deeply agrarian roots of its beautiful countryside. At just 140 miles long and between 2 and 40 miles wide, depending on where you're standing, it is the smallest of the Canadian provinces. It's where agriculture meets aquaculture, with little space in between. Here the terroir turns soft, with rolling hills of bucolic beauty cascading endlessly to where red and white sand beaches dip into the aqua waters of the Gulf of St. Lawrence and the Northumberland Strait. This is a place inhabited by generations of people tied to the food, land, and sea, and it's an artists' paradise too.

The provincial marketing campaign proclaims PEI to be Canada's Food Island, and it's not hard to see why. Almost every acre, both on land and at sea, is given over to food production. There are seemingly endless iron-rich red fields of potatoes, grains, and corn, and smaller-scale organic farms forming a patchwork quilt of colours. Other crops of note are the gloriously sweet strawberries of Penny's Farm & Garden, the deeply aromatic and delicious honey of Canoe Cove, and the crisply tart stalks of rhubarb found in almost every farm, garden plot, and backyard across the island. You'll also find dairy farms producing incredibly rich creams to be crafted into delicious products like the traditional Goudas from Glasgow Glen Farm or the famous Cows Creamery ice cream—a must-have on a hot sunny day. All across the undulating grassy green knolls, cattle ranchers are rearing the province's famous Blue Dot beef.

The aquatic offerings are equally impressive as the internationally acclaimed Malpeque oyster jostles for position with a certain red-headed lass as the island's most famous inhabitant. And for good reason: one taste of aqua farmer Johnny Flynn's glorious sweet and briny Colville Bay variety, in their beautiful deep-green shells, is all you'll need to understand why they call these treasures the fruits of the sea. Come for the oysters and stay to enjoy the plump, tender blue mussels that appear on almost every menu across the province, or the delicate scallops that need nothing more than to be lightly seasoned and basted with a bit of island-bred butter. As in all of the Atlantic provinces, traditional lobster dinners are held in almost every village community hall, and the camaraderie of donning a large bib and cracking into a juicy crustacean among a crowd of soon-to-be friends while the fiddle players lay down a jig is one of the greatest joys we experienced here.

Given the incredible natural abundance, it's no surprise that the province is also a hotbed of innovative restaurants and notable chefs. The immensely popular Blue Mussel Café has people lined up out the door for a taste of its traditional-fare-with-a-twist menu, while the kitchens at both The Pearl Eatery and Dalvay By The Sea offer diners an elegant cuisine showcasing the best of island seasonality. In Charlottetown, chef Irwin MacKinnon digs deep into homegrown flavours at Papa Joe's, while chefs like Lucy Morrow and Jane Crawford marry tradition and trend to craft some of the most uniquely creative dishes in town. And over at The Inn at Bay Fortune, chef Michael Smith offers guests a unique dining experience during his FireWorks Feast, where his love for PEI is evident in every bite. This vibrant culinary scene is an endless cycle of small-scale organic farms and fisheries collaborating with restaurants to feed people. In turn, these restaurants bring compost back to the farms to support the start of another growing season.

Come to PEI, taste the food, meet the chefs, and you'll quickly understand the strength of this tiny but impressive province. Canada's Food Island? We agree.

Crumpets

1½ cups milk

1 Tbsp sugar

2 tsp quick rise yeast

1 cup flour

1 tsp baking powder

½ tsp fine sea salt

4 Tbsp butter, divided

Jam, for serving

The English influence on PEI is unmistakable, so it's no wonder that crumpets slathered in jam are a staple here. This quick and easy recipe cooks up in minutes. The key is to make sure your batter is the right consistency and to grease the egg rings really well so the crumpets don't get stuck on the inside. Put on the kettle for a pot of tea and you'll be sitting down to breakfast in no time.

In a small pot over medium heat, warm the milk until it reaches 110°F to 120°F. Remove from the heat. Sprinkle the sugar over top and stir to combine, then sprinkle the yeast over top and allow it to sit for 10 minutes to bloom and start to froth.

In a mixing bowl, whisk together the flour, baking powder, and salt. Make a well in the centre of the flour and pour in the milk-yeast mixture. Starting in the centre and working outwards, whisk to incorporate all the flour. It will be quite watery, which is fine. Cover with a tea towel and let rest for 30 minutes in a warm, draft-free place, until bubbles start forming on the top and the batter has risen a little.

In a large, heavy-bottomed cast iron skillet over medium heat, melt 2 tablespoons of the butter. Use about 1 teaspoon of the remaining butter to generously grease the inside of four egg rings. Place the egg rings in the skillet. Scoop a generous ¼ cup of batter into each of the rings and let cook for 5 minutes, until bubbles start to appear on the surface and the sides look like they're setting. Using tongs, remove the rings from the crumpets and flip them over. Cook for an additional 30 to 45 seconds, to just brown and set the other side. Allow the rings to cool slightly, grease them again with butter, and repeat with the remaining batter.

To serve, generously butter the crumpets and slather them with jam.

STORAGE: The crumpets will keep in an airtight container in the fridge for up to 1 week or in the freezer for up to 3 months. To reheat, simply pop in the toaster for a few minutes and serve as described above.

Cream Biscuits & Honey

MAKES 8–10 BISCUITS

These cream biscuits are the perfect canvas for the fresh churned butter and complex honeys found across agrarian PEI. One of our favourite honey producers is Canoe Cove Honey, run by husband and wife team Mickael and Jennifer Jauneau. With just over two hundred hives, they have a deep passion for their bees, which support South Shore farmers with pollination services as well as creating unique flavour variations in their honey. The trick, as Mickael explains, is to extract from the hives multiple times a year. "At first it was because we didn't have the space or time to harvest just once a year," he says, "but now it's by choice." Having multiple harvests means that the flavours of the varying nectars collected by the bees are preserved and change with the seasons, giving wild blueberry honey in spring and evolving wildflower variations in summer and early autumn. Serve with an extra slathering of honey or your favourite preserve.

2 cups flour

1 Tbsp baking powder

¼ cup cold butter, cubed

1 egg

¾ cup heavy cream, plus more for wash

¼ cup + 2 Tbsp honey, divided

Preheat the oven to 400°F. Line a baking sheet with parchment paper.

In a mixing bowl, place the flour and baking powder. Whisk to sift. Add the butter. Using two knives or a pastry blender, cut in the butter until the mixture resembles coarse oatmeal.

In a small bowl, beat the egg and then whisk in the cream. Add the cream mixture and the ¼ cup of honey to the flour and mix with a wooden spoon to combine. The dough will be moist and slightly sticky, and will come together to form a stiff ball.

On a lightly floured surface, shape the dough into a circle about 1 inch thick. Press a 3-inch round cookie cutter into the dough to cut out circles and place them 1 inch apart on the prepared baking sheet. Re-form the remaining dough into a circle and cut out the remaining biscuits.

Brush the tops of the biscuits with the remaining 2 tablespoons of honey mixed with 2 tablespoons of hot water, making it more spreadable.

Bake for 10 minutes, until the tops are golden and crisp.

STORAGE: The biscuits will keep in an airtight container at room temperature for up to 4 days, although they are best enjoyed warm from the oven.

DEALING DAIRY

Driving down the dusty rolling back roads of PEI, flicking through the handful of island radio stations on the car's stereo, we're inundated with delightful crave-inducing jingles for locally produced ice cream, butter, and cheese. The ads are all for the ADL—Amalgamated Dairies Ltd.—a sixty-five-year-old dairy cooperative owned by over 160 of the island's dairy farmers, producers, processors, and retailers working at every level of the supply chain to keep the industry thriving. As we pull into Glasgow Glen Farm in New Glasgow, we're charmed by the sight of a beautiful barn conversion housing both a wood-fired bakery and the island's famous Gouda shop. Owner Jeff McCourt purchased the business in 2014 from Martina ter Beek, the original Cheese Lady and PEI's first artisanal cheesemaker. Jeff now produces just over 40,000 pounds of cheese a year and supplies more than thirty restaurants, as well as farmers' markets and retailers. Even with this volume, he doesn't export off-island.

Jeff leads us to the cheese cellar, a delightfully cool place to be on a scorching-hot July day. As he walks us through his Goudas—including a scrumptious stout-infused wheel and the gorgeous aged, smoked rounds—Jeff explains that all of the milk that he works with comes directly from his neighbours at Abelaine Farms. In Canada, each province regulates its local dairy industry, and PEI is unique in allowing direct farm-to-dairy delivery. This means that Jeff, in collaboration with the farmer, can choose feed types and schedules to control the butter fat content and protein in the milk

he uses while still being regulated and approved by the ADL. Since he's a chef by trade, it's no surprise that the details matter to him: having exactly the right milk is essential for consistency and quality in the cheese. Jeff explains, "It's all about working together. Abe Buttimer grows hay on my back field for the cows, then sends me his milk for cheese. It's all about the circles."

When we arrive at Abelaine, Abe and his wife Elaine are out tending their herd. Their passion for their craft is immediately evident as the happy Holsteins come to say hello for a head scratch while we walk through the barn and pastures. The cows here wear activity monitors to ensure their welfare 24/7, and they eat only first-cut hay, fresh grass, homegrown barley, and freshly fermented silage. The Buttimers have been farming their whole lives—they both grew up on dairy farms—and they're currently directors on the ADL board. For them, like Jeff at Glasgow Glen, the cycle of raising healthy, happy cows to deliver superior milk for the neighbouring cheesemaker is of utmost importance. Knowing where their milk is going, how it's being treated, and having control over the process is what it's all about.

After a delicious Glasgow Glen lunch of wood-fired pizza topped with Jeff's favourite Gouda, we head on our way. As we drive along, another ADL advertisement comes on the radio: "Come get an ice cream made with fresh PEI cream!" On this sultry summer day, it's the best idea ever, and we start looking for the closest stand. The dairy on PEI is truly irresistible.

Fish Cakes *with* Bacon Bourbon Tomato Jam

SERVES 4

Mercator Vineyards' Tidal Bay

Perched on the edge of the bay in North Rustico, the Blue Mussel Café is as picturesque inside as it is out. There are big windows overlooking the harbour, the white-washed tables are filled with customers chatting over tasty meals, and the fresh ocean air wafts in, blending seamlessly with the smell of the dishes coming out of the kitchen for a full-on sensory experience. The hour-long wait to get in is entirely worth it. Owner Christine McQuaid comes to greet us, explaining as she's clearing tables that given what is locally available, freshness here is not just a luxury, but also the only sensible choice. The restaurant serves only the freshest seafood, often having multiple deliveries a day from producers in peak season. Creative yet simple, and always delicious, these fish cakes with their bacon-y tomato jam are just a taste of what this local gem has to offer.

Bacon Bourbon Tomato Jam:

6 strips bacon

1 small Spanish onion

2 cloves garlic

1 cup chopped tomato

2 sprigs thyme

1 sprig rosemary

½ tsp dried chili flakes

1 oz bourbon

½ cup maple syrup

¼ cup balsamic vinegar

For the Bacon Bourbon Tomato Jam: Chop the bacon into small pieces, about 1 inch long. Chop the onion and mince the garlic. Place the bacon pieces in a skillet over medium heat and fry until the fat has rendered and the bacon is starting to crisp, 3 to 4 minutes. Add the onions and garlic and cook until translucent and soft, about 2 to 3 minutes. Add the tomatoes, thyme, rosemary, and chili flakes. Using a spoon or spatula, gently mash the tomato to draw out all juices. Allow the mixture to come to a boil, and reduce by half, stirring occasionally. Deglaze the pan with the bourbon, scraping up any brown bits from the bottom. Add the maple syrup and vinegar, turn down the heat to medium-low, and simmer, stirring constantly, until the mixture has reduced by one-third and is quite thick, just pulling away from the bottom of the pan. Remove from the heat and allow to cool slightly. Transfer to a blender and blend until almost completely smooth. Transfer to an airtight container and allow to cool before placing in the fridge until ready to use.

(continued)

Fish Cakes:

½ lb white fish fillet

2 Tbsp dry white wine

1 lemon, zest and juice

1 lb russet potatoes, peeled and cubed

¼ cup mayonnaise

2 Tbsp grainy Dijon mustard

2 Tbsp chopped cilantro

2 Tbsp chopped parsley

Sea salt and black pepper

1 cup flour

2 eggs

1 cup panko-style breadcrumbs

1–2 cups neutral oil, for frying

For the Fish Cakes: Place the fish in a small pot, add just enough cold water to cover it, and then pour in the wine and lemon juice. Set over low heat and simmer until the fish is naturally flaking and fully cooked through, 5 to 8 minutes. Remove from the heat, drain the water, and place the fish in a small mixing bowl. Place in the fridge until ready to assemble.

Cook the potatoes until fork-tender, 5 to 7 minutes. Using a masher or hand mixer, mash the potatoes in the pot. Mix in the mayonnaise and mustard, and then add the lemon zest, cilantro, and parsley. Using a wooden spoon or spatula, mix in the fish and season with salt and pepper to taste.

Transfer the mixture to a bowl and place in the fridge, uncovered, for 30 minutes to chill and set. When you're ready to cook, remove the potato mixture from the fridge and form it into eight patties.

Prepare a dredging station to coat the fish cakes. In one shallow bowl, place the flour; in a second, whisk the eggs; and in a third, place the breadcrumbs.

To prevent your fingers from becoming too sticky while dredging or breading, use one hand for handling the dry ingredients and the other for the wet. Dip one fish cake in the flour and turn to coat, then dip it in the egg and coat in breadcrumbs. Place on a plate and repeat with the remaining fish cakes. If you like, you can freeze the fish cakes in an airtight container at this point.

To Serve: In a skillet over medium heat, heat ½ inch of oil. Fry the fish cakes until golden and crisp, 2 to 3 minutes per side. Give the oil 1 to 2 minutes to return to temperature between batches.

Serve immediately with a dollop of the jam.

STORAGE: The fish cakes will keep in an airtight container in the fridge for up to 3 days once cooked or in the freezer for up to 3 months. Allow frozen fish cakes to thaw in the fridge before cooking. The jam will keep in an airtight container in the fridge for up to 1 week.

Recipe contributed by Jamie Power, Blue Mussel Café

Fresh Whipped Tartar Sauce

MAKES 1½ CUPS

Every Atlantic cook has their own version of tartar sauce, and nothing compares to a freshly whipped batch. The choice of seasonings is both wide and loudly debated—from fresh dill to horseradish, paprika to mustard, capers to green relish—and although we tried many versions, we're sure we didn't manage to try them all. Our personal favourite so far is to make it with eggs instead of mayonnaise, as this makes for a light and fluffy sauce perfect for dunking crisp chips or fried fish in, or mixing with lobster for a simple sandwich spread, or . . . Actually, the list is endless. The seasoning mix in this recipe is our combination of choice, but feel free to make it your own!

2 egg yolks, at room temperature

2 Tbsp lemon juice, at room temperature, divided

1 Tbsp white wine vinegar

1 tsp creamy Dijon mustard, at room temperature

1 cup neutral oil

1 tsp sea salt

1 tsp white pepper

½ tsp paprika

2 medium dill pickles

1 Tbsp capers

2 Tbsp chopped dill

Warm a heavy-bottomed mixing bowl under hot running water and wipe dry. Add the yolks and whisk for 30 seconds to 1 minute, until they are a light to creamy pale-yellow colour and starting to leave ribbons behind as you whisk. Add 1 tablespoon of the lemon juice, the vinegar, and mustard and whisk for 1 minute to fully combine and emulsify. Starting with droplets at a time, slowly begin to add the oil, whisking constantly to ensure the yolk is absorbing it. Once 1 to 2 tablespoons of the oil have been absorbed and the mixture is light in colour and thickened slightly, pour in the rest of the oil in a very fine, steady stream, whisking constantly. The mixture will be very thick, creamy white, and the consistency of thickly whipped cream. Whisk in the remaining 1 tablespoon of the lemon juice, the salt, pepper, and paprika.

Dice the pickles and roughly chop the capers, squeezing them to drain off any excess juices. Using a spatula, mix the pickles, capers, and dill into the egg yolk mixture. Chill, covered, in the fridge for at least 1 hour to allow the flavours to develop before serving.

STORAGE: The tartar sauce will keep in an airtight container in the fridge for up to 2 weeks.

Recipe pictured on page 12

Grandma's Mustard Pickle

MAKES 4 CUPS

2 large cucumbers, skin on

1 white onion

1 red bell pepper

1 cup grated green cabbage

2 Tbsp pickling salt

1 cup sugar

1 cup distilled vinegar

1 Tbsp black or yellow mustard seeds

¼ cup flour

3 Tbsp prepared mustard

2 tsp ground turmeric

Tart and bright, in more ways than one, these mustard pickles are nostalgia in a jar. Emily's grandma made them every summer when the vegetables were at their best and always talked about how she had learned the recipe from her mother during her childhood on a farm. Pickles are a staple in any East Coast pantry, and these are tart, sweet, and a little saucy. They make a perfect pairing for a charcuterie board to balance the richness of cheese or pâté, or try them as a spread on a roast beef sandwich or a simple glaze for seared pork medallions. This recipe is easily quadrupled to stock up the cupboards, or easily pared down to make just enough for a meal if desired.

Sterilize two (2-cup) Mason jars, lids, and rings by washing them in the dishwasher or boiling them in water for 5 minutes. Set aside to air-dry. This will only take a few minutes.

Finely slice the cucumber and onion and dice the bell pepper. Toss them in a large mixing bowl with the cabbage to combine. Sprinkle the picking salt over top and gently mix to combine. Let sit, covered, at room temperature for 10 to 12 hours. Drain the vegetables, squeezing out as much liquid as possible.

In a large pot, whisk together the sugar, vinegar, and mustard seeds. Add the vegetables and bring to a boil over high heat. Turn down the heat to medium and gently boil, uncovered, for 30 minutes, stirring occasionally.

In a small mixing bowl, combine the flour, mustard, and turmeric. Adding 1 tablespoon of water at a time, whisk until a light, lump-free slurry forms. Add the slurry to the pot of vegetables and, stirring constantly, cook over medium heat until fully combined and the cooked vegetables are starting to thicken slightly. Bring back to a rolling boil and boil for 1 minute.

Pour the hot cooked vegetables into the prepared jars, leaving ¼ inch of headspace. Clean the rims, place the lids on the jars and tighten the rings down. Let sit at room temperature to cool for 24 hours. The lids will seal and pop. If a lid doesn't seal, store the jar in the fridge immediately.

STORAGE: The sealed jars will keep in a dark cupboard for up to 3 months. Once opened, they will keep in the fridge for up to 1 month.

Recipe pictured on page 12

CULTIVATING OYSTERS

Five years of growth, with countless touch points along the way, culminating in the delivery of one pleasurable, tasty moment: that is the life of an oyster, by far the most celebrated of PEI's seafoods. Years ago, a blight came through the waters surrounding the province and killed almost all of the oysters, except the Malpeque Bay strain. These became the seed oysters for the rest of the island and are now the prominent variety cultivated throughout PEI. Each bay, with its tidal influences, seaweeds, and available sunlight, offers oyster farmers the opportunity to fine-tune their cultivation, resulting in a wide variety of flavours and sizes. Most of the PEI oysters are thus named after the bay in which they're raised, but the Malpeque is the foundation for all. As one of the few aquaculture sectors that are continuously increasing their stocks, these humble bivalves are quite the local heroes.

At the oyster farm in Colville Bay, Johnny Flynn of the Colville Bay Oyster Company, strolls up the beach in his rubber boots, jeans, and a red sweatshirt cut off at the elbows—probably to avoid the inconvenience of soggy sleeves, given that he spends so much time reaching into the water. He gives us a firm handshake, a smile, and an invitation to hop into the boat heading out to the open waters of the bay. He lowers a basket and drags it gently along the bottom of the ocean, stirring the silt slightly in the crystal clear waters. When the basket comes up, it's filled to the brim with beautiful, deep-green oysters—a unique attribute endowed by the oyster's main food source: a phytoplankton that grows in the bay. Johnny explains that "each oyster filters 50 gallons of water per day to capture and feed off the algae. It's the reason why most of the sheltered PEI bays are so pristine." The high tidal movements constantly pull in the cold Atlantic waters, creating the perfect environment for the oysters to live in and delivering an endless source of nutrients for the oysters to absorb.

Oysters spawn once a year, producing millions of spat each time, and repeat the process three or four times before being harvested. In the uncontrolled conditions of open water, less than 1% of the spat typically become full-size oysters, so Johnny has developed a protected nursery in which to cultivate the Colville Bay variety. He mixes lime and concrete together to cover the cones and then places them in the bay to attract the spat, which attach themselves to the cones and start to grow into tiny oysters. After six months the baby oysters are knocked off, placed into big, tea bag–like sacks, and set to grow in the sheltered waters of the bay. For two years, the oysters grow undisturbed, protected from predators. The floats are turned over every week so that the oysters can be checked and allowed to absorb some sunshine. Every few months they are "tumbled" to knock off the thin edges of the shells, encouraging them to grow deep pockets and succulent forms. They're also checked for shape, sized for growth, and moved into increasingly larger bags. Once the oysters' shells are fully formed and large enough to not be a target for predators, they're spread out in the bay and left to grow naturally for another two to three years.

Being a lobsterman and local restauranteur as well, Johnny lives his life by the sea. He loves the ocean and is grateful for all that it has given to his family. "If you respect her and take care of her, she will take care of you too," he explains, and it seems the sea has indeed taken care of the Flynns. Almost all of Johnny's family are employed in this family business in one way or another. It's important to Johnny that there are ample opportunities for his family to stay on the island and prosper. The humble little Colville Bay oyster is more than enough to allow Johnny's family to thrive while investing in a sustainable industry, their community, and the island's economy at large.

Back on shore, Johnny reaches into a basket and pulls out an oyster the size of his palm. "These were spread here three years ago," he explains. "They're five years old now, mature and ready for market." He takes an oyster knife from his pocket and pops the beautiful green shell open, revealing the sweet, creamy flesh inside. The taste is as delicious as anticipated: sweet and rich with a slightly briny, cucumber-like taste and a gentle tang of minerals. They taste of the sea, of the earth, and of all the care that went into their cultivation. It's a taste Johnny and his family should be proud of, and as he pops another open and offers it to us, his beaming grin at our delight proves they are.

Freshly Shucked Oysters *with* Rhubarb Mignonette

SERVES 2

Jost Vineyards' Selkie Rosé

When we first met oysterman Johnny Flynn, our full day of interviews was delightfully disrupted as he ushered us out onto the oyster boats to learn about oyster cultivation. Upon arriving back to shore, we were invited to come along for a full tour of Eastern PEI, the area that he proudly calls home. It's easy to see why Johnny is so delighted with the place—it's incredibly beautiful!

Rhubarb and oysters may sound like strange bedfellows, but they actually marry perfectly. The crisp tang of the fruit paired with the rich creaminess of a fresh PEI oyster is one of the greatest flavour-meets-texture combinations we have encountered, and it is definitely one of our favourite ways to enjoy both. We especially love Johnny's Colville Bay variety. Deep-pocketed, perfectly briny, and light on the mineral finish, these creamy delights show why PEI oysters are prized worldwide.

---

3 Tbsp finely diced rhubarb

2 Tbsp peeled and finely diced cucumber

1 Tbsp finely chopped shallot

½ cup champagne vinegar

1 Tbsp sugar

½ tsp sea salt

12 freshly shucked oysters

2 Tbsp freshly grated horseradish

1 lemon, cut into 12 thin wedges

In a 1-cup Mason jar, place the rhubarb, cucumbers, and shallots. Pour the vinegar over top and then add the sugar and salt. Close the lid and shake gently until the sugar and salt have dissolved. Chill in the fridge for at least 1 hour before serving.

When ready to serve, place the shucked oysters on a bed of crushed ice and serve with the mignonette, horseradish, and lemon wedges.

STORAGE: The oysters need to be enjoyed the day they are shucked. The mignonette will keep in an airtight container in the fridge for up to 1 week.

Heirloom Tomato Sandwich *with* Black Garlic Butter

SERVES 4

Gahan's 6 Hours of Sun Cider

Is there anything better than a tomato sandwich in the peak of the summer season? Honestly, we think not. Fresh white bakery bread slathered in whipped black garlic butter and topped with thickly sliced ripe tomatoes is elegant simplicity at its finest. Black garlic is aged for twenty-one days under specific temperature and humidity conditions, then rests for five days to air out, creating the best version of roasted garlic, still in the bulb. It's not fermented, as is often assumed. At Eureka Garlic in Norboro, Amy Picketts explains how their turban garlic is soft and easily mashes into a paste, unlike the hard black garlic that's commercially available. When paired with fresh-from-the-vine PEI tomatoes, it is utter perfection!

½ cup butter, softened

1 bulb black garlic

8 thick slices white bakery bread

4 fresh heirloom tomatoes

Sea salt and black pepper

Place the butter in a small bowl. Using a whisk or a hand mixer, whip it until it's smooth and light. Squeeze in the bulb of garlic and continue to whisk until combined.

Generously smear the butter on one side of each slice of bread, getting right to the edges. Slice the tomatoes thickly and lay them on the bread to cover it. Sprinkle with salt and pepper to taste and serve immediately.

STORAGE: The sandwiches are best enjoyed the day they are made. The black garlic butter will keep in an airtight container in the fridge for up to 2 weeks.

Golden Beet & Apple Soup

SERVES 4

Newman Estate Winery's Seyval Blanc

2 lb golden beets, greens removed
  and beets cut in half

2 Tbsp butter

½ cup diced onion

1 lb sweet apples, peeled, cored,
  and quartered

¼ cup apple cider vinegar

2 Tbsp sugar

5 cups chicken or vegetable stock

Sea salt and black pepper

1 Tbsp liquid honey

½ cup Greek yogurt

Flat-leaf parsley or dill fronds, for
  serving

This may sound like a strange combination, but believe us, the deep earthiness of the golden beets is a perfect pairing for the sweet, crisp flavour of fresh late-summer apples. We like to triple the recipe and freeze some for the colder autumn months—just be sure to omit the honey and yogurt until you thaw and are ready to eat the soup. If you can't find golden beets, purple ones will work just as well and make for a gorgeous deeply pink soup.

Preheat the oven to 375°F.

Wrap the beets in a double layer of aluminum foil and crimp the package to seal. Roast for 1 hour, or until fork-tender. Remove from the oven and let rest until the beets are cool enough to handle. Once cooled, the skins of the beets should slide off easily. Roughly chop the beets into 1-inch chunks and set aside to cool.

In a large soup pot over medium heat, melt the butter and then add the onions. Stirring often, sauté the onions for 6 to 7 minutes, until softened and translucent. Add the apples, vinegar, and sugar and continue to cook for another 1 to 2 minutes. Add the beets and stock. Bring to a boil over medium-high heat, turn down the heat to medium and simmer until the apples are softened and begin to break down, 15 to 20 minutes. Remove the soup from the heat and let cool completely.

Once the soup is cooled, blend it until it is creamy and smooth. Return the soup to the pot and warm through. Season with salt and pepper to taste.

To serve, divide the soup between four serving bowls. Stir the honey into the yogurt and place a dollop in the middle of each bowl of soup. Top with parsley or dill fronds.

STORAGE: The soup, without the honey and yogurt, will keep in an airtight container in the fridge for up to 1 week.

Scallop Crudo

SERVES 4

*Double Hill Cidery's Nomad
 Sparkling Cider*

When chef Lucy Morrow took over the kitchen at Terre Rouge, now called Terra Rossa, in downtown Charlottetown at just twenty-three years old, she dove in headfirst. She has since become a culinary rock star, offering the very best of seasonal meals at her local pop-up dinners. Her success is rooted in her passion for creating and collaborating as well as showcasing the very best that PEI has to offer. Lucy lights up when she talks about organic farm-to-table cuisine. Her vibrancy is contagious as she describes the province's changing food scene, and the importance of developing relationships with the farmers and producers who fill her kitchen with the best ingredients available. This scallop dish is a perfect example of Lucy's philosophy: Keep it simple yet innovative, and above all, fresh and delicious!

½ cup white vinegar

1½ tsp honey

½ tsp sea salt

1 small radish

1 small shallot

½ stalk rhubarb

½ stalk celery

8 fresh Digby scallops, shelled
 (page 55)

In a small bowl, whisk together the vinegar, honey, and salt until the honey and salt dissolve. Chill, uncovered, in the fridge until needed.

Finely dice the radish, shallot, rhubarb, and celery. Keep each ingredient separate until ready to serve so the flavour of the shallot doesn't overwhelm the other flavours too much.

When you're ready to serve, wash and pat dry the scallops. Slice the scallops in half or into thirds, making small medallions. Chill in the freezer for 5 minutes. Toss the radish, shallot, rhubarb, and celery pieces together in a small bowl.

Remove the scallops from the freezer and place three or four slices in the centre of a shallow serving bowl or plate. Spoon just enough of the vinegar mixture over the scallops to cover the bottom of the bowl. Repeat with the remaining scallops. Divide the minced vegetables evenly between the plates, sprinkling them over the scallops. Serve immediately.

STORAGE: This dish is best enjoyed the moment it's made. The vinegar mixture will keep on its own in an airtight container in the fridge for up to 2 weeks.

Recipe contributed by Lucy Morrow

Beach Chair Mussels

SERVES 2–4

PEI Brewing Company's Beach Chair Lager

2 Tbsp olive oil

1 Tbsp butter

½ cup diced sweet onion

2 cloves garlic, thinly sliced

1 tsp sea salt

2 tsp honey

1–2 tsp hot sauce

1 (473 ml) can PEI Brewing Company's Beach Chair Lager

2 lb fresh PEI blue mussels in shells, bearded

½ cup chopped parsley

Crusty bread, for serving

Mussels and lager are a classic East Coast combination, and our top choice of beer for this recipe is PEI Brewing Company's Beach Chair Lager. With a perfect balance of hops and malt, this homegrown brew pairs perfectly with the sweet, sumptuous mussels that grow in abundance around the island. The resulting liquor is so delicious, you'll want to be sure you have lots of crusty bread on hand to soak up every last drop.

In a Dutch oven over medium-high heat, place the oil and butter. Once the butter has melted, add the onions and garlic and sauté for about 3 minutes, until the onions become translucent. Add the salt, followed by the honey and hot sauce, and simmer for 1 to 2 more minutes. Slowly pour in the beer, making sure it doesn't foam, and bring the mixture to a low boil.

Add the mussels and cover the pan. Steam the mussels for about 7 minutes, until they are all open. Discard any that don't open. Portion the mussels into serving bowls, top each with a few ladlefuls of the steaming liquor, garnish with parsley, and serve immediately with lots of crusty bread. Serve immediately.

Grilled Potato & Corn Salad

Somehow there always seem to be leftover potatoes on the table after a hearty summer meal shared with friends and family. This recipe is a great way to enjoy them as a perfect lunch or snack the next day. Served cold or warm, it's a summer favourite either way.

2 ears of corn, husk on

1 small potato (such as Yukon Gold or Kennebec)

1 lb (about 4 cups) baby potatoes

½ cup olive oil, divided

⅓ cup vegetable stock

3 Tbsp grainy Dijon mustard

2 Tbsp white wine vinegar

1 Tbsp dill, plus more for garnish

Sea salt and black pepper

Preheat the grill to high heat or the oven to 425°F.

Soak the ears of corn in a large bowl of warm water.

Meanwhile, bring a large pot of lightly salted water to a boil over high heat. Peel and cube the small potato and boil in the salted water until soft and cooked through, 4 to 5 minutes. Using a slotted spoon, transfer the potato cubes to a bowl and set aside to cool completely.

Drain and rinse the baby potatoes under cold running water, pat dry with a towel, and then toss with 2 tablespoons of the oil.

If using a grill: Transfer the baby potatoes to a grill basket and place them on the grill. Place the ears of corn on the grill beside the basket. Grill until the baby potatoes are well browned and the corn is charred, 15 to 20 minutes.

If using the oven: Line a rimmed baking sheet with parchment paper and roast the baby potatoes and corn for 15 to 20 minutes.

In a medium bowl with an immersion blender, or bowl of a blender, or blender, blend the boiled potato cubes, the remaining oil, the stock, mustard, vinegar, dill, and salt and pepper to taste until the mixture is creamy and smooth.

Transfer the grilled potatoes to a serving bowl. Discard the husk from the ears of corn and, using a sharp knife, slice the kernels off the cob in strips and add to the serving bowl. Toss with the dressing until well coated. Garnish with dill and serve immediately.

STORAGE: This salad is delicious served cold as well as hot and will keep in an airtight container in the fridge for up to 1 week.

GROWING POTATOES

The PEI potato might be the most humble and yet honoured ingredient to come from Atlantic Canada. This tiny island produces 25% of Canada's potato crop, growing over one hundred different varieties that ship to more than twenty countries. It is the largest commercial crop grown here and a significant contributor to the province's economy.

One of the things that makes PEI ideal for growing potatoes is its iconic deep-red soil, which has a very high mineral content and a unique concentration of iron. The soil also has a perfect concentration of moisture, balanced with light and heat, which allows the farmers to grow crops of quality potatoes with consistent yields. The proximity to the sea keeps the plants aerated, with the ocean breeze naturally keeping diseases at bay. Over 85,000 acres of potatoes cover the landscape, and almost every road on PEI is within view of a potato field. The pastoral landscape lends itself well to the rolling red furrows, topped with bright-green bushy plants and waving white and purple flowers.

As we sit at the picnic table in his barn, Bill Cousins explains that white flowers indicate white or yellow potatoes and purple indicate purple potatoes. It seems intuitive, although somehow not obvious at first glance. Bill grew up on his family farm in Kensington, PEI, so the iron in the soil runs deep in his blood too. When he first started growing potatoes in 1977, the processing side was just developing and most potatoes were sold directly from the farmer to consumers. Now it's the opposite: the processors essentially control the industry, as they manage all of the distribution. If the processors decided to leave, there wouldn't be a market for this beloved crop.

It's mid-July, and Bill and the other farmers are in desperate need of rain. He's doubtful now that the harvest will yield enough to produce a profit. His goal, if conditions are optimal, is to grow in excess of 18 tons of potatoes per acre. "There is still hope," he says, "if the rains come." Having planted purchased seed potatoes, his expectation of plant to harvest is a weight ratio of one to ten. As the cost to plant is consistent, the higher the yield the better the profits. Most of what is grown is table stock: round white, long white, yellow, and russet potatoes, which came to the island in the 1970s. Kennebec potatoes, the first to be harvested, are the preferred variety for commercial french fries.

Even though the iron in the soil has the perfect mineral composition for growing potatoes, as the climate is changing the crop is shifting too. Hotter, longer summers and wetter, longer springs have pushed harvest later, making farming even more of a challenge. When the average sale price for the farmer is about 10 cents a pound, every potato matters, and losing crop to drought and frost can be devastating. The processor has specifications for the size and weight of the potatoes, and if those aren't met when the potatoes are being sorted, the potatoes become cattle feed and the year's income is lost.

PEI is a small province, and thus the amount of land a company or individual can own is highly regulated to prevent monopolies. In many ways this creates more camaraderie among the farmers, but there are challenges too. Crop rotation to keep the soil healthy is crucial, and planting potatoes in the same field year after year isn't sustainable. With a limited number of acres on which to grow, working together as a community is the only viable option for farmers. The extensive and expensive equipment is often shared, as is the harvest of potatoes from the land.

Later in the year, while driving by a field during harvest, we pull over to take some pictures and a man waves us over to find out what we're doing. He motions for us follow him down the road, where we find a mountain of potatoes being sorted and piled in a barn for winter storage. The lot is filled with willing workers, happy and jovial; the harvest is indeed a good one. The rains came when they needed it most, and the potatoes are coming in to feed families across Canada for yet another year.

Lobster Potato Nachos

SERVES 4

Moth Lane Brewing's Weizen Up B'ye

This recipe combines roasted potatoes and the decadence of a lobster dinner into one simple, delicious comfort food! PEI potatoes, with their crisp outside, fluffy, light texture, and deep, earthy flavour, are second to none for this dish. These are a popular request at game night, so we're making them all the time . . . which is OK with us!

2 large baking potatoes

4 Tbsp olive oil, divided

1 tsp sea salt

1 tsp black pepper

½ tsp dried parsley

½ tsp dried oregano

4 strips bacon

1 lb freshly cooked lobster meat

2 Roma tomatoes

1 green bell pepper

2 cups grated cheddar cheese

1 cup Greek yogurt

2 Tbsp lime juice

½ tsp sea salt

½ tsp smoked paprika

2 Tbsp chopped cilantro

Hot sauce (optional)

Place the baking rack on the lowest shelf and preheat the oven to 400°F. Line a baking sheet with parchment paper.

Wash and scrub the potatoes, leaving the skins on. Using a mandolin, slice the potatoes ¼ inch thick. If you're using a knife, slice them as thinly as possible. Place the potato slices in a single layer on the prepared baking sheet. Drizzle with 2 tablespoons of the olive oil and shake the pan slightly to coat the slices as evenly as possible. Turn the potatoes over and drizzle with the remaining oil. Sprinkle with the salt, pepper, parsley, and oregano. Bake for 20 minutes, until crispy, golden brown, and curling at the edges.

While the potatoes are in the oven, line a plate with paper towel. In a skillet over medium heat, fry the bacon for 5 to 8 minutes, until crispy. Transfer to the prepared plate to drain off any grease. Let the bacon cool slightly. Once it is cool enough to touch, crumble the bacon and set aside. Chop the lobster meat, tomatoes (discarding the seeds), and bell pepper into bite-sized pieces, and move to a plate in preparation for assembly.

Let the potatoes cool slightly on the baking sheet. Line an ovenproof serving plate with parchment paper. Arrange one-third of the potatoes in a single layer on the plate and sprinkle with one-third of the lobster, tomatoes, peppers, and cheese. Repeat the layers twice more, ending with a layer of cheese. Move the oven rack to the middle of the oven and preheat the oven to 350°F. Bake the nachos for 10 minutes, until the cheese is fully melted.

Meanwhile, in a small bowl, whisk together the yogurt, lime juice, salt, and paprika until fully incorporated. Add the cilantro and hot sauce to taste, if using.

When the nachos are done baking, turn on the broiler and crisp up the cheese until bubbly and golden brown.

Remove the nachos from the oven. Top with a dollop of lime cream, place more on the side for dipping, and serve immediately.

Smoked Cheddar & Oyster Pot Pies

SERVES 6

Rossignol Estate Winery's L'Acadie Blanc

The oysters from PEI are arguably some of the best in the world. Sweet, creamy, and with just the perfect amount of brine, they lend themselves just as well to savoury cooked dishes as they do to being slurped straight from the shell. And, yes, they're perfect in these cheesy pot pies. Cows Creamery's Appletree Smoked Cheddar pairs perfectly with the sweet oysters and salty bacon. This is comfort food at its best.

---

2 cups freshly, shucked oysters, liquor reserved

4 thick strips bacon, cut into bite-sized pieces

¼ cup dry white wine

2 Tbsp lemon juice

3 Tbsp butter

1 medium onion, diced

½ cup diced carrots

½ cup diced celery

1 clove garlic, minced

¼ cup flour

¾ cup chicken stock

¾ cup whipping cream

2 cups grated smoked cheddar cheese (we like the Appletree Smoked Cheddar by Cows Creamery)

1 Tbsp Old Bay Seasoning

1 tsp black pepper

½ tsp ground nutmeg

Sea salt

1 (1 lb) package puff pastry

1 egg

Place the baking rack on the lowest shelf of the oven and preheat the oven to 400°F.

Chop the oysters into 1-inch chunks, place in a bowl, and reserve ⅓ cup of the oyster liquor.

In a large pot or Dutch oven over medium heat, fry the bacon until crispy and golden brown, 6 to 7 minutes. Transfer to a paper towel–lined plate. Drain off all but 3 tablespoons of fat from the pot.

Deglaze the pot by adding the wine and lemon juice, stirring to scrape off any bits from the bottom. Add the butter, followed by the onions, carrots, and celery, and sauté for 3 to 4 minutes. Add the garlic and cook for 1 minute more. Stirring constantly, add the flour and cook for an additional 2 to 3 minutes, until the flour begins to bubble. Continuing to stir, slowly add the stock. Add the reserved oyster liquor and cream, stirring to incorporate. Add the cheese, Old Bay Seasoning, pepper, nutmeg, and salt to taste. Stirring constantly, cook until the mixture thickens to a consistency of a thick pancake batter, 3 to 4 minutes.

Remove the pot from the heat and stir in the oysters and bacon. Lightly grease six (12-ounce) ramekins. Divide the mixture evenly between them. Cut the pastry into six circles slightly larger than the ramekins. Top each ramekin with a circle of pastry. In a small bowl, whisk the egg with 1 tablespoon of water. Using a pastry brush, spread this egg wash over the pastry.

Bake until browned and bubbly, 30 to 35 minutes. Let stand for 15 minutes. Then serve immediately.

Cider-Braised Pork Tacos *with* Rhubarb Salsa

SERVES 6

*Annapolis Cider Company's Rhubarb
Ginger Cider*

This is our favourite dish to serve on a cool evening in early June. Rhubarb is at its peak then and longing to be enjoyed to the fullest, like in this tangy, tart salsa alongside tender and delicious pork tacos. The Rhubarb Ginger Cider from the Annapolis Cider Company is the perfect braise for the meat, as it enhances the subtle sweetness of the pork—just be sure to enjoy a pint of it while you eat.

Braised Pork:

2–3 lb boneless pork shoulder

2 tsp ground cumin

2 tsp ground coriander

1 tsp sea salt

½ tsp black pepper

¼ cup olive oil

1 small red onion, sliced

1 red bell pepper, sliced

2 cloves garlic, crushed

1 bay leaf

½ cup chopped cilantro

3 cups Rhubarb Ginger Cider

Rhubarb Salsa:

3 stalks rhubarb, diced

1 small red onion, diced

1 small jalapeño, seeded and diced

¼ cup lime juice

Pinch of sea salt

½ cup chopped cilantro

For the Braised Pork: Pat the pork shoulder dry with paper towel. In a small bowl, combine the cumin, coriander, salt, and pepper. Evenly coat the pork with this rub. Place the pork in an airtight container and chill in the fridge for at least 2 hours, or up to 24 hours, to allow the spices to infuse into the meat. Remove the meat from the fridge 30 minutes before cooking. When you're ready to cook, cut it into 3- to 4-inch cubes.

Preheat the oven to 350°F.

In a Dutch oven over medium heat, place the oil. Add the onions, bell peppers, and garlic and sauté until translucent and starting to brown, 2 to 3 minutes. Add the pork and cook, stirring often, until the vegetables are well browned and the meat is seared on all sides, 5 to 7 minutes. Add the bay leaf, sprinkle the mixture with the cilantro, and then pour the cider over top. Bring to a boil. Cover and roast in the oven until the meat is falling apart and very tender, 1½ to 2 hours. Check the liquid level every so often. If at any point it appears to be low, add ¼ to ½ cup of water, or cider if you have any left over. Remove the pork from the oven and discard the bay leaf. Shred the meat using tongs or two forks, and transfer to a serving platter.

For the Rhubarb Salsa: While the pork is cooking, toss the rhubarb, onion, and jalapeño together in a mixing bowl. Drizzle with the lime juice, add the salt, and mix. Add the cilantro and stir until fully combined. Cover and chill in the fridge for at least 1 hour, or until ready to serve, to let the flavours develop.

(continued)

Cilantro Lime Crema:

1 cup Greek yogurt

1 tsp ground cumin

½ tsp sea salt

2 Tbsp lime juice

½ cup chopped cilantro

To Serve:

2 large avocados

18 tortillas

For the Cilantro Lime Crema: In a small mixing bowl, whisk together the yogurt, cumin, salt, and lime juice until completely smooth. Add the cilantro and stir until fully combined. Cover and chill in the fridge for at least 1 hour, or until ready to serve, to let the flavours develop.

To Serve: Peel and pit the avocado and slice lengthwise. Place one or two tortillas on each serving plate, lay a slice of avocado on each one, and top with a generous helping of braised pork, salsa, and crema. Or put all the elements on the table in individual dishes and let everyone build their own!

STORAGE: The pork will keep in the fridge in an airtight container for up to 4 days. The salsa and crema will keep in separate airtight containers in the fridge for up to 1 week. Once assembled, the tacos are best enjoyed the day they are made.

133

Crispy Fried Chicken *with* Pad Thai Fries

SERVES 4 (MAKES ABOUT
1½ CUPS OF BUTTER
AND 1½ CUPS OF MAYO)

Red Island Cider's Father Walker's
  Dry Cider

"Play with your food, make it fun, be playful, enjoy it!" is chef Jane Crawford's philosophy in a nutshell. The energy with which she creates is palpable, even when sitting across the table from her, talking all things culinary over a pint or two. Combining traditions, cultures, and techniques, finding contrast in flavour and texture, then infusing all of it into simple, everyday fare is where her genius shines. This is her version of chicken and potatoes. We can only dream of being back in her kitchen, sharing much laughter alongside this dish.

Pad Thai Butter:

1 cup packed brown sugar

1 cup salted butter

½ cup tomato paste

½ cup white vinegar

½ cup sriracha

Sesame Cilantro Mayo:

1 bunch cilantro

2 cloves garlic

¼ cup sesame oil

1 cup mayonnaise

Sweet Basil Vinegar:

1 cup basil

2 Tbsp white vinegar

2 Tbsp sugar

Kosher salt

Peanut Brittle:

1 cup chopped peanuts

½ cup sugar

For the Pad Thai Butter: In a saucepan over medium-high heat, combine all of the butter ingredients. Bring to a boil, and continue boiling, stirring constantly, until the sauce has reduced by one-third. Set aside to cool.

For the Sesame Cilantro Mayo: Roughly chop the cilantro (and stems) and transfer to a blender or food processor. Add the garlic and sesame oil and purée until smooth. Pour into a small bowl and fold in the mayonnaise until evenly combined. Chill in the fridge, covered, for about 30 minutes or until ready to use.

For the Sweet Basil Vinegar: Roughly chop the basil and transfer to a blender or food processor. Add the vinegar, sugar, and salt to taste, and purée until the sugar and salt have dissolved and the liquid has fully incorporated. Pour into a jar or small bowl and chill in the fridge, covered, for about 30 minutes or until ready to use.

For the Peanut Brittle: Line a rimmed baking sheet with parchment paper. In a small skillet, mix together the peanuts and sugar. Place over medium heat, stirring constantly, until the sugar has melted and the nuts are coated. Transfer to the prepared baking sheet and allow to cool completely. Place the brittle on a cutting board and, using a sharp knife, chop until it has the consistency of fine gravel. Place in a small bowl and set aside.

(continued)

Pad Thai Fries:

4 large Kennebec potatoes

¼ cup olive oil

Crispy Fried Chicken:

1 cup rice flour

¼ cup chili flakes

2 Tbsp kosher salt

2 Tbsp ground cinnamon

2 Tbsp garlic powder

8 boneless chicken thighs

Vegetable oil, for frying

To Serve:

2 green onions, chopped on a bias, for garnish

Fresh bean sprouts, for garnish

Cilantro, for garnish

Toasted sesame seeds, for garnish

For the Pad Thai Fries: Preheat the oven to 425°F. Line a baking sheet with parchment paper.

Scrub the potatoes and slice them into matchsticks. Fill a large bowl with lightly salted water, soak the potatoes for 10 minutes to remove some of the starch, and then drain and toss to dry. Coat the potatoes in the oil and place them on the prepared baking sheet. Bake for 30 to 40 minutes, turning once about halfway through, until golden and crisp.

For the Crispy Fried Chicken: While the fries are baking, in a small bowl, combine the flour, chili flakes, salt, cinnamon, and garlic powder. Pat the chicken dry and dredge each piece in this flour mixture to coat completely. Place the pieces on a plate. In a heavy-bottomed skillet, heat ½ inch of oil over medium-high heat. Line a plate with paper towel. Shallow-fry until the chicken is fully cooked and golden brown. Remove from the oil and set aside on the prepared plate.

To Serve: As soon as the fries come out of the oven, toss them in enough pad Thai butter to evenly coat. Divide the fries between four serving plates. Sprinkle the fries with the brittle, some green onions, and a generous drizzle of the mayo. Place two pieces of fried chicken on top of the fries on each plate and drizzle with the vinegar to finish. Garnish with bean sprouts, cilantro, and a few toasted sesame seeds. Serve immediately.

STORAGE: This dish is best enjoyed as soon as it's assembled. However, there will be lots of leftover pad Thai butter. You can put it on everything from fried rice to pork tenderloin. It will keep in an airtight container in the fridge for up to 5 days. The mayo will also keep in an airtight container in the fridge for up to 5 days, the vinegar will keep in an airtight container in the fridge for up to 2 weeks, and the brittle will keep in an airtight container at room temperature for up to 2 weeks. The chicken and fries will keep in the fridge in separate airtight containers for up to 3 days. Warm the fries in the oven to keep them crisp.

Recipe contributed by Jane Crawford

Blue Dot Beef Wellington

SERVES 4

Rossignol Estate Winery's
  Marechal Foch

The historic Dalvay By The Sea hotel in Prince Edward Island National Park is a warm and welcoming yet stately building. Large armchairs sit on the porch, and the heavy walnut doors invite you in. Originally built as a vacation cottage in 1895, it is still used as such by guests, many of whom have been coming to Dalvay for over thirty years. With an eye to innovation while staying true to tradition, the inn has earned its status as one of the most elegant culinary experiences in the province. Chef Ryan Janssens honours the island's ingredients, constantly changing the menu based on what fish was caught that morning, although the classic dishes are always available as well. This Beef Wellington, made with Blue Dot Reserve PEI certified beef, is a perfect example of one of those classics.

---

3 cups button mushrooms

2 shallots

3 cloves garlic

½ cup butter

3 tsp sea salt, divided

1½ tsp black pepper, divided

3 sprigs thyme, leaves only

2–3 lb Blue Dot Reserve beef
  tenderloin

2 Tbsp olive oil

6 slices prosciutto

1 (8 oz) square puff pastry

1 egg

Preheat the oven to 350°F. Line a rimmed baking sheet with parchment paper.

Roughly chop the mushrooms and shallots and spread them evenly on the prepared baking sheet. Roast until the vegetables are tender and the juices have released, about 20 minutes. Allow to cool slightly. Transfer to a food processor and add the garlic, butter, 1 teaspoon of the salt, and ½ teaspoon of the pepper. Purée until smooth. Transfer to a small bowl. Fold the thyme leaves into the mushroom mixture. Cover and place this mushroom duxelles in the fridge to cool completely.

Remove the beef from the fridge about 30 minutes before you plan to cook it, to allow it to come to room temperature. Pat dry with a paper towel and season well with the remaining 2 teaspoons of salt and 1 teaspoon of pepper. In a heavy-bottomed skillet over high heat, heat the oil. Sear the beef until all sides are brown and golden, 1 to 2 minutes per side. Remove from the pan and allow to rest on a plate to cool.

Lay a large piece of plastic wrap on the counter. Overlap the pieces of prosciutto over top. Spread the prosciutto with the mushroom duxelles, then place the tenderloin in the centre and roll the prosciutto around the beef, using the plastic wrap as a guide to help you tighten it into a log.

(continued)

Roll out the puffed pastry until it is a rectangle 2 inches longer than the tenderloin, 1 inch wider than the circumference of the beef, and between ¼ and ½ inch thick. Unwrap the beef from the plastic wrap and place it on the long edge of the pastry closest to you. Roll up the log in the pastry and fold over the ends, fully encasing the tenderloin in the pastry.

In a small bowl, beat the egg. Seal the edges of the pastry and, using a pastry brush, brush the entire roast with the egg wash. Place on a plate and chill, covered, in the fridge for at least 1 hour, or up to 24 hours.

Preheat the oven to 400°F. Bake the beef Wellington for 20 to 30 minutes, until a thermometer inserted in the centre reads 120°F—perfect for medium-rare—and the pastry is golden. Allow the meat to rest for 10 to 15 minutes before serving, as the beef will increase in temperature by 10°F to 15°F once removed from the oven.

STORAGE: The beef Wellington will keep in an airtight container in the fridge for up to 4 days, although it is always best enjoyed the day it's made.

Recipe contributed by Ryan Janssens, Dalvay By The Sea

RAISING BEEF

The rolling quilt-like pastoral farmland of PEI is punctuated with decorative cattle roaming the landscape. The largest farm has approximately 250 head, but the average is only about 50, which affords the farmers more time to care for and attend to their animals. Cattle farming is a growing industry on PEI, where the abundant grain, potatoes, and fertile ground provide rich, healthy feed and ideal conditions. It's a wonderfully cyclical system where the cows are fed on premium crops and in turn provide organic fertilizer that helps enrich the soil and enhance simple farming practices.

Walking down the laneway of the farm at Dexter Cattle Company on a hot and dusty summer day, we approach the edge of a low-lying fence from which owners Mike and Evelyn Lafortune call out to their herd. The cattle are lazing along the fringe of the field, enjoying the shade afforded by the neighbouring forest. At the sound of her greeting, the cows come trotting over, nuzzling up to Evelyn as she gives their heads a scratch. They're tiny, even beside her petite frame, reaching only about mid-chest. Shorter than most cattle, and sporting coats in a variety of colours from auburn red to deep black, these Dexters are a unique breed that produce an intensely flavourful meat. The Lafortunes' herd are strictly grass-fed and grass-finished, which means they are never fattened on grains. They never see the inside of a barn and are instead free to graze the farm's fields year round. Mike explains that "a cow's favourite temperature is –5°C," and with cool treed forests providing shelter from sun and wind, they not only enjoy the long summer days but also are happy to stay outdoors in the winter, roaming the snow-covered fields and munching on the harvested first-cut organic hay the Lafortunes supply.

Mike and Evelyn fully embrace the farm-to-table philosophy and, as such, they refuse to be middlemen, selling only to consumers for home use instead of to restaurants, stores, or a processing facility. They personally take the mature cows to the abattoir and walk with them through the process, monitor the hanging and butchering, and then bring the meat home to be distributed to their customers through a community supported agriculture (CSA) program. These cows are loved, and the taste of the beef is reflective of the care that is taken in raising them. By taking the cattle straight from field to plate, Mike and Evelyn are able to keep and tend their herd to the highest standard and provide an incredible, high-quality beef directly to families across PEI at an affordable price.

On a larger scale, there's the Atlantic Beef Products (ABP) processing facility, which lies just outside of Charlottetown, PEI. It's the largest processor in the Atlantic region, yet only 0.5% of Canada's beef comes through it. The company cannot compete with the supply numbers across the rest of the country, so instead they strive to stay ahead of the curve in quality. For marketing purposes, the ABP worked with the provincial government to create certification parameters that include humane handling, small herd size, and full traceability from pasture to plate.

Once the cows have been slaughtered and hung to age for forty-eight hours, the beef is graded. The meat inspector comes through and makes a cut in the side just below the shoulder into the rib cage. Allowing the meat to cure before grading is important as the fat is able to solidify allowing the marbling, colour, and muscle texture to be evaluated. Meat that is deemed Blue Dot Reserve status, the highest standard in PEI, will fetch the highest price for the farmer. Along with the physical characteristics of the meat, Blue Dot Reserve cattle must also be raised hormone-free on small family farms and fed on the highest-quality grain, fodder, grass, and potatoes. Blue Dot Reserve standards are so high that only about one-third of the Canadian Triple A (AAA) grade beef is considered worthy of the rank. This top-quality beef is mostly used in the commercial food industry, with top Atlantic restaurants such as Masstown Butchers (Nova Scotia), Dalvay By The Sea, Fogo Island Inn (Newfoundland), The Inn at Bay Fortune, Mallard Cottage (Newfoundland), and Raymonds Restaurant (Newfoundland) having it in regular rotation on their menus.

The ABP also employs a full tip-to-tail philosophy, which means almost every part of every animal is processed and utilized in some form—only about 1% of each cow will go to waste. For example, the hides are sent for tanning and made into coats and leather goods, and the blood is used to make energy drinks and iron supplements. Even the surfactant, a mucus-like substance that prevents the areolae in the lungs from sticking together, is extracted, sent to pharmaceutical companies, and made into life-saving drugs for premature babies in neonatal intensive care units.

Seated in the beautiful dining room at Dalvay By The Sea, enjoying their delectable Beef Wellington (page 137), we're struck by just how incredible these animals are. Experiencing the care, attention, and love that this island gives its bovine residents gave us a greater understanding of the culinary superiority of PEI-raised beef. From a small, grass-fed CSA program to the larger but meticulously run Atlantic Beef Products plant, the cattle here live under the highest standards, are treated with the ultimate respect, and produce some of the most delicious beef we have ever had the good fortune to taste.

Saltwater Brined Beef *with* Black Garlic Tapenade

SERVES 4

Luckett Vineyards' The Old Bill

It may seem counterintuitive to take dry-aged meat and then brine it, but trust us, this is so delicious that it's worth the work. The dry-aging process naturally tenderizes the meat, slowly removing excess juices, so when it's brined before cooking, the beef absorbs the exact flavours you want it to. The sweet, spicy brine complements the tender, enhanced meaty flavour of the steaks, especially when paired with the sweet richness of PEI black garlic. Enjoy with a glass of The Old Bill red wine. Aged for two years, the deep black fruit flavour and tannic qualities of the wine are remarkably present and blend perfectly with the complexity of the beef and sweet salty tapenade.

Saltwater Brined Beef:

4 dry-aged (28–30 days) 8 oz
  beef steaks

3 Tbsp sea salt

¼ cup olive oil

¼ cup maple syrup

2 tsp hot sauce

Tapenade:

1 bulb black garlic

2 tsp capers

1 sun-dried tomato

1 Tbsp lemon juice

1 Tbsp olive oil

For the Saltwater Brined Beef: Generously sprinkle the steaks on all sides with the salt, then place in a large resealable plastic bag. Add ¼ cup of water. Remove as much air as possible and seal the bag. Brine in the fridge for 12 hours.

Transfer the steaks to a shallow baking dish or deep-sided plate, shaking off any excess liquid.

In a small bowl, whisk together the oil, maple syrup, and hot sauce. Generously brush the steaks with the mixture on both sides and let rest at room temperature for 1 hour. The steaks will absorb the marinade. Brush the steaks with any remaining marinade.

For the Tapenade: Peel the garlic cloves, roughly chop, and place in a small mixing bowl. Chop the capers and mince the sun-dried tomato and add both to the bowl. Drizzle in the lemon juice and oil and stir to combine. Let sit at room temperature for 1 hour to allow the flavours to develop.

Preheat a grill to high heat and brush with a little heat-tolerant oil. Dry-aged meat doesn't contain much blood, so it's best cooked on the rarer side. Cook to desired doneness (see page 70). Remove the steaks from the grill, place on a cutting board, and cover with foil. Allow to rest for 10 minutes. This will allow them to reabsorb the juices and finish cooking. The steak will increase in temperature by about 10°F during the resting phase.

Serve the steaks as soon as they have rested, with the tapenade on the side.

STORAGE: The tapenade will keep in an airtight container in the fridge for up to 1 week. The steaks will keep in an airtight container in the fridge for up to 3 days.

Island Beef Short Ribs

SERVES 4

Newman Estate Winery's Lucie
Kuhlmann Red

8–10 beef chuck short ribs

¼ cup Montreal steak spice

¼ cup packed brown sugar

½ cup olive oil

10 strips bacon, diced

1 large onion, chopped

2 stalks celery, chopped

2 large carrots, chopped

10 cloves garlic, roughly chopped

2 cups dry red wine

4 sprigs rosemary

1 bay leaf

1 (6 oz) can tomato paste

2 cups beef stock

1 tsp black pepper

Creamy Horseradish Whipped
Potatoes (see right), optional

Growing up on a farm on PEI, chef Irwin MacKinnon accidentally fell in love with food. With both parents coming home hungry after a long day of work, he started cooking for his family at a young age. He loved the garden, and raising cows, pigs, and chickens gave him a unique appreciation of where food came from. This has translated into his now many years of cooking at Papa Joe's in Charlottetown, a homegrown place that serves something for everyone. Their goal is to serve what their customers want, whether it's fine dining or simple diner fare. Irwin's favourite meals to cook are still those his mom loves, including these simple, hearty, and incredibly delicious short ribs.

Preheat the oven to 350°F. Line a rimmed baking sheet with parchment paper.

In a large bowl, toss the short ribs with the steak spice and sugar, and then drizzle with the oil until the ribs are thoroughly coated. If there is any spice mixture left, carefully pat it over the ribs. Place the ribs, evenly spaced, on the prepared pan. Roast for 30 minutes.

In a large, heavy-bottomed ovenproof pot or Dutch oven over medium heat, place the bacon with about ½ cup of water. Cook, stirring frequently, until the water evaporates, the fat starts to render, and the bacon becomes crisp, 5 to 7 minutes. Add the onions, celery, and carrots and continue to cook until the vegetables begin to brown, 3 to 4 minutes. Add the garlic and cook until fragrant, about 1 minute. Add the wine, rosemary, and bay leaf. Bring to a boil and reduce for 5 minutes to begin to concentrate the flavour. Add the tomato paste and stir well to combine. Remove from the heat.

Arrange the ribs vertically in the braising liquid, fitting them close together. Add the stock. The ribs should be completely covered. Sprinkle the pepper over top, place the pot back on the heat, and bring to a boil. Cover the pot and transfer to the oven. Turn down the oven to 325°F. Cook the ribs for about 3 hours, or until completely tender.

Using tongs, remove the cooked ribs from the braising liquid, place them on a large serving platter, and tent with foil to keep warm. Place the pot with the braising liquid on the stovetop. Using a ladle, skim off the surface fat. Bring to a boil and reduce for about 15 minutes. Remove from the heat, let cool slightly, and, strain through a fine-mesh strainer into a clean pot. Using an immersion blender, purée the liquid. Season to taste with salt and pepper.

Serve with potatoes, if desired, and the braising liquid.

Creamy Horseradish Whipped Potatoes

5 waxy potatoes (such as Yukon Gold
  or new potatoes)

½ cup whipping cream

¼ cup cream cheese, cubed

3 Tbsp prepared horseradish

2 Tbsp butter

1 tsp salt

The tang of horseradish is the perfect complement to these creamy mashed potatoes, bringing balance and brightness to this classic side dish.

Bring a large saucepan of salted water to a boil over high heat. Peel the potatoes, chop them into 1-inch cubes, and boil for 7 to 10 minutes, just until tender. Drain and place them in a large mixing bowl. Add the cream, cream cheese, horseradish, butter, and salt. Using a handheld electric mixer, whip the potatoes until completely smooth.

STORAGE: The ribs will keep in an airtight container in the fridge for up to 3 days. Leftovers make great eggs Benedict or hot beef sandwiches for lunch. Potatoes will keep in an airtight container in the fridge for up to 3 days.

Recipes contributed by Irwin MacKinnon, Papa Joe's

Black Currant Buttermilk Doughnuts

MAKES 8 DOUGHNUTS

Red Island Cider's Halcyon Cider

Doughnuts are one of those things that people tend to shy away from making, believing them to be too complicated for a make-at-home treat, but really, nothing could be simpler—or more delicious! Here buttermilk keeps the crumb moist and supple while adding its trademark delectable tang, complementing the sweet tartness of the currants. If you have the time and want to be really adventurous, steep some black currant leaves in the buttermilk before adding it to the recipe. The leaves taste just like the fruit and add an extra pop of flavour. The black currant leaves also make a delicious tea, for a whole black currant affair.

Doughnuts:

2 eggs

½ cup buttermilk

⅓ cup honey

1 Tbsp baking powder

½ tsp baking soda

2½ cups flour

½ cup dried black currants

Neutral oil, for frying

Glaze:

2 cups icing sugar

½ cup black currant jam

1 Tbsp whipping cream

STORAGE: The doughnuts are best enjoyed the day they are made, but will keep in an airtight container at room temperature for up to 3 days.

For the Doughnuts: In a mixing bowl, whisk together the eggs, buttermilk, and honey until fully combined and frothy. Add the baking powder and baking soda and mix to combine, then add the flour and fold two to three times, until just mixed. Add the black currants and continue to mix until a soft dough forms.

Turn the dough out onto a well-floured surface and shape it into a disc about ¾ inch thick. Using a 3-inch cookie cutter, cut out rounds from the dough. Then, using a small cookie cutter or the metal icing tip from a piping bag, cut out a centre hole approximately ½ inch in diameter. Re-form the dough and repeat until all the dough is used.

In a heavy-bottomed skillet or pot over medium-high heat, heat 1 inch of oil to 375°F, using a candy thermometer to monitor the temperature. Turn down the heat to medium to prevent the oil from getting too hot. Using tongs, slip two to three doughnuts at a time into the hot oil, ensuring they have space to move, aren't overcrowded, and aren't sticking to the bottom of the pan. Flip after 1 minute of cooking. They will be golden brown and may have cracked open a bit, which is perfect. The cracks will allow the glaze to seep in. Cook for 1 more minute, then transfer to a wire rack with parchment underneath it to cool and set. Give the oil 1 to 2 minutes to return to temperature between batches. Repeat with the remaining doughnuts.

For the Glaze: In a shallow bowl, whisk together the glaze ingredients.

When the doughnuts are cool enough to touch, dip each one in the glaze and place back on the wire rack for 10 minutes, allowing the glaze to set and any excess to drip off.

Serve as soon as the glaze is set.

Red Currant Ice Cream

MAKES 1 (5- BY 9-INCH) LOAF TIN

Matos Winery's Rosé

2 cups milk

1 cup whipping cream

8 egg yolks

2 cups sugar, divided

1 tsp vanilla extract

2 cups red currants

2 Tbsp cornstarch

1 Tbsp lemon juice

STORAGE: The ice cream will keep in an airtight container in the freezer for up to 3 months.

Tart, sweet, and unmistakable, red currants are as much a part of PEI as the red soil. Their season being all too short, this is a great way to preserve them to enjoy all summer long. Using fresh local milk and cream makes this ice cream the perfect snack to enjoy while sitting on the front porch reading *Anne of Green Gables*. You'll need an ice cream maker for this.

In a saucepan over medium heat, heat the milk and cream until simmering. Do not let them come to a boil. While the milk mixture is warming, in a mixing bowl, whisk together the egg yolks and 1 cup of the sugar until very frothy and creamy, and yellow in colour. Temper the yolks by adding 1 cup of the warm milk mixture to the yolk mixture and stirring to combine. Add another cup of the milk mixture, then slowly add the warmed yolk mixture to the pot of milk, stirring as you pour. Return to medium heat and, stirring constantly, bring the milk to a simmer. It's ready as soon as it is thick enough to coat the back of a spoon. Remove from the heat and stir in the vanilla. Pour through a fine-mesh strainer into a mixing bowl or large liquid measuring cup to remove any lumps. Cover with plastic wrap, making sure it touches the surface of the warm liquid to prevent a skin from forming. Place in the fridge to cool completely, at least 6 hours and no longer than 2 days.

Prepare your ice cream maker according to the manufacturer's instructions. While the ice cream base is cooling, in a small saucepan, mash the red currants gently with the back of a spoon. In a mixing bowl, mix the remaining 1 cup of sugar and the cornstarch until no lumps remain. Add to the pan along with the lemon juice. Place the saucepan over medium heat and slowly bring to a boil, stirring constantly. Boil for 1 minute and then remove from the heat.

Pour this compote through a fine-mesh strainer, pressing the berries and juice through and removing any skins and seeds. Cover with plastic wrap and allow to cool in the fridge.

When the ice cream base is fully chilled, add it to your ice cream maker and churn as directed.

Using a spatula, scrape the ice cream into a 5- by 9-inch loaf tin. Working quickly, spoon half the compote mixture over top, fold a few times to incorporate, and then top the ice cream with the remaining compote and swirl to make a pretty design on the top and incorporate into the ice cream as well. Place in the freezer to chill completely, at least 6 hours. Cover the ice cream once it has hardened or serve immediately.

Carrot Halva

SERVES 4

Red Island Cider's Ginger Brett House
  Cider or

Deep Roots Distillery's Spiced Apple
  Liqueur

Carrot Halva:

2 cups grated carrot

2 cups milk

4 whole cloves

4 allspice berries

4 cardamom pods

1-inch piece cinnamon, smashed

1 cup sugar

1 Tbsp butter

Cream Cheese Mousse:

1 (8 oz) package cream cheese, at
  room temperature

½ cup icing sugar

1 Tbsp finely grated lemon zest

2 tsp vanilla extract

1 cup chilled whipping cream

"If you cook for people with love, you feed their body, mind, and soul," says chef Steven Wilson of The Pearl Eatery in North Rustico. He then sits back and smiles at us from across the table, and it's obvious food is much more than just ingredients for him—it's the connection to who he's feeding and the place he's cooking from. "Understanding hospitality and the reality that food is family enriches the community and inspires collaboration, which keeps the industry growing."

This carrot halva encapsulates all that Steve loves about food: familiar flavours, uncomplicated methods, and a unique process. Put those together and you have one incredible dish.

For the Carrot Halva: In a heavy-bottomed saucepan, combine the carrots and milk. In a small skillet over medium heat, cook the spices, stirring frequently, until fragrant. Transfer the spices to an empty loose-leaf tea bag or wrap them in a small piece of cheesecloth and tie with a string. Add the spices to the carrot mixture.

Place the saucepan over medium-low heat and, stirring frequently, simmer until the carrots have absorbed almost all of the milk. This will take anywhere from 1 to 2 hours.

Discard the spices. Stir in the sugar and continue cooking until the mixture forms a cohesive mass, the carrots are very tender, and all the milk has been absorbed, an additional 20 to 30 minutes.

Remove from the heat and stir in the butter. Transfer to a sheet pan, spreading the carrot mixture evenly across it. Chill in the fridge, uncovered, for at least 1 hour. It should be completely cold.

For the Cream Cheese Mousse: In a mixing bowl, using a handheld electric mixer, beat the cream cheese, icing sugar, zest, and vanilla until light and fluffy. In a separate bowl, but using the same beaters on the mixer, whip the cream. Add it to the cream cheese mixture and gently mix together until fluffy and well combined. Cover and chill in the fridge for at least 30 minutes to set.

(continued)

Pistachio Walnut Brittle:

1½ cups sugar

1 Tbsp corn syrup

½ cup chopped walnuts

¼ cup chopped pistachios

1 tsp sea salt

To Serve:

8 sprigs mint

For the Pistachio Walnut Brittle: Line a baking sheet with parchment paper. In a heavy-bottomed pot over medium-high heat, bring the sugar and corn syrup to a boil in 1 cup of water. Using a pastry brush dipped in cold water, brush down the inside of the pot during cooking to prevent crystallization. When the sugar reaches a deep caramel colour, remove the pot from the heat. Stir in the walnuts, pistachios, and salt and spread the mixture onto the prepared sheet. Allow to cool fully at room temperature for 30 to 45 minutes.

Place the brittle on a cutting board and, using a sharp knife, chop it into pieces, then add to a food processor fitted with the steel blade and chop until the brittle has the consistency of fine gravel.

To Serve: Spread a generous spoonful of the mousse across each dessert plate. On each plate, using a pair of steel kitchen soup spoons, form a quenelle with the carrot halva and lay it across the mousse on one side. Form another quenelle and place it on the other side, parallel to the first one. Insert a mint sprig in one end of each quenelle to create the image of the carrot. Garnish with the nut brittle and serve.

STORAGE: The halva and mousse will keep in separate airtight containers in the fridge for up to 1 week. The brittle will keep in an airtight container at room temperature for up to 2 months.

NOTE: You will have extra mousse and brittle. Although these are both delicious served on their own, you can also pair them with a fruit compote for a light dessert.

Recipe contributed by Steven Wilson, The Pearl Eatery

BACKYARD RHUBARB

When you picture foraging, you typically think of wandering through the woods, uncovering wild mushrooms on the forest floor, or plucking fiddleheads in the early days of spring—not picking rhubarb in your own backyard. However, rhubarb is common in PEI, as almost every home has a rhubarb patch. Originally brought to North America by European immigrants, it now grows prolifically across the province and gives a connection to the land that most people enjoy even if they're not actively involved in growing their own food.

Two people who are very much involved in growing local PEI produce are cousins Kyle Panton and Curtis Penny, co-owners of the fully organic One Vision Farms. Curtis grew up on his family's generational conventional farm, Penny Lane, where his passion for growing delicious fruits and vegetables started young. As an adult looking to provide his family with the healthiest and most nourishing food possible, he began growing wholly organic produce in his own backyard. Curtis inspired his cousin Kyle, a local chef, to start cooking with these backyard vegetables, and Kyle loved Curtis's produce so much that he started bringing it into the restaurant. Other chefs began noticing the quality of the produce, and the cousins, wanting to make a firmer connection between restaurant and farm, started selling and sharing their vision more broadly. The connection between naturally grown food and superior flavours was clear to them, and so One Vision, a community supported agriculture (CSA) box program, was born. One Vision provides both restaurants and locals with quality organic produce. Kyle and Curtis's ultimate goal is to connect people to the land and allow producers to see the results of their work through beautiful dishes shared daily around the island.

Since launching in 2012, One Vision has grown from Curtis's backyard to a 7-acre parcel that is part of the larger family farm, and the cousins are now supplying fresh greens to most of the restaurants in Charlottetown. Curtis is a true student of the land, pulling in creativity and inspiration from many seemingly unrelated sources to find ways to control pests naturally and grow consistently delicious and beautiful crops. They grow rotating organic crops using fish fertilizer and large black tarps to kill weeds, and white mesh canopies to keep the bugs away while providing sunlight and moisture throughout during the growing season.

Seeking respite from the sun inside one of the barns, Curtis shows us a massive pile of freshly cut and gorgeously pink rhubarb. Unlike their other specialty items, this isn't a cash crop for them, but even here on a commercial farm, it's an important component of the culinary year. Their hope is that the more communities learn about and enjoy the foods that grow around them, the more they'll want to cultivate deeper relationships with the land and with farmers.

As it grows prolifically across PEI, rhubarb is for many an easy backyard connection between the land and the foods that it supplies. As we concern ourselves with the basics of learning, knowing, and caring about where our food comes from, the relationships between earth and growing, producer and chef become readily apparent. In the case of PEI, rhubarb, a humble backyard vegetable, has become celebrated across the province in jams and jellies, cakes and pies, even liqueurs and local ale. More than just a bushy weed, rhubarb is a tie to the past, a current celebration, a connection to the land that is easily available, and oh, so delicious!

Rhubarb Buttermilk Cake

MAKES 1 (9-INCH) ROUND
CAKE

Jost Vineyards' Riesling

Rhubarb Buttermilk Cake:

¼ cup butter

¼ cup olive oil

¾ cup packed brown sugar

¾ cup sugar

1 egg

2 cups flour

2 tsp baking powder

1 tsp ground ginger

1 tsp ground cardamom

½ tsp ground nutmeg

½ tsp ground cinnamon

¼ tsp fine sea salt

1 cup buttermilk

2½ cups chopped fresh or frozen
  rhubarb

Crumble Topping:

½ cup packed brown sugar

2 Tbsp flour

¼ cup butter, slightly chilled, cubed

1 Tbsp icing sugar

This cake is filled with tart rhubarb and tangy buttermilk and is easy to whip together. It holds its moisture and is just as delicious after sitting on the counter for a few days, or pulled from the freezer when unexpected company arrives, as it is right from the oven. With rhubarb being so abundant in spring, this cake is the perfect way to use up freshly frozen stalks for when the craving hits later, after the growing season is over.

For the Rhubarb Buttermilk Cake: Preheat the oven to 350°F. Prepare a 9-inch round baking pan by coating it evenly with a little olive oil.

Using a stand mixer fitted with the paddle attachment, cream the butter and oil, then add the sugars and mix until fully combined. Add the egg and whisk to fully incorporate. The batter will be pale in colour and fluffy in texture.

Over a piece of parchment paper (much easier than dirtying a second bowl!), sift the dry ingredients together. Add half of the dry ingredient mixture to the batter, then ½ cup of the buttermilk. Repeat with the remaining dry ingredients and buttermilk, mixing well and scraping down the bowl after each addition. Gently fold in the rhubarb until it is evenly distributed and coated in batter. The batter should be smooth, with only the rhubarb adding lumps.

Using a spatula, pour the batter into the prepared baking pan, scraping out the bowl. Spread the batter evenly in the baking pan and tap it a few times on the counter to let out any air bubbles and allow it to settle.

For the Crumble Topping: In a clean bowl, combine the sugar with the flour. Add the butter. Using two knives or a pastry blender, cut in the butter until the mixture has a coarse, crumbly texture and there is no dry flour left. Spread the topping evenly over the batter.

Bake until a toothpick inserted in the centre comes out clean, the topping is golden, and the cake has risen in the centre, 45 to 50 minutes.

Remove from the oven, run a knife around the outside, dust with icing sugar, and try to not steal a piece the moment it's out of the oven . . . but we won't blame you if you do.

STORAGE: This cake will keep in an airtight container at room temperature for up to 5 days or, once it has cooled to room temperature, you can wrap it tightly in plastic wrap and store it in the freezer for up to 6 months.

Roasted Rhubarb Crumble

SERVES 6

Lightfoot & Wolfville's Pinot Rosé or

Annapolis Cider Company's Geneva Crab Rosé

Roasted Rhubarb:

6 large stalks rhubarb

¼ cup cornstarch

¼ cup rosé wine

1 cup honey

2 tsp ground cardamom

Crumble Topping:

1 cup oats

¾ cup flour

¾ cup packed brown sugar

1 tsp ground nutmeg

½ tsp ground allspice

½ tsp ground ginger

1½ cups cold butter, cubed

STORAGE: The crumble will keep, covered, in the fridge for up to 3 days.

You know spring is officially in full swing when the rhubarb pops up and fresh strawberries start appearing at farmers' markets across the province. As much as we love a good strawberry rhubarb pie, there is something incredibly satisfying about a hearty, rich crumble—and no need to fuss about with pastry. Roasting the rhubarb concentrates the flavour and increases the natural sweetness of the fruit. When combined with the lightly spiced cardamom, sweet honey, and the complexity of the rosé, it is pure perfection. Our favourite rosés to use here are Lightfoot & Wolfville's Pinot Rosé and Jost Vineyards' Selkie Rosé. Or, for a uniquely flavourful combination, use Annapolis Cider Company's Geneva Crab Rosé.

For the Roasted Rhubarb: Preheat the oven to 375°F. Line a rimmed baking sheet with parchment paper.

Roughly chop the rhubarb into 1-inch pieces. Spread it evenly on the prepared baking sheet and roast until the edges are brown and the rhubarb has softened, about 15 minutes. Allow to cool slightly.

While the rhubarb is roasting, in a small bowl, whisk together the cornstarch and wine until completely smooth. Whisk in the honey and cardamom to make a smooth, creamy paste.

Prepare a 2- to 3-quart baking dish by coating it evenly with a little olive oil. Carefully pick up the corners of the parchment paper the roasted rhubarb is resting on and pour the rhubarb and its juices into the baking dish. Drizzle the honey-cornstarch mixture over top and give the baking dish a shake and a few taps on the counter to allow the rhubarb to settle and the honey mixture to run through the fruit. As the dish cooks and the fruit warms, the honey will loosen, so if it doesn't look like it has settled much that's ok.

For the Crumble Topping: In a small bowl, combine the oats, flour, sugar, and spices. Add the butter. Using two knives or a pastry blender, cut in the butter to pea-sized pieces and until the mixture has a coarse, crumbly texture. Spread evenly over top of the rhubarb. Place the dish on a rimmed baking sheet to catch any drips, as the juice might bubble over.

Bake until the fruit is bubbling and the topping is golden brown, 35 to 40 minutes. Let sit for 10 minutes to cool before serving.

CRAFTED: MEET THE BREWERS, DISTILLERS, AND VINTNERS OF ATLANTIC CANADA

One can't speak to the foods of Atlantic Canada without also mentioning the incredible array of microbrewers, distillers, and vintners that abound throughout the region. Utilizing the very best in local ingredients, each with their own distinct approach to their craft, these artisans are gaining international recognition, earning awards at some of the world's most prestigious competitions. Steinhart Distillery's Steinhart Gin was awarded the Best Classic Gin in the World at the 2019 World Gin Awards in London, UK—no mean feat for a small distillery in Antigonish, Nova Scotia, on the way to Cape Breton Island. Steinhart is also known for incorporating local flavours in unique ways, such as with their haskap gin. Glenora Distillery, also in Nova Scotia, is not only North America's first traditionally crafted single malt whisky maker, but also the first outside of Scotland. Halifax-based Compass Distillers' rotating GiNS lineup features locally grown seasonal Nova Scotian ingredients. Ironworks Distillery has a wood-fired copper still named Birgitta, and their blended Rum Boat Rum is aged at sea right in the Lunenburg Harbour, in Nova Scotia, while Moonshine Creek Distillery in Waterville, New Brunswick, has crafted the aptly named Canadiana, a spirit similar to white rum but derived from syrup collected in Saint-Quentin, New Brunswick, the Maple Syrup Capital of Atlantic Canada. Meanwhile, the Prince Edward Distillery has produced an award-winning vodka made exclusively with PEI potatoes, and The Newfoundland Distillery Company is making waves with their Chaga Rum.

Likewise, the microbrewery scene has exploded in the past few years, and gastro pubs with in-house brewing can be found in every city and small town across the provinces. Some standouts are the YellowBelly Brewery in St. John's, Newfoundland, which often features wild-food-inspired brews, and Big Spruce Brewing in Cape Breton Island, whose Cereal Killer is one of the best stout beers around. Moncton's famous Tide & Boar gastropub has ever-rotating taps of house-brewed ales, lagers, porters, and stouts on offer, and in Charlottetown, both Hopyard and Upstreet Craft Brewing made our "best place to try a flight" list for their dizzying array of options on tap. Of course, beer is not the only local thing brewing. Cideries such as Nova Scotia's Annapolis Cider Company, No Boats On Sunday, and Noggins Corner Farm are utilizing the abundance of apples in the province to craft gorgeously dry, crisp ciders, while Double Hill Cidery out of PEI creates a wide range of foraged wild fruit ciders.

The wines of Nova Scotia's Annapolis Valley, both the locally branded Tidal Bay blend and their sparkling wines, are gaining worldwide recognition. Winery tours throughout the region leave hourly from Wolfville during the summer season and are a great way to visit the plethora of gorgeous vineyards, many of which feature tasting rooms and world-class restaurants.

The following are a few of our favourite producers, but the list is in no way comprehensive. We encourage you to search out new artisans and create your own go-to list.

Wineries

NOVA SCOTIA
Benjamin Bridge
Domaine de Grand Pré
Gaspereau Vineyards
Jost Vineyards
Lightfoot & Wolfville
Luckett Vineyards
Mercator Vineyards

PEI
Matos Winery
Rossignol Estate Winery

NEW BRUNSWICK
Dunhams Run Estate Winery
Magnetic Hill Winery
Richibucto River Wine Estate
Sunset Heights Meadery
Winegarden Estate

NEWFOUNDLAND
Auk Island Winery
Rodrigues Winery & Distillery

Breweries

NOVA SCOTIA
Big Spruce Brewing
Garrison Brewing Company
Horton Ridge Malt & Grain
  Company
Saltbox Brewing Company

PEI
Barnone Brewery
Island Honey Wine Company
Moth Lane Brewing
PEI Brewing Company
Upstreet Craft Brewing

NEW BRUNSWICK
Bigtide Brewing Co.
Foghorn Brewing Company
Graystone Brewing
Loyalist City Brewing Company

NEWFOUNDLAND
Dildo Brewing Co.
Port Rexton Brewing Co.
Quidi Vidi Brewery
YellowBelly Brewery

Distilleries

NOVA SCOTIA
Compass Distillers
Glenora Distillery
Ironworks Distillery
Steinhart Distillery

PEI
Deep Roots Distillery
Island Honey Wine Company
Prince Edward Distillery

NEW BRUNSWICK
Distillerie Fils du Roy
Moonshine Creek Distillery
Sussex Craft Distillery

NEWFOUNDLAND
The Newfoundland Distillery
  Company

Cideries

NOVA SCOTIA
Annapolis Cider Company
Chain Yard Urban Cidery
No Boats On Sunday
Noggins Cider

PEI
Double Hill Cidery
Red Island Cider
Riverdale Orchard & Cidery

NEW BRUNSWICK
Gagetown Cider Co.
Red Rover Craft Cider
Yip Cider

NEWFOUNDLAND
Newfoundland Cider Company

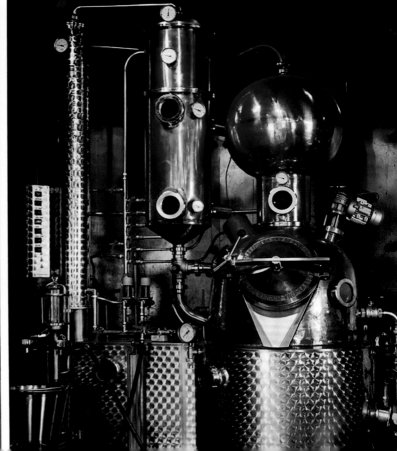

New Brunswick

Recipes

Though it's often thought of as a "drive-through" province for those on their way to the more seafaring of the Atlantic provinces, you only have to get off the highway to fully understand that New Brunswick has it all: agrarian marshlands, quaint seaside towns, deep dark forests, and bustling artisan city scenes. From the delightful seaside village of St. Andrews by-the-Sea, with its beautiful murals and artisan shops, to the hip urban scene in Fredericton, we were constantly enchanted by the people, the scenery, and of course, the food. Fredericton's Farmers' Market was second to none, and, Saint John City Market held so many delicious treasures that we needed an extra bag for our trip home.

The largest of the Atlantic provinces, New Brunswick is as diverse as the people who live there. It is the cultural crossroads where the Mi'kmaq and Maliseet First Nations taught foraging lessons to the early Acadian farmers, who passed those lessons on to the subsequent waves of British immigrants. When the Acadian people first arrived in the coastal region of New Brunswick, they brought with them their farming practices, many of which are still used today. Intricate dikes were built to keep the sea water at bay, allowing these settlers to farm grains, legumes, corn, flax, and hemp below sea level. As a result, we now reap cranberries, ancient marsh grasses, and waterfowl on these traditional lands. Further out to the coast you'll find all of the treasures you'd expect from a Maritime province: lobster, oysters, mussels, sea urchin, crab, and many varieties of fish. Several of the best seafood dishes in the region can be found here, with those at Saint John Ale House being of particular note.

Out on the island of Gran Manan, located at the mouth of the Bay of Fundy, you'll find a different kind of harvest as multigenerational farmers pull myriad sea vegetables by hand from the shadowy beds below the bluffs of Dark Harbour. Deeply purple and packed with umami, the dulse harvested here is considered the finest in the world (see page 209).

However, the coastal region makes up only a small percentage of the province, with the greater area covered in rolling grain fields and dense forest. The climate here is harsher, the land less populated than the rest of the low-lying Maritime region, and hunting and fishing are a large part of the domestic culinary scene. Game such as venison, moose, and bear live alongside the New Brunswick rivers and lakes, spots beloved by fly fishermen around the world. Within the forests you'll find wild mushrooms, berries, and fiddleheads waiting to be foraged, as well as the magic elixir drawn from the sugar maples and boiled down into sweet golden syrup.

As the least touristy of the Atlantic provinces, New Brunswick is a hotbed of homegrown pride. Young farmers and restaurateurs, having travelled and worked throughout Canada and abroad, are returning home in droves to start businesses that focus not only on serving and creating locavore fare, but also on creating jobs throughout the community.

Next time you find yourself driving through New Brunswick, we encourage you to exit the highway, drive into the towns and villages, and discover the immense beauty of this incredibly diverse and delicious province.

Scrambled Eggs & Lobster

SERVES 4

Once you get off the main highways of New Brunswick, beautiful sights and foods abound. This simple dish, suggested by a local lobsterman, is a favourite after a long morning at sea. For years, lobster was considered poor man's food, an essential protein that was begrudgingly added to children's lunch boxes and a staple ingredient in simple everyday dishes. Now, even though this coveted crustacean is enjoyed worldwide, lobster is still appreciated as an everyday food in kitchens across the Atlantic region, and this simple way of preparing it highlights the delicious elegance it can afford.

6 eggs

½ cup heavy cream

4 Tbsp olive oil, divided

1 Tbsp grainy Dijon mustard

2 tsp sea salt

2 cups cooked lobster meat

1 Tbsp parsley, for garnish

In a mixing bowl, whisk together the eggs, cream, 2 tablespoons of the oil, the mustard, and salt until fully combined and frothy.

In a large skillet, warm the remaining 2 tablespoons of oil over medium heat and then add the egg mixture. Immediately sprinkle the lobster meat evenly over the egg. Gently scramble the eggs, using a spatula to lift the egg up from the bottom of the pan and fold it over the lobster, breaking apart any larger pieces. Continue to fold and stir until the egg is no longer runny, 1 to 2 minutes.

Transfer to serving plates. Sprinkle each plate with a little parsley to garnish and serve immediately.

Brayon Ployes

1 Tbsp baking powder

1 tsp baking soda

1 cup boiling water

1½ cups buckwheat flour

1 cup all-purpose flour

1 tsp sea salt

Butter, for frying

Ployes are a delicious breakfast food traditionally eaten by les Brayons, the francophone people located in and around the Edmundston, New Brunswick, area. Not quite pancakes, crepes, or crumpets, but a little bit of all three, these buckwheat ployes are a savoury griddle cake. They look very similar to a crumpet because of the bubbles that form on the top on one side, they resemble a pancake as they don't contain yeast, and the batter is quite thin, hence the crepe similarity. The trick for perfect ployes is to allow the baking powder to soak in the boiling water for a few minutes, which removes the pasty flavour. Cook them in a hot pan—cast iron works best—for even heat distribution and consistency. Slather in molasses or maple syrup for the sweet-toothed in the family.

In a small bowl or liquid measure, combine the baking powder, baking soda, and boiling water. Let sit for 5 minutes.

In a large mixing bowl, whisk together both flours and the salt. Pour in the water mixture and, stirring constantly, slowly add an additional cup of warm tap water to form a loose batter. Let sit for an additional 3 minutes.

Preheat the oven to 325°F. Once it comes to temperature, turn it off.

Place a heavy-bottomed skillet or griddle over medium-high heat and add a pat of butter to lightly grease it. When the butter is bubbling and the pan is hot, ladle ⅓ cup of batter onto the hot pan, swirling with the back of the ladle to spread it evenly across the pan if needed. Let cook until the top is bubbling and firm to the touch, 1 to 2 minutes. Using a spatula, remove the ploye from the pan, place it on a plate, and put it in the oven to keep warm. Repeat with the remaining batter.

STORAGE: These are best enjoyed the day they are made but will keep in an airtight container in the fridge for up to 3 days. To reheat, place them in a toaster or quickly reheat in a frying pan with a little bit of butter over medium heat.

GROWING GRAINS

We tend to think of Canadian cereal grains, especially wheat, as coming from the Western provinces and not the Atlantic coast. In reality, vast amounts originate in the Eastern provinces. While the "bread basket" prairies predominately focus on producing larger volumes of commercial crops, the smaller farms across New Brunswick and PEI, along with parts of Nova Scotia, concentrate on growing small quantities of specialty grains like red millet, heritage Marquis wheat, Red Fife wheat, buckwheat, malting barley, and unique varieties of rye and spelt. It's a question of scale, and Atlantic Canada grain farmers are perfectly set up to plant smaller acreages of specialty varieties. Collectively, there's a healthy market for both specialty and mass-produced grain across Canada, which is known as a high-quality cereal grain producer in the global marketplace.

Sitting at the white Formica table in Maurice Girouard's kitchen, a forty-minute drive north of Moncton, we're spellbound as he shares stories of this, his father's farm, often pointing out the large picture window that looks onto the surrounding green fields. This is the land he grew up on, and when his father passed away in 1986, Maurice retired from engineering and took up farming in order to keep the fields open. By 1993 he was fully certified as an organic cereal grain farmer in New Brunswick.

As we wander around the property, we note Maurice's deep affection for the farming equipment. These machines and the physical processes they employ—the "mechanics of farming," as he calls it—are both his passion and his primary tools for keeping the farm fully organic. Instead of spraying for weeds, he uses a special cultivator fitted with sweep blades to pull fast-growing weeds up from the roots without disturbing the crop. A harrow tills the ground before a packer sets the seeds, ensuring they are planted at the same level in the soil to grow at an even rate, which also helps combat weed growth. On larger farms, the goal is to reduce the time you need to be on the fields for a more efficient process called single-pass farming—often towing multiple pieces of equipment behind the tractor at one time. Single pass farming is needed for many reasons in Ontario and Western provinces: not only is there a very short window for planting wheat (typically four days), but larger farms just don't have time to till, harrow, plant, and go over the fields many times in order to get the seeds in the ground. For a small organic farm such as Maurice's, this is not the case. Many passes are needed and the land continually needs to be cared for in order to encourage the plants to grow.

If a larger conventional farmer produces 25 to 30 bushels per acre, they will have had a great year, but a small organic farm needs much more than that to break even. Due to the care and time farmers like Maurice put into their fields, their yield might be as high as 60 bushels per acre. Maurice smiles as he says, "It's a passion project, really." From keeping the faithful tractors running to implementing intentional crop rotation and tillage to keeping the fields fertile with rotation and fallow seasons, it's obvious his goal is to create nutrient-rich, flavourful grains that can be enjoyed throughout Atlantic Canada.

Much of the organic grain grown in Atlantic Canada lands at Speerville Flour Mill, in Speerville, New Brunswick. Supporting the industry by paying top dollar for quality crops is part of owner Todd Grant's philosophy. "If we don't have farmers, I don't have a mill," he says. Todd works the entire milling process in-house. The grain is dried and sifted for size, the vetch (fodder crop which grows alongside or underneath the tall wheat) is removed, and then the grain is sifted again through a gravity table before being milled and labelled with the classically old-school iconic logo proudly featuring New Brunswick wheat. Oats are rolled through stainless rollers, and, although they're not crafted with the use of a hand crank, they're as close to hand-rolled oats as you can get. The rolling process is time-consuming but preserves the oats more fully and creates the highest-quality product, which, as Todd explains, "is always the goal."

Aside from the mill, he has also created a seed bank to assist local farmers in keeping and cultivating the most popular heritage grains. Acadian wheat is a prime example. He found some seeds over twenty years ago and has laboured to revitalize and propagate this ancient local variety ever since. Supporting the small organic farmers, cultivating those relationships, and allowing the farmers to increase the value of much desired crops is what keeps the business alive and the market growing. "If I didn't love what I do, I wouldn't be in business," proclaims Todd. "Know your food, tie yourself to it. It's the best way to understand how to be a sustainable link in the ever-changing and ever-growing food chain." Given the delights we've tasted here, these small-scale Atlantic farmers understand their place in the food chain well, and the amazing heritage grains they're growing are proof that ingenuity and hard work really do result in the most delicious products.

Brown Bread *with* Dulse Butter

MAKES 2 (5- BY 9-INCH)
LOAVES AND 2 CUPS DULSE
BUTTER

*Foghorn Brewing Company's Old Forte
Winter Warmer*

Crosby's Molasses, the beloved Canadian brand, has its roots in Saint John, New Brunswick. While it has many uses, its deep mineral tones pair well with the natural nuttiness of the wheat and are amplified by the flavour of local oats, which also add their own texture. You can have fresh loaves of this traditional brown bread pulled from the oven in just over two hours, as using quick rise yeast shortens the first rise significantly. Serve with a slather of dulse butter alongside Maple Baked Beans (page 198), Beans Basquaise (page 199), or just on its own for breakfast.

Brown Bread:

2 cups boiling water

1 cup oats

¼ cup butter

2 Tbsp sugar

2 tsp sea salt

2 cups whole wheat flour

Olive oil, for drizzling

1 Tbsp quick rise yeast

¾ cup molasses

3 cups all-purpose flour, sifted,
  plus more for dusting

Dulse Butter:

1 cup butter, softened

¼ cup ground dulse

For the Brown Bread: In a mixing bowl or liquid measure, combine the boiling water with the oats, butter, sugar, and salt. Let sit for at least 15 minutes, until the water has cooled to 115°F.

In the bowl of a stand mixer fitted with the dough hook, use a fork to combine the whole wheat flour and yeast. Add the oat mixture and begin to mix on the lowest speed. While the mixer is running, slowly pour in the molasses in a fine stream until it is fully incorporated into the dough. The mixture will be quite wet. Start to spoon in the all-purpose flour ½ cup at a time, continuing to mix after each addition, to form a soft dough. Let mix for an additional 5 minutes, then stop the mixer and remove the dough hook. Drizzle the dough with a little olive oil and turn it to coat in the oil, scraping off any extra bits of dough from the side. Cover with plastic wrap and let rise for 10 minutes in a warm, draft-free place.

Remove the dough from the bowl and divide it in half. Shape each half into an oval, tucking the ends under to form a long, even loaf. Grease two (5- by 9-inch) loaf tins with butter and place a loaf in each tin. Cover with a damp tea towel and place in a warm, draft-free place to rise for 1 hour, or until the loaf is about 2 inches above the edge of the loaf tin.

When there are 10 to 15 minutes left in the rise time, adjust the oven racks so one is in the middle and one is on the lowest rung. Place a baking dish filled with water on the lowest rack. Preheat the oven to 350°F.

When the dough is done rising, place each loaf tin on the centre rack. Bake for 40 to 45 minutes, until the bread is golden and crisp on top and sounds hollow when tapped.

(continued)

Remove from the oven, run a knife around the outside, and let rest in the pans for 10 minutes before removing and allowing to cool completely on a wire rack.

For the Dulse Butter: Using a stand mixer fitted with the whisk attachment, whisk the butter on medium speed until light, fluffy, and almost doubled in volume. Stop the mixer, scrape down the sides of the bowl, and add the dulse. Start mixing on the lowest speed, then gradually increase the speed to fully incorporate the dulse. Stop the mixer again, scrape down the sides of the bowl, and whisk again on medium-high speed for 30 seconds. Stop the mixer and transfer the butter to a storage container. A wide-mouth Mason jar is perfect for this.

When the bread is cool, slice, toast, and slather it with dulse butter to serve.

STORAGE: The bread will keep in an airtight container at room temperature for up to 3 days or wrapped tightly in plastic in the freezer for up to 3 months. The dulse butter will keep in an airtight container in the fridge for up to 2 weeks.

Sea Buckthorn Hot Pepper Jelly, Chow Chow, & Quick Pickles Charcuterie Board

SERVES 6

Richibucto River Wine Estate's Eterno

From duck pâté and rillettes to moose and venison sausages, the creativity with which home salumists are presenting cured game is quite astounding, and artisanal shops from across the region sell delicious local meats perfect for your next spread.

When done properly, a charcuterie board is a thing of beauty. The secret lies in the accompaniments, and in Atlantic Canada that is always a few jars of homemade pickles and preserves. Every home has a store of pickled ingredients, and other acidic delights that live on the table to balance the rich, delicious food that appears on the plate. These are a now in constant rotation when we lay out a charcuterie spread (see page xx).

Quick Pickles:

½ English cucumber (see note, page 180)

4 cloves garlic

¼ cup chopped dill

2 Tbsp sugar

2 Tbsp sea salt

2 tsp mustard seeds

¾ cup white wine vinegar (see note, page 180)

Chow Chow:

4 green tomatoes

1 small white onion

3 cloves garlic

2 tsp pickling salt

¼ tsp smoked paprika

¼ cup sugar

½ cup apple cider vinegar

For the Quick Pickles: Using a mandolin, slice the cucumber thinly and transfer to a clean 2-cup Mason jar. Peel and roughly chop the garlic.

In a small pot, place the garlic, dill, sugar, salt, and mustard seeds. Pour the vinegar over top and bring to a simmer over medium-high heat. Add ¼ cup of water and stir to dissolve the sugar and salt. Pour everything into the Mason jar, scraping out any bits of dill that may have been left behind in the pot. Let sit on the counter for 15 minutes to cool, then seal tightly with the lid and ring. Place in the fridge to chill completely, about an hour. They can be served as soon as they are chilled.

For the Chow Chow: Chop the tomatoes and onion and crush the garlic. In a medium bowl, whisk together the salt and paprika until evenly combined. Add the tomatoes, onion, and garlic, toss to combine, and then let sit for 15 minutes to allow the juices to extract from the tomatoes. Transfer to a pot, mix in the sugar and vinegar, bring to a rolling boil over high heat, and boil for 2 minutes. Let the mixture cool for a few minutes. Transfer to a blender and blend until it is smooth. Pour into a clean 2-cup Mason jar and seal tightly with the lid and ring. Let sit at room temperature to cool, then transfer to the fridge until ready to serve.

(continued)

Sea Buckthorn Hot Pepper Jelly:

1 lb chili peppers (a variety of red chili peppers works well)

4 cups sugar

¾ cup sea buckthorn juice (see page 223)

1 (85 ml) pouch liquid pectin

To Serve:

3–4 (8 oz each) portions of your favourite charcuterie

2–3 (2 oz each) portions of your favourite cheeses

2 Tbsp grainy mustard

2 Tbsp creamy mustard

Crackers, crostini, and breadsticks

For the Sea Buckthorn Chili Pepper Jelly: Sterilize two (2-cup) or four (1-cup) Mason jars, lids, and rings by washing them in the dishwasher or boiling in water for 5 minutes. Set aside to air-dry. This will only take a few minutes.

Wearing gloves, wash the chilies and discard the stems, membrane and seeds. Finely chop the flesh. You should have about 2½ cups of diced chilies. Place the chilies in a large pot, and add the sugar and sea buckthorn juice. Bring to a simmer over medium heat, stirring constantly until the sugar has dissolved. Increase the heat to high and, still stirring, let the mixture come to a rolling boil, and boil for 1 minute. Remove from the heat and immediately add the pectin. Stir well to combine. Continuing to stir, skim off any foam that has formed on the surface. Stir for about 5 minutes, then let rest for 2 minutes. Pour the jelly into the prepared jars, leaving ¼ inch of headspace. Clean the rims, place the lids on the jars and tighten the rings down. If serving immediately, let a jar cool on the counter for 15 minutes, then place in the fridge to chill, about an hour. To preserve, let sit at room temperature to cool for 24 hours. The lids will seal and pop. If a jar doesn't seal, keep it in the fridge and use it first.

To Serve: Arrange the meats and cheeses on a plate, or a slate or wooden board. Arrange the mustards either in generous dollops directly on the plate or in small dishes. Serve with the quick pickles, chow chow, and sea buckthorn chili pepper jelly in separate dishes or their jars, and a basket of crackers, breadsticks, and crostini on the side.

STORAGE: The quick pickle and chow chow will keep in in the fridge for up to 1 month. The jelly will keep in a cool, dark cupboard for up to 1 year. Once opened, the jelly will keep for up to 1 month in the fridge.

NOTE: For the quick pickles, using vegetables other than cucumbers is a fun way to make your plate more colourful. Beets, carrots, turnips, and even blueberries are delicious. Substituting half the vinegar for malt vinegar adds a flavour twist for the quick pickles.

Dulse-Spiced Popcorn

SERVES 4

Dunhams Run Estate Winery's Lily In The Pink

½ cup grated Parmesan cheese

2 Tbsp dulse flakes

1 tsp garlic powder

¼ cup neutral oil

¼ cup popcorn kernels

¼ cup melted butter

The nutritional value of dulse is quite remarkable: it's high in magnesium, potassium, phosphorous, zinc, vitamins A, B, C, E . . . It's like eating a multivitamin! Sprinkling some over popcorn for an afternoon snack or movie night is a great way to sneak in extra nutrients for the kids, and the salty flavour from the dulse means no added salt is necessary!

In a small bowl, combine the cheese, dulse, and garlic powder.

In a large pot with a lid, heat the oil over medium-high heat just until a drop of water sprinkled into the pan sizzles and evaporates.

Add the popcorn kernels and gently shake the pot with the lid on, keeping the pot over but not touching the heat. The popcorn will start to pop. When the popping sounds start dwindling to one or two odd pops, remove the pot from the heat and carefully lift the lid, preventing any extra condensation from dripping onto the kernels.

Pour the popcorn into a large bowl, drizzle with the butter, and toss well to coat. Sprinkle with half the prepared seasoning and toss again. Distribute into serving bowls and sprinkle the remaining dulse seasoning, dividing evenly. Enjoy immediately.

STORAGE: The popcorn is best enjoyed as soon as it's made.

Bottled Quahogs

MAKES 2 PINTS

Loyalist City Brewing Company's Three Sisters Pale Ale

When chef Jesse Vergen decided to open a restaurant in Saint John, it was long before "farm-to-table dining" was a popular catchphrase. Drawing inspiration from the close-knit community he grew up in, building a sustainable dynamic relationship between farm and restaurant became his obvious focus for Saint John Ale House. "We support the farmers because we know them," he explains. "In a small town like this, you can actually make a difference, having a bigger effect on the greater surrounding economy." In turn, he is able to create dishes with the very best in local ingredients, sourced by his own hand or from foragers and farmers he considers neighbours.

Jesse has been digging quahogs, large local clams hand-harvested from the Fundy shores, since he was a kid, and when these gems are pickled, they are nothing short of spectacular. He tells us that the juice can be used to give a kick to a classic Caesar, or clams added to a chowder for a punch of briny flavour. We find the bottled quahogs make a wonderful standalone weekend cabin snack, are a perfect addition to any charcuterie board, and make for an excellent appetizer when served on crostini with chèvre, pepper jelly, and lemon zest.

10 lb hand-dug quahogs, scrubbed and rinsed

½ cup pickling salt

⅓ cup lemon juice

STORAGE: The quahogs will keep sealed in a cool, dark place for up to 3 months. Once opened, they will keep for 1 week in the fridge.

Recipe contributed by Jesse Vergen, Saint John Ale House

Sterilize two (2-cup) Mason jars, lids, and rings by washing them in the dishwasher or boiling in water for 5 minutes. Only use new lids in this canning procedure. Place the jars in simmering water to keep them hot.

In a large stockpot over medium heat, bring 4 litres of water to a simmer. Add the quahogs, salt, and lemon juice and cook until all the shells are open, 3 to 5 minutes. Discard any unopened quahogs. Strain the liquid into a bowl through a colander or cheesecloth and quickly remove all the meat from the shells. Pack each jar with hot meat, leaving 1 to 2 inches of space between the meat and the rim of the jars. Add the strained clam juice, making sure to remove all the air bubbles from the jar with a metal skewer. If you don't have enough liquid to cover the quahogs, just add salted boiling water.

Place the lids on the jars, tighten the rings down, and process the jars in a pressure canner at 10 psi for 1 hour. Let the canner cool to zero pressure and then let the jars rest for 24 hours on a counter. When you hear them pop, you'll know the seal is depressed and holding well. If a jar doesn't seal, keep it in the fridge and use immediately.

Haskap Pickled Eggs

SERVES 4

🍷 *Lightfoot & Wolfville's Blanc de Blancs Brut*

After spending the morning fishing on the Saint John River, we have a new appreciation for the delicacy that is wild Acadian sturgeon caviar. Cornel and Dorina Ceapa, owners of Acadian Sturgeon and Caviar Inc., took the time to give us a tour of their farm and wild fishery, followed by an incredible sturgeon-filled feast. While sustainability and freshness are buzzwords for some, we saw first-hand how they take the practice of both very seriously. Cornel has a PhD in sturgeon biology, and caring for and keeping the sturgeon stocks strong is a passion that runs deep in this family business. The caviar is never harvested without processing the entire fish, and preserving the product means nothing more than packing it on ice so it can be served as fresh as can be.

These pickled eggs are as delicious as they are beautiful! The haskap berries impart not only a gorgeous deep-burgundy colour, but also an earthiness that pairs perfectly with the salty-smooth Acadian caviar topping.

---

2 cups fresh or frozen haskap berries, crushed with juice retained

2 cups white vinegar

2 Tbsp sugar

1 Tbsp sea salt

8 eggs

2 Tbsp mayonnaise

2 Tbsp sour cream

1 tsp Dijon mustard

1 tsp lemon juice

3 Tbsp wild sturgeon caviar

In a medium pot over medium-high heat, bring the crushed haskap berries along with their juice, vinegar, sugar, salt, and ½ cup water to a boil. Stir to dissolve the sugar and salt into the brine. Remove from the heat and let sit at room temperature, uncovered, for at least 30 minutes.

Fill a medium pot with water, add the eggs, cover, and bring to a boil over medium-high heat. When the water comes to a boil, turn off the heat and let sit for 12 minutes. Prepare an ice bath. Place the eggs in the ice bath to chill for at least 30 minutes. Once chilled, peel the eggs and transfer them to a 4-cup Mason jar. Fill the jar with the haskap brine, ensuring the eggs are covered. Place in the fridge to chill for at least 24 hours, or up to 1 month.

When you're ready to serve, remove the eggs from the brine and cut the eggs in half lengthwise. Remove the yolks and add them to a bowl with the mayonnaise, sour cream, mustard, and lemon juice. Mash together to form a smooth mixture. Fill a piping bag with the egg yolk mixture and pipe it into the egg white halves. Cover loosely and chill in the fridge for 30 minutes to set. To serve, place the eggs on a platter and top each with about ½ tsp of wild sturgeon caviar.

Fiddlehead Fritters *with* Golden Yogurt

SERVES 4

Red Rover Craft Cider's Spring Cider

Fiddlehead Fritters:

1 cup flour

1 tsp baking powder

1 tsp fine sea salt

½ tsp black pepper

½ tsp paprika

½ cup diced onion

½ cup milk

1½ cups trimmed fiddleheads, blanched

Neutral oil, for frying

Golden Yogurt:

¾ cup Greek yogurt

1 Tbsp lime juice

1 Tbsp ground turmeric

1 tsp ground cumin

½ tsp ground coriander

½ tsp fine sea salt

STORAGE: The fritters are best enjoyed they day they are made, although they will keep in an airtight container in the fridge for up to 3 days. The yogurt will keep in an airtight container in the fridge for up to 5 days.

Good food doesn't need to be complicated, and fiddleheads are a prime example. Whether you've sautéed them in olive oil with salt and pepper, tossed them with some scrambled eggs, or added them to a creamy soup, these glorious little green buds epitomize the value of simplicity. These fritters are one of our favourite ways to enjoy fiddleheads. They're delicious dunked in a softly spiced golden yogurt that complements the fresh green bite of the fiddleheads hidden inside.

For the Fiddlehead Fritters: In a large mixing bowl, whisk together the flour, baking powder, salt, pepper, and paprika. Add the onion and toss until the onion is well coated with the flour mixture. Stirring constantly, slowly add the milk to form a thick batter. Gently fold in the fiddleheads until they are just coated in the batter.

In a heavy-bottomed skillet or pot over medium-high heat, heat 2 inches of oil to 375°F, using a candy thermometer to monitor the temperature. Turn down the heat to medium when the oil reaches temperature, to prevent it from getting too hot. Using two spoons, gently place three to four fritters in the hot oil. Using tongs, nudge the fritters to ensure they have space to move, aren't overcrowded, and aren't sticking to the bottom of the pan. Allow to cook for between 60 and 90 seconds before flipping. They will be golden brown. Cook for 1 more minute or so, then transfer to a wire rack with parchment paper underneath it and allow any excess oil to drip off. Repeat with the remaining fritters.

For the Golden Yogurt: In a small bowl, whisk together all of the yogurt ingredients until smooth.

Serve the fritters on a platter with the yogurt on the side.

NOTE: As fiddleheads are foraged wild, here is an outline to safely prepare them for eating.

- Remove the brown husk from the fiddleheads and trim the ends.
- Rinse thoroughly in cold water, to remove any dirt and extra bits of husk.
- Bring a lot of water to a rolling boil and prepare an ice bath.
- Blanch the fiddleheads for 15 minutes. Drain the fiddleheads, discarding the boiling water, and immediately place fiddleheads in ice bath to stop them from cooking.
- Use as directed in recipe, or place in freezer bags and freeze to preserve for up to a year.

FORAGING FIDDLEHEADS

Walking through the thick, marshy New Brunswick forest on a spring day, engulfed by the varying dappled shades of green, we're struck by the feeling of rebirth that surrounds us. The snow is all but gone, the ground is soft, and the large pine and spruce trees, along with the smaller birch trees, are all beginning to bud. Fiddlehead season has arrived: the ground is covered in wild ferns and the bounty to be harvested is plentiful. Fiddleheads are the tiny bright-green, almost emerald, leaves that grow from the rich black soil at the base of ostrich ferns in the early days of spring. Fiddleheads aren't cultivated, so the easiest way to enjoy these morsels is by sourcing them at your local farmers' market or foraging for them during an adventurous walk in the woods.

Foraging is a way of life for many in New Brunswick, stretching back long before the days when the Mi'kmaq First Nation taught the Acadians traditional methods of identifying plants to forage and ways to preserve food, many of which are now being infused into the local cuisine. In meeting several Acadian chefs—and getting to taste their incredible foods—we saw first-hand how this history has created a unique bond between the people and the land. Cheyenne Joseph, a Mi'kmaq chef and teacher, shared stories of how, although these cultures have evolved over time, the foundations are steadfast. She explains that because the eastern side of Canada was exposed to colonialization first, many Indigenous food traditions were lost, but what remains is the sense of community, connection, and a resurgence of communal eating with a deepening tie to Earth's wild foods.

There is a reclamation happening as new ways of infusing traditional ingredients with modern practices become more and more common; collaboration and community develop as people forage together, sharing meals that showcase all that the forests and land provide.

The good news for those new to the craft is that fiddleheads are probably one of the safest and easiest things to forage for, making them a great place to start a foraging journey. The ostrich fern, once you learn to identify it, is fairly easy to spot. These fiddlehead ferns are typically found close to a river or stream, as they like cool, wet, rich soil. They're bright green and loosely covered with a papery brown husk, and they look like the scroll of a violin or fiddle—hence the name. They typically grow in clumps with six to eight (1-inch) heads per plant. They are often found alongside bracken and other ferns, which aren't the best for eating. Those ferns also look different from the ostrich ferns: bracken have fuzzy stems, are more of a brown colour, are bent in shape like a shepherd's staff instead of having a tightly curled head, have only one stem instead of clumps, and have a perfectly round stem instead of the deep U-shaped groove that the ostrich fern possesses.

When you're foraging, please remember to harvest only half of the fiddleheads per plant; this will ensure that the fern thrives throughout the season. If all of the sprouts are taken, the plant won't be able to sprout any leaves that year, thus restricting its growth and ability to feed itself with sun and rain. If we take care of the Earth and respect her limits, she will in turn shower us with delicacies in abundance.

Fiddlehead Soup & Salmon Toasts

SERVES 4

 Lightfoot & Wolfville's Sauvignon Blanc

"New Brunswick really does have it all," says chef Pierre Richard as we sit around a table at Little Louis' Fine Cuisine (locally just known as Little Louis') in Moncton. "The terroir here really puts that into perspective." This is a land that has wilderness, forest, and marsh, and is surrounded by an ocean, lakes, and rivers to make everything flourish. Pierre pulls out a piece of goose tongue, a local grass that grows in the marshes. He picked it this morning on his way to the restaurant to add to his evening dinner service, blanched in the same way as spinach. Being Acadian himself and wanting to honour his culture as well as its beautiful historic connection to the Mi'kmaq communities, Pierre is constantly incorporating foraged foods into his cuisine. This fiddlehead soup recipe is no exception.

To prepare fiddleheads properly for this soup, see the cooking note on page 188.

Fiddlehead Soup:

1 small white onion

2 stalks celery

1 small fennel bulb

¼ cup butter

1 tsp sea salt

2 cloves garlic

½ cup dry white wine

2 Tbsp flour

2 cups vegetable stock

2 cups whole milk

½ tsp black pepper

½ tsp grated nutmeg

2 cups trimmed fiddleheads, blanched

1 cup baby spinach

For the Fiddlehead Soup: Chop the onion, celery, and fennel. In a large saucepan over medium heat, melt the butter and sauté the vegetables for 1 to 2 minutes. When the onions are just softening and the celery is vibrant green, sprinkle the salt over top. Add the garlic and continue to sauté and sweat the vegetables until the onion is fully translucent, an additional 3 to 4 minutes. Deglaze the pan with the wine, scraping up any bits that may have stuck to the bottom of the pot, and cook until almost all the liquid has been absorbed. Sprinkle in the flour, stir to combine, and cook for about 1 minute, creating a roux. Slowly add the stock, whisking constantly until the mixture is smooth, then gradually add the milk, still whisking constantly. Increase the heat to high and bring to a boil. Boil for 30 seconds, then turn down the heat to low and continue to cook, still stirring, until the mixture has thickened slightly. Season with the pepper and nutmeg. Simmer, covered, for 15 minutes, stirring occasionally. Add the fiddleheads and spinach, then remove from the heat and let sit for 5 minutes to finish cooking and allow the spinach to wilt. This will give the soup a vibrant green colour.

Using an immersion blender or a traditional blender in batches, blend the soup until it is creamy and smooth. Season to taste. Return to the pot to keep warm until you're ready to serve.

Salmon Toasts:

8 slices rustic bread

2 tsp capers

2 Tbsp butter

¼ cup mayonnaise

2 Tbsp grainy Dijon mustard

8 pieces smoked Atlantic salmon

1 small red onion

To Serve:

½ cup Greek yogurt, for garnish

Black pepper

Grated nutmeg

For the Salmon Toasts: Lightly toast the bread slices. In a small skillet, sauté the capers until crisp, 2 to 3 minutes, then remove from the heat. Spread each slice of toast with butter, mayonnaise, and mustard (in that order). Top each slice with a piece of smoked salmon. Finely slice the red onion and garnish each toast with a few strips of onion and fried capers.

To Serve: Ladle the soup into serving bowls, garnish with a dollop of yogurt and a sprinkling of pepper and nutmeg, and serve alongside the smoked salmon toasts.

STORAGE: The soup, without the garnishes, will keep in an airtight container in the fridge for up to 5 days. The toasts are best enjoyed the day they are made.

Recipe contributed by Pierre Richard, Little Louis' Fine Cuisine

Three Sisters Soup

SERVES 4

Graystone Brewing's Burning Rock Red

1 small butternut or acorn squash

2 Tbsp butter

¼ cup diced white onion

2 cloves garlic, minced

1 tsp curry powder

1 tsp ground cumin

½ tsp sea salt

1 cup canned beans (such as navy, black, kidney, or a mixture), drained and rinsed

½ cup canned corn, drained

4 cups chicken stock

"The three sisters are squash, beans, and corn," says Cheyenne Joseph, known in the Atlantic culinary world as Mi'kmaq Mama. "They are the foundational focus of many Indigenous seed savers, groups of people who are saving their food heritage by working to find and cultivate heirloom seeds, propagating crops, and encouraging the growth of healthy food diversity." Her passion is using these traditional ingredients in modern dishes that everyone can make at home. This soup is simple and delicious, and can be made in a flash with everyday pantry items.

Preheat the oven to 375°F. Line a rimmed baking sheet with parchment paper.

Peel the squash, cut it into 1-inch cubes, and place on the prepared baking sheet. Roast for 30 minutes, until fork-tender. Remove from the oven, allow to cool slightly, and then transfer to a bowl and mash or purée with an immersion blender. Set aside.

In a large saucepan over medium-low heat, melt the butter. Add the onions and garlic and cook until tender, 3 to 5 minutes. Stir in the curry powder, cumin, and salt, and cook for 1 minute. Add the beans, corn, and stock and bring to a boil. Turn down the heat to low and cook, covered, stirring occasionally, for 15 to 20 minutes. Stir in the squash and cook for 5 to 7 minutes, until the mixture is bubbling and steaming hot. Remove from the heat and serve.

STORAGE: The soup will keep in an airtight container in the fridge for up to 5 days.

Recipe contributed by Cheyenne Joseph, Mi'kmaq Mama

Tricolour Beet & Lentil Salad

SERVES 4

🍷 *Magnetic Hill Winery's Illusions*

2 lb mixed candy cane, golden,
  and sugar beets

1 cup dried French lentils

1½ tsp sea salt, divided

¼ cup olive oil

2 Tbsp white wine vinegar

1 cup Greek yogurt

2 Tbsp lemon juice

1 tsp ground cumin

Beet microgreens, for garnish

We have to admit, we simply adore root vegetables—beets most of all—and this recipe is a great way of serving them up, whether they're freshly harvested or straight from the root cellar. Topped with seasoned yogurt and made hearty with lentils, this is a wonderful main course for vegetarians or the perfect side dish to pair with Whole Trout en Papillote (page 207).

Preheat the oven to 375°F.

Scrub the beets. Using a paring knife or vegetable peeler, peel the candy cane beets. Slice the beets into wedges and set aside. Repeat with the golden beets, and then the sugar beets. Continue to keep the colours separate. Wrap each colour separately in aluminum foil so the colours don't bleed. Roast until fork-tender, 30 to 45 minutes,. Remove from the oven and allow to cool slightly.

While the beets are cooking, rinse the lentils well, place in a medium pot, and add just enough water to cover them. Cover the pot and bring the water to a boil, then turn down the heat to low and set the lid slightly ajar. Simmer until all the water is absorbed and the lentils are fork-tender, 30 to 45 minutes. Remove from the heat and fluff with a fork. Drizzle 1 tsp of the salt, the oil, and vinegar over top, and mix well with a wooden spoon to evenly coat the lentils.

In a small bowl, whisk together the remaining ½ teaspoon of salt, the yogurt, lemon juice, and cumin until fully combined.

Spoon the lentils onto a serving platter, arrange the beets on top, and drizzle with the yogurt dressing. Garnish with microgreens and serve.

STORAGE: This salad is lovely served warm or chilled. Once dressed with the yogurt, it's best enjoyed the day it's made, although the various components will keep in separate airtight containers in the fridge for up to 1 week.

Maple Baked Beans

SERVES 4

Gaspereau Vineyards' Lucie Kuhlmann

Dried edible beans are such a wonderful part of New Brunswick cuisine. Although not commonly grown commercially in New Brunswick today, they are steeped in tradition and remain a staple in Acadian and Mi'kmaq diets. Maple syrup adds a distinctly Canadian flavour to this dish, reducing the amount of molasses normally needed. These baked beans are wonderful on their own but also make a perfect side to Island Beef Short Ribs (page 144) or Moose Roast with Irish Red Ale Gravy (page 290). The sauce can be made ahead of time and frozen. Just thaw in the fridge, add the beans, and dinner will be ready in no time!

---

8 thick strips bacon

1 large white onion

2 cloves garlic

1 small red or serrano chili pepper

2 Tbsp olive oil

1½ cups crushed tomatoes

¾ cup maple syrup

¼ cup molasses

2 tsp chili powder

2 tsp celery seeds

1 tsp smoked paprika

1 tsp ground cinnamon

1 (19 oz) can navy beans, rinsed and drained

1 (19 oz) can black beans, rinsed and drained

Sea salt and black pepper

Line a small plate with paper towel.

Cut the bacon into 1-inch pieces. Finely chop the onion and garlic. Wearing gloves, wash the chili and discard the stems, membrane and seeds. Finely chop the flesh.

In a large, heavy-bottomed pot over medium heat, sauté the bacon until crisp and golden. Transfer the bacon to the prepared plate. Leave the grease in the pot and add the oil.

Add the onions to the pot and sauté for 3 minutes, just until translucent. Add the garlic and chilies and sauté just until the garlic is soft and starting to brown, 2 to 3 minutes. Add the tomatoes, maple syrup, and molasses. Stirring well to combine, bring to a boil. When it starts bubbling, turn down the heat to low. Add the chili powder, celery seeds, paprika, and cinnamon, mixing well to combine. Simmer, uncovered, for 10 minutes.

Add the bacon and beans to the pot, and season with salt and pepper to taste, stirring to combine. Partially cover the pot and allow to simmer, stirring often, until the sauce is thick and the beans have softened, 30 to 45 minutes. If the beans appear too thick, add ¼ cup of water to the pot and continue to simmer. If they are too watery, continue to cook until the liquid reduces to your desired consistency.

STORAGE: The beans will keep in an airtight container in the fridge for up to 1 week.

Beans Basquaise

SERVES 6

Annapolis Cider Company's Old-Fashioned Gravenstine

"Be a good student of the land and what it produces," says chef Michel Savoie of Les Brumes du Coude, as he shares with us the essentials of being an Acadian chef in New Brunswick. In his restaurant, where he educates both locals and travellers about the uniqueness of Acadian cuisine, he uses 90% local ingredients and everything is made from scratch. As we're chatting, he runs to the kitchen to stir a pot and then hurries back to sit down again. We ask about his favourite local ingredient and he beams: "Beans, edible beans!" His twist on poulet basquaise, a slow-braised chicken ragout that is often enjoyed in the autumn when bell peppers are at their peak, is a celebration of his beloved beans.

2 cups dried lima or white navy beans

1 large white onion

2 large carrots

3 red bell peppers

2 stalks celery

3 tomatoes

4 cloves garlic

¼ cup olive oil

6 chicken legs

1 tsp sea salt, plus more to taste

8½ cups chicken stock

¼ cup chopped parsley

4 sprigs thyme

2 bay leaves

1 tsp chili flakes

Olive oil, for garnish

Grated hard cheese, for garnish

Rinse the beans well, place them in a large mixing bowl, cover with at least 3 inches of water, and let soak at room temperature for 8 to 12 hours.

When you're ready to cook, roughly chop the onion, carrots, bell peppers, celery, and tomatoes. Crush the garlic, but leave the cloves whole. Set aside.

In a large Dutch oven or heavy-bottomed ovenproof pot over medium heat, heat the oil. Pat the chicken legs dry and sear well on all sides until the skin is golden and crisp, for a total of 10 to 15 minutes. Transfer the legs to a plate, cover and refrigerate.

Preheat the oven to 350°F.

Add the onions to the pot and sauté until soft and translucent, 3 to 5 minutes. Sprinkle the salt over top. Sautéing for 3 to 5 minutes after you add each vegetable, add the carrots, then the peppers, celery, tomatoes, and finally the garlic. Don't rush this step. Allowing the vegetables to soften and caramelize naturally adds to the character of the dish.

Drain and rinse the beans and add them to the vegetables, followed by the stock. Add the parsley, thyme, and bay leaves, stir, cover the pot, and roast in the oven until the beans are just tender. If they have a bit of crunch that is ok, but they should still be quite soft. This will take 45 minutes to 1 hour.

(If you don't have an ovenproof pot, you can sear the chicken and sauté the vegetables in a large skillet. Transfer the vegetables to a roasting pan, or a slow cooker, add the beans and stock, and continue as directed. If you're using a slow cooker, cook on low for 6 hours.)

(continued)

Remove the lid, and add the chili flakes and more salt to taste. Add the chicken legs, nestling them into the top of the beans. Bake for an additional 20 to 25 minutes (or, if you're using a slow cooker, cook for 1 hour more). Check the legs with a meat thermometer to ensure they register 165°F and are cooked through. Test the beans to ensure they are tender. The dish may need to cook for another 10 minutes. Once the chicken is done and the beans are tender, remove from the oven and cover.

Let rest at room temperature for 1 hour to allow the flavours to develop and the beans to absorb even more of the liquid. Discard the bay leaves before serving. Serve warm or cold, with the beans in a bowl, topped with a chicken leg, and a good glug of oil and some grated cheese scattered over top.

STORAGE: The beans and chicken can be kept in airtight containers in the fridge for up to 4 days.

Recipe contributed by Michel Savoie, Les Brumes du Coude

Fish & Potatoes

SERVES 4

Red Rover Craft Cider's Summer Cider

½ lb salt cod

1 small stalk celery

1 small carrot

¼ white onion

2 cloves garlic, divided

2 sprigs thyme

2 sprigs parsley

1 bay leaf

½ tsp black peppercorns

½ tsp coriander seeds

2 cups whole milk

1 large or 2 small potatoes (Yukon Gold are best)

16 small new potatoes

8 Tbsp olive oil, divided, plus more for garnish

2 Tbsp capers

2 Tbsp chopped herbs (such as chives and parsley), for garnish

Sea salt

Jennie Wilson fell in love with food when she met Peter Tompkins, and it didn't take long for her to share his passion for culinary adventures as well. After living in Toronto for years, they felt the pull to move home to Fredericton and open their own restaurant—thus 11th Mile was born. Their philosophy is simple: Go the extra mile for your customers, feed people in a loving way, and give back to the community every chance you have. "We wanted to make a difference and the opportunity for impact was here." Their love for the province carries over into their simple, yet innovative dishes that use the best of local ingredients and perfectly exemplify why this place they call home really does have it all.

This brandade, a salt cod emulsion usually made with potatoes, is the perfect expression of creativity mixed with a sense and taste of place.

Chop the salt cod into small pieces and place them in a small bowl. Cover with at least 2 inches of cold water, cover with plastic wrap, and soak in the fridge for 6 hours. Change the water and repeat this process three times, until the fish is fully hydrated and the salt has soaked out. It usually takes about 24 hours of soaking.

Slice the celery, carrot, and onion into 1-inch pieces. Smash 1 garlic clove, leaving the clove whole. Mince the second clove of garlic and set aside.

In a saucepan, place the celery, carrots, onions, the smashed garlic, thyme, parsley, bay leaf, peppercorns, coriander seeds, and milk. Bring to a simmer over low heat and cook for 15 minutes, allowing the flavours to infuse. Remove from the heat and allow to cool for 30 minutes.

Meanwhile, preheat the oven to 425°F. Line a rimmed baking sheet with parchment paper.

Peel the potato and chop it into 1-inch cubes. Rinse them, then place them in a small pot of salted water and bring to a boil over medium-high heat. Cook until fork-tender, 5 to 8 minutes. Remove from the heat, keeping the potatoes in the water until you're ready to use them. In a second pot, place the small new potatoes and cover them with ½ inch of water. Bring to a boil over medium-high heat and cook until just tender, 5 to 8 minutes. Remove from the heat and drain.

(continued)

Transfer the small new potatoes to the prepared baking sheet. Using the bottom of a glass, press each potato until it is about ¾ to 1 inch thick. Drizzle with 2 tablespoons of oil. Bake until the potatoes are crisp and golden, about 30 minutes.

Strain the milk mixture into a bowl and return the milk to the saucepan. Set the vegetables aside for another use—they work great as a side dish or in soup.

Rinse the salt cod one final time and squeeze out as much water as possible. Add the cod to the milk, bring to a simmer over medium heat, and cook for 10 minutes. Using a slotted spoon, transfer the cod to a food processor fitted with the steel blade, along with the reserved minced garlic and ¼ cup of the milk. Pulse to combine. Drain the potato cubes, add to the food processor, and pulse to combine. With the food processor running, slowly add the remaining 6 tablespoons of oil through the feed tube and keep mixing until a thick, creamy purée, about the consistency of a thick aioli, forms. Transfer to a bowl and cover to keep warm until ready to serve.

In a small skillet, fry the capers for 3 to 4 minutes, until crisp.

To serve, divide the brandade between four plates. Top each serving with four crispy potatoes and garnish with crisped capers, fresh herbs, a sprinkle of salt, and a good glug of olive oil to taste.

STORAGE: The baked potatoes will keep in the fridge in an airtight container for up to 1 week. The brandade will keep in the fridge in a separate airtight container for up to 3 days.

Recipe contributed by Peter Tompkins, 11th Mile

Whole Trout en Papillote

SERVES 4

Luckett Vineyards' Rosetta

6 cloves garlic

4 bay leaves

4–5 lb cleaned whole trout

2 lemons

4 Tbsp olive oil, divided

1 tsp sea salt

½ tsp black pepper

Small handful of sea buckthorn
  berries (optional)

Fly-fishing is a popular late-summer and early-autumn activity in northern New Brunswick. You'll know the season is open when you see the waterside roads lined with trucks and the lakes dotted with people in hip waders. This dish is the ultimate reward for a wonderful morning spent fishing. Tart and tangy from the addition of lemon and easy to prepare, this fish is hearty yet simple. If you're enjoying this later in the season, the addition of a few fresh sea buckthorn berries to the cavity makes it beyond delicious.

Preheat the oven to 400°F.

Line a baking pan large enough to hold the fish without crowding with enough parchment paper (about twice the width of the pan) to easily fold over and seal the fish.

Smash the garlic cloves with the back of a knife, leaving them whole. Place the bay leaves in a parallel line along the centre of the parchment and lay the fish on top.

Slice the lemon into rounds about ¼ inch thick.

Using a knife, open the fish gently, scatter the garlic evenly throughout the cavity, and lay the slices from one lemon evenly over top of them. Drizzle the cavity with 2 tablespoons of the oil and season with the salt and pepper. Sprinkle with sea buckthorn berries, if using. Drizzle the fish with the remaining 2 tablespoons of oil and rub it into the skin. Place the remaining lemon slices along the length of the top of the fish, then seal the parchment by bringing the long ends together over the fish and folding them downwards and over themselves. Twist the ends of the paper and tuck them under the fish, making a little roasting packet.

Bake for 30 minutes. Carefully open the packet (there will be steam!), and let the fish rest for 10 minutes. Place the fish on a serving platter, remove the lemon rounds before serving, and discard the bay leaves (note they may stick to the skin underneath).

Serve immediately on a platter.

STORAGE: The fish is best enjoyed the day it's made, but it will keep in an airtight container in the fridge for up to 3 days.

GATHERING DULSE

Dulse seaweed grows at an incredible pace along the shores of Grand Manan, a small island located in the Bay of Fundy just off the New Brunswick–Maine border. Grand Manan is one of the few places on the planet where this prized sea vegetable grows in such abundance. The west side of the island, below the tall cliffs of Dark Harbour, offers perfect conditions for the deeply purple beds that move softly in the current. Shaded from the sun, with a constant flow of clean, cold water brought in by the Fundy tides, dulse from here is said to be the best in the world.

Walking the shores of Dark Harbour on Grand Manan at dawn, we're awestruck at the effort that goes into gathering this most unusual crop. It is not an activity for the faint of heart. Harvest time is a two-week window on either side of the full and new moon cycles, when the tides are at their most extreme. The seaweed can only be picked during the lowest of tides, as it grows on the rocks at the edge of the intertidal zone. The female plants are almost invisible; the male plants grow the iconic large purple leaves. These leaves are always picked off the root stock by hand, as the use of any tools—scissors included—is impossible not only because of the topography but also because they would damage the plant beds. Once collected, the dulse roots begin to produce again, replenishing the crop completely every couple of weeks. Roughly 1 million pounds of dulse is collected from Grand Manan annually.

We watch as the harvesters don hip waders and scramble over the rocks, picking the sea vegetables under the moonlight, filling large food-safe burlap bags until their wooden dories are almost too heavy to float. The dulse is then brought up and laid out to dry in sheets under the heat of the morning sun. The leaves are gently torn and overlapped in long rows, and as they dry, they create a carpet. After a few hours they are rolled and flipped (see page 178), and then taken to the buyer.

While we're chatting with Jayne Turner of Atlantic Mariculture Ltd., a few harvesters arrive with bundles of freshly dried dulse on their shoulders. Each roll is weighed and checked for quality. "Anyone can harvest dulse," Jayne says. "It's competitive, but it's not regulated like the fishing industry, and since it's naturally sustainable, there isn't really a need." Once the dulse arrives, the goal is to keep it pure, with as few touch points as possible—only nine or ten times by two to three small groups of people—as it travels from harvest to package. "That's also what makes it special," Jayne explains. "It's a people-filled industry."

Jayne hands us a nutritional information document on dulse that's pages long. Rich in iodine and loaded with minerals, eating dulse is like taking a multivitamin; it has character inside and out, as do the people of Grand Manan. This beautiful seaweed, the crown jewel of sea vegetables, is not only the finest found anywhere in the world, it is also reflective of the culture, the people, and the land. It's no wonder it's found in such a unique and special place.

Dulse Salt–Seared Pork Chops *with* Roasted Garlic Mornay

SERVES 2

*Richibucto River Wine Estate's
Radiant Red*

1 bulb garlic

4 Tbsp olive oil, divided

2–3 dulse leaves (see note)

2 Tbsp sea salt

2 pork loin chops, bone in

1 Tbsp flour

¾ cup milk

1 cup grated Jarlsberg cheese

STORAGE: The sauce will keep in an airtight container in the fridge for up to 1 week. The pork chops will keep in an airtight container in the fridge for up to 3 days. You can also sprinkle the dulse salt on the chops and then freeze them to allow the salt to more fully tenderize the meat. Thaw completely before cooking.

NOTE: If you don't have dried dulse leaves at home, substitute 2 tablespoons of flaked, ground or dulse powder.

Dulse is the essence of the sea: it smells like the ocean and tastes like sea salt. When blended with the richness of a mornay, a cheesy béchamel sauce, poured over pork chops, you'll find the best of surf and turf on your plate.

Preheat the oven to 375°F. Carefully cut off the top of the bulb of garlic, exposing the cloves. Place the bulb on a piece of aluminum foil and drizzle the tops of the cloves with 1 tablespoon of the oil, allowing it to seep into them. Pull up the corners of the aluminum foil and twist at the top, ensuring that the bulb will stay upright. Roast until tender and soft, 20 to 30 minutes.

Chop or tear the dulse leaves into small pieces and place them in a mortar along with the salt. Using the pestle, grind the dulse and salt together until a fine mixture forms. It will be burgundy in colour. You might still have some pieces or flakes of dulse visible. That's ok.

Evenly rub 1 teaspoon of the mixture onto each side of the pork chops, ensuring they are well covered. Chill the pork chops in the fridge for 20 to 30 minutes to allow the dulse salt to tenderize the meat.

In a heavy-bottomed ovenproof skillet or cast iron pan over high heat, add 1 tablespoon of the remaining oil. Once hot, and the oil is easily flowing around the pan, sear the chops, one at a time, until well browned and just a hint of pink remains. This will take about 2 minutes per side. Nestle the chops together in the pan and place in the oven for 5 minutes to allow them to finish cooking. Allow the chops to rest for 4 to 5 minutes before serving.

In a small pot, whisk together the remaining 2 tablespoons of oil and the flour until completely smooth and creamy. Place over medium heat and allow the mixture to bubble. Once it starts bubbling, remove from the heat, add the milk, and whisk until the milk is fully incorporated. Return to the heat and continue to cook until the mixture is thick and bubbles are forming. Add 1 teaspoon of the remaining dulse salt, squeeze in the whole bulb of roasted garlic, and whisk to combine, breaking up any large clumps of garlic. Remove from the heat. Stir in the grated cheese, let rest for 1 minute, allowing the cheese to melt, then whisk to combine fully.

To serve, place each chop on a serving plate and top with a generous pour of mornay sauce. Serve with extra sauce on the side.

Cranberry Hoisin Duck Breast
with Fresh Cranberry Relish

SERVES 4

*Lightfoot & Wolfville's Small Lot
Sparkling Rosé or Mercator Vineyards'
Upper Ridge Marquette*

Glaze:

3 shallots

¼ cup butter

½ tsp sea salt

2 cups fresh or frozen cranberries

Zest and juice of 1 navel orange

½ cup packed brown sugar

½ cup red wine vinegar

¼ cup hoisin sauce

8 sprigs thyme

4 sprigs savory

2 bay leaves

Duck Breasts:

4 duck breasts

¼ cup olive oil

Duck served with cranberries is a delicious combination, as the bright, tart tang of the berries perfectly complements the rich, full flavour of the meat. When we make this on a cool autumn day, the kitchen smells intoxicating and has us dreaming of the holiday season to come. This is perfect with Wild Mushroom & Barley Risotto (page 283), followed by Molasses Pie (page 304) for dessert.

For the Glaze: Dice the shallots. Place a saucepan over medium heat and melt the butter. When it starts to sizzle, add the shallots and sprinkle them with the salt. Allow them to caramelize, stirring occasionally but not too often, then add the cranberries and sear on all sides. They will start to pop after a few minutes. Stir in the orange zest and juice, followed by the sugar, vinegar, hoisin sauce, thyme, savory, and bay leaves. Simmer the sauce until the glaze easily coats the back of a spoon and the berries have burst, 7 to 10 minutes. It will be very fragrant. Remove from the heat and allow to cool completely.

Strain through a fine-mesh strainer over a bowl, using the back of a spoon to squeeze out all the remaining juice from the cranberries. Discard the pulp and transfer the strained glaze to a large resealable plastic bag or airtight container large enough to hold the duck breasts without crowding.

For the Duck Breasts: Pat the duck breasts dry and place them in the glaze, turning to coat. Marinate in the fridge for 24 hours, turning once halfway through to coat again.

About 30 minutes before you're ready to cook, remove the breasts from the fridge [as per earlier food-safety notes]. Preheat the oven to 350°F.

Remove the breasts from the glaze marinade, shaking off any excess. Set the glaze aside. Place a large ovenproof skillet over medium heat and add the oil. Place the breasts fat side down in the pan to sear until deep golden, 2 to 3 minutes, then flip and sear the other side until deep golden, 1 to 2 minutes. Using a pastry brush, coat both sides of each breast with glaze and discard the rest. Bake for 10 minutes. Remove from the oven and let sit in the pan, covered, to rest and finish cooking. For medium-rare, the duck's internal temperature should be 140°F; for well done, 170°F.

(continued)

213

Relish:

1 small orange

2 cups fresh cranberries

¼ cup maple syrup

2 Tbsp sugar

½ tsp sea salt

½ tsp ground nutmeg

¼ tsp ground cloves

To Serve:

Fresh greens

For the Relish: While the duck is resting, slice the orange in half, then into wedges, removing the peel, pith, and any seeds. Place the orange wedges, cranberries, maple syrup, sugar, salt, nutmeg, and cloves in a blender. Pulse to break up the orange and cranberries, then blend until the orange pieces look like zest and the relish is almost completely smooth.

Serve the glazed duck breasts with a dollop of relish and fresh greens on the side.

STORAGE: Leftover relish will keep in an airtight container in the fridge for up to 1 month. Leftover duck will keep in an airtight container in the fridge for up to 3 days.

COLLECTING CRANBERRIES

Juiced or sauced, whipped into a curd, or dried into craisins, cranberries are loved across Canada. Yet they're rarely recognized as local to the Atlantic region. Here in New Brunswick, where the floodplains of the Saint John and Miramichi Rivers offer the perfect growing conditions, seven varieties are produced on almost 1,000 acres, with an annual harvest of over 10 million pounds. New Brunswick is now Canada's third-largest producing province, but until the early 1990s, only 25 acres were planted for intentional cranberry agriculture. Realizing that the land between the Miramichi River and the Northumberland Strait, which is along the Bay of Fundy, created the perfect habitat for the fruit to grow, the government created an incentive program to promote the sector. Crown land was leased and farmers received subsidies to help with planting costs and equipment purchases.

Sitting in Mel Goodland's truck, headed down the lane to his cranberry bog, he tells us how he accidentally came to love cranberries. Bayview, his 30-acre farm at Coast Cranberries Ltd. in Dorchester, is beautiful—and not just because the Bay of Fundy offers glorious views off in the distance. The fields are planted on a natural spring-fed ditch system that was put in place hundreds of years ago by the early Acadians, the architectural lines of which are still perfectly formed and lovely in their rhythmic structure. Today the cranberry bogs are covered in a carpet of tiny pink flowers just beginning to bloom. The shrubs are a natural ground cover that will only grow to around 8 inches tall. Their diminutive size allows producers to pick the berries easily in the autumn with machines that look like second cousins to domestic lawnmowers. The fruits are fed through the mechanical tracks into burlap sacks,

cleaned of leaves and debris, and packed into wooden shipping crates. On average, the Goodlands will gather 20,000 pounds of cranberries per acre, although in a good year they can fetch up to 30,000 pounds an acre.

At Coastal Cranberries Ltd. they grow two varieties of cranberries: Ben Lear and Stevens. Ben Lear have a deep-red colour and ripen earlier in the season. These popular berries are picked dry instead of being collected through the traditional flooding system, and are ready in time for Canadian Thanksgiving. Stevens come later in the season, are variegated in colour, and are plumper, meatier, and tarter. They are also dry-harvested, but only on the first pass. The mechanical harvesters pick the berries at the top of the plant, close to the surface, which is about 50% of the available fruit. Any berries left in the fields are wet-harvested—this means that the bogs are completely flooded and the waters stirred, forcing the remaining berries to float to the top so that they can be skimmed together and collected. Wet-harvested berries are best juiced or dried and must be preserved quickly, as the water they absorb through the harvest decreases their shelf life significantly.

As the cranberry industry grows in the province, word is spreading that these incredibly healthy and delicious berries are indeed local. In addition to their commercial distribution, fresh cranberries are now sold at many New Brunswick farmers' markets, allowing the public access to the freshest fruit possible. If you're fortunate enough to come upon such a stand, be sure to enjoy the freshly picked fruit while stockpiling some to preserve in the freezer. They are chock-full of antioxidants, incredibly tasty, and a welcome addition to many a sweet and savoury dish.

Cranberry Bread Pudding *with* Dark Chocolate & Thyme

SERVES 4–6

Winegarden Estate's Marechal Foch

10 thick slices sourdough bread or
  croissants

1½ cups fresh or frozen cranberries

4 oz chopped dark chocolate

6 eggs

1 cup heavy cream

½ cup sugar, divided

2 sprigs thyme

2 tsp orange zest

1 tsp vanilla extract

Whipped cream or ice cream,
  for serving (optional)
  (Emily likes vanilla)

Cranberries add an invigorating pop to this rich, cream-filled bread pudding. As perfect as it is for dessert, our favourite way to serve it is for brunch, as it needs to sit in the fridge overnight. When you wake up, all you need to do is bring the pudding to room temperature, put it in the oven, and start the coffee! If you're feeling really fancy, use croissants instead of the sourdough for an extra-flaky, decadent version.

Grease a 9-inch square baking pan with butter and set aside.

Cut the bread into cubes, leaving the crust on. Layer the bread, cranberries, and chocolate in the prepared baking dish so the berries are evenly distributed throughout. The dish will appear full, which is perfectly ok.

In a mixing bowl, whisk together the eggs, cream, and ¼ cup of the sugar until fluffy and light golden. In a small bowl, combine the remaining ¼ cup of sugar with the thyme and zest. Use your fingers, rub the mixture together to remove the leaves from the sprigs of thyme, discarding the stems, and extract the oil from the zest. The mixture will look quite sandy. Add it to the egg mixture along with the vanilla and whisk well to combine.

Pour the egg mixture over the bread mixture. Gently press down on the bread so it fully absorbs the egg mixture. Cover with plastic wrap and place in the fridge for 6 hours, or up to 18 hours.

Remove from the fridge 1 hour before baking to allow the pudding to come to room temperature. Remove the plastic wrap.

Preheat the oven to 350°F.

Lightly grease some aluminium foil, or a heatproof cover, cover the pudding, and bake for 45 minutes. Remove the cover and bake until the top is golden brown and a toothpick inserted in the centre of the pudding comes out clean, an additional 15 minutes.

Let sit for 5 minutes to set, then serve with a dollop of whipped cream or ice cream, if desired.

STORAGE: The pudding will keep, covered, in the fridge for up to 4 days.

Bee Balm Poached Peaches

SERVES 4

Lightfoot & Wolfville's Scheurebe

For a quality restaurant kitchen, you have to grow relationships with producers and have talented chefs to make creative dishes with oft-unexpected ingredients. We witnessed this first-hand at Rossmount Inn, the property Chris Arnie and his wife Graziella purchased over twenty years ago and restored to its current beauty. We were blessed with a few extra hours at Rossmount, as Chris had to leave unexpectedly to run to Saint John to pick up a fish someone had just caught, which was then added to the menu that very evening. On his return he explained that teaching, sharing, and being curious are all part of their ethos, as is staying close to the food chain, feeding the earth, foraging, and exploring the nuances of seasonality. Even the colours on the menu matter. Late-summer menus, for example, are full of the aesthetic vibrancy of harvest, as you'll see with these poached peaches. Serve them alongside a few scoops of Red Currant Ice Cream (page 148), with some Sage & Flax Shortbread (page 83) on the side, for a deliciously decadent dessert.

10 dried bee balm flowers

2 cups sugar

1 Tbsp lemon juice

4 ripe peaches

¼ cup off-dry white wine

Place the bee balm flowers in a medium bowl. Heat 2 cups of water to almost a boil—it should be the perfect temperature to make tea. Pour the water over the flowers, sprinkle the sugar over top, and stir until the sugar is fully dissolved, 2 to 3 minutes. Let sit for 5 minutes, then stir in the lemon juice. Let sit, covered, at room temperature for 2 days. Place the syrup in a small pot and bring to a simmer. Simmer for 5 minutes, then strain out the flowers and place the syrup in a sterilized Mason jar.

Slice the peaches in half and discard the pits. Place the peaches cut side up in a stainless steel pot that will easily fit the peach halves without crowding. Add the bee balm syrup, wine, and, if needed, just enough water to cover them. Partially cover the pot with the lid, allowing some steam to escape, and bring to a boil over medium-high heat. Immediately turn the heat down to medium-low and carefully simmer until soft. If the peaches are ripe, this shouldn't take more than 5 minutes. Let the peaches cool slightly, then remove from the syrup and slip off their skins. Place back in the syrup to cool. Serve peaches warm with a few spoonfuls of syrup.

STORAGE: The peaches will keep in an airtight container in the fridge for up to 5 days. The syrup will keep in the fridge for up to 2 months.

Recipe contributed by Chris Arnie, Rossmount Inn

Chocolate Sea Buckthorn Meringues

MAKES ½ DOZEN LARGE OR
I DOZEN SMALL MERINGUES

*Foghorn Brewing Company's
Coffee Stout*

Bright, tart, and packed with antioxidants, sea buckthorn is common in the cosmetics industry but less well-known in most kitchens. We're sure that is about to change, as we just can't get enough of these incredibly delicious berries. Beth Fowler and Clay Bartlett of Big Sky Sea Buckthorn Orchard and Winery farm over 20 acres of sea buckthorn in Chipman, New Brunswick, all of it organically grown and hand-harvested. They cut the thorny branches and carefully pick the berries from the stems to make wines, juices, jellies, and powders, and to distill into essential oils. Sea buckthorn juice is pulpy and quite oily, which makes it perfect for using in rich curds. Swirled into a sweet, crunchy chocolate meringue, it's absolute perfection.

½ cup sea buckthorn juice

⅔ cup + 4 Tbsp sugar, divided

2 Tbsp cornstarch, divided

½ cup dark or semisweet chocolate chips

3 egg whites

1½ tsp cream of tartar

½ tsp fine sea salt

In a small saucepan, whisk together the sea buckthorn juice, the 4 tablespoons of sugar, and 1 tablespoon of the cornstarch until smooth. Place over medium heat, bring to a boil, and boil for 30 seconds. Transfer to a small dish and cover with plastic wrap, making sure it touches the surface so a skin doesn't form. Set aside to cool.

In a small saucepan over low heat, begin to melt the chocolate chips, stirring constantly. Remove from the heat once half of the chocolate has melted. Keep stirring until smooth and creamy, being careful not to burn. Set aside to temper and cool.

Place the egg whites in a stand mixer fitted with the whisk attachment and allow to come to room temperature.

Preheat the oven to 275°F and place a rack in the centre of the oven. Line a baking sheet with parchment paper.

(continued)

In a small bowl, whisk together the remaining ⅔ cup of sugar, the remaining 1 tablespoon of cornstarch, the cream of tartar, and salt. Begin to beat the egg whites on low speed. Slowly increase the speed to medium-high as they increase in bulk. When they have doubled in bulk and are just starting to form peaks, begin to slowly sprinkle in the sugar mixture, with the machine still running on medium-high. Once all the sugar has been added, beat the egg whites on high speed for an additional 2 to 3 minutes. Stop beating. Rub a bit of meringue between your thumb and index finger. If you feel any graininess between your fingers, beat for 1 more minute. Continue to check, beating as necessary, until the egg whites feel completely smooth and have glossy and beautiful stiff peaks. Detach the bowl from the stand mixer.

Drizzle the melted chocolate over the meringue and use a spatula to fold it once or twice to create a swirl. Do not fully incorporate. Using a large ice cream scoop or two spoons, drop large baseball-sized spoonfuls onto the prepared baking sheet, about 2 inches apart. Using a fork, swirl in the sea buckthorn curd through the meringues to make a contrasting swirl to the chocolate and round out the meringues. Try to keep them tall, as they naturally fall slightly when cooling.

Bake for 30 minutes. Turn down the heat to 250°F without opening the door and bake for an additional 15 to 20 minutes, until the tops are golden and just starting to crack. If you are using a convection oven, the golden look might appear sooner. This doesn't mean the meringues are fully done—the airflow just causes them to brown a bit sooner. Turn off the oven and allow the meringues to cool and set slowly as the oven cools, for 1 hour. If your oven naturally holds its heat well, crack the door a little.

STORAGE: The meringues will keep in an airtight container at room temperature for up to 3 days or in the freezer for up to 2 months. They will sweat and become soggy if stored in the fridge.

SUGARING-OFF MAPLE

The majestic maple tree is the source of two truly Canadian things: our iconic syrup and the big, beautiful leaf on our flag. The Atlantic provinces have sugar maple forests that produce a delicious sap that is unique in both sweetness and flavour profile. The sugary sap is created when water that is absorbed in the trees' root systems mixes with natural starches and is converted to sugar thanks to some hardworking enzymes. This only happens a few weeks a year, which is why many people across Atlantic Canada consider March to be Maple Month.

Of course, March also means an incredible amount of work for those in the industry. "The days of the true sugar shack in the woods are all but gone," explains Andrew Crawford of Royal View Maples. We're standing in his barn, where he's making preparations for the sugaring-off, the process of making syrup from the sap of the sugar maple trees. As buckets of raw sap are no longer collected by hand, there is no need for multiple evaporators to be out in the sugar bush. Instead, every year Andrew, his wife Colleen, and son Jordan tap the trees on their property and collect the syrup in lines that run to a central evaporator in their barn. Once the syrup is in the lines, a combination of gravity, due to the farm's hillside location, and a light vacuum pump keep the sap moving. The intent of the vacuum is not to apply suction to the trees, but to prevent the liquid from sitting in the lines. When the sap arrives at the evaporator, it is heated, evaporating the water and leaving behind the concentrated sugar known as maple syrup.

Although the trees produce the sap naturally, tapping them for syrup involves a lot of manual labour. A small hole is drilled in the tree trunk and then a spout is tapped in by hand. You can't tap a tree in the same place every year, as the spigot leaves a scar where the syrup flows from, so each year the taps need to be removed. Andrew pulls a slab of wood from a shelf, showing us a round from an old fallen tree that his grandfather tapped for many years. You can see the history in the rings and count the years between tappings. It takes only a few years for a hole to fully mend, but the trees do need time to rest and heal. Andrew explains that they will often leave a tree to rest for a year or two just to make sure that it is healthy and growing well. If there is a big storm or a noticeable decrease in sap volume in any area of the sugar bush, they may choose to leave the whole section for a season to let the trees continue to grow and thrive before tapping again, thus creating a sustainable rotating system across their land. "We have to look after the trees. They're our livelihood," he explains.

Once the sap is collected, it's time to make syrup. It takes about 40 gallons of sap to make 1 gallon of maple syrup. The grading process is based on a combination of light transparency and flavour. Typically, in the early season, cooler sap is more subtle; as temperatures warm, the syrup becomes richer and darker. The grade of the syrup is not dependent on its colour, however, but on the ability of light to pass through it. Grade A syrup has a light transparency of between 44% and 75% or higher, grade B between 27% and 43.9%, and grade C less than 27%. Within the grades there are subcategories as well. For example, a Canadian #1 grade A can run from a soft golden colour with a delicate flavour to a much darker and stronger-tasting syrup.

Since everyone tends to have their own favourite flavour profile, we think tasting them all is the best option. A deep-flavoured, robust syrup is a Canadian staple, especially when consumed on pancakes on a warm and inviting maple farm—and pouring hot amber syrup on snow to make taffy is part of many an Atlantic childhood. It's no wonder that maple syrup is considered a part of our Canadian identity.

Maple Walnut Butter Tarts

MAKES 1 DOZEN TARTS

*Sunset Heights Meadery's
Scuttlebutt Mead*

Some days we wonder if there is anything more Canadian than rich, sweet, and delicious butter tarts. We enjoy them all year long, although we especially love this version during the holiday season when the local walnuts are finished curing and in early spring when the syrup harvest has just come to a close. These delectable tarts are perfectly maple-forward but not overly sweet, and the lovely crunch of nuts adds balance to their gooeyness.

Pastry:

2 cups cake and pastry flour

2 Tbsp brown sugar

½ tsp baking powder

½ tsp fine sea salt

⅔ cup cold butter, cubed

¼ cup ice-cold water

Butter Tart Filling:

2 eggs

¾ cup packed brown sugar

½ cup maple syrup

¼ cup melted butter

1 tsp red wine vinegar

1 cup chopped walnuts

For the Pastry: In a large mixing bowl, whisk together the flour, sugar, baking powder, and salt. Add the butter in pieces and, using two knives or a pastry blender, cut it into the flour mixture until it has a coarse oatmeal texture. Gently stir in the water and form the dough into a soft ball. Wrap in plastic wrap and chill in the fridge for 30 minutes.

For the Butter Tart Filling: In a separate bowl, whisk together the eggs and brown sugar until well combined. Add the maple syrup, butter, and vinegar and whisk well until fully emulsified.

Preheat the oven to 400°F. Lightly grease a muffin tin with oil and add paper liners.

Roll out the tart pastry and cut out twelve rounds about 4 inches in diameter. Gently press each round into a paper liner in the muffin tin. Divide the walnuts evenly between the pastry shells. Fill each tart shell two-thirds full with butter tart mixture, being careful not to spill it over the sides, as it will stick while cooking and make it difficult to remove the tarts.

Bake until the tarts are golden and the filling is rounded and puffed, 12 to 15 minutes. Remove from the oven and immediately run a butter knife or small spatula around the outside of each tart. Allow to cool completely in the pan before removing.

STORAGE: The tarts will keep in an airtight container at room temperature for up to 5 days.

Winter Spiced Oatcakes

MAKES 9 OATCAKES

Sussex Craft Distillery's Northern Comfort Maple Rum Liqueur

½ cup butter

1 cup oats

¾ cup flour

½ cup packed dark brown sugar

2 tsp ground ginger

1 tsp ground nutmeg

1 tsp ground cardamom

½ tsp ground allspice

6 oz white chocolate, chopped

STORAGE: The chocolate-dipped oatcakes will keep in an airtight container at room temperature for up to 1 week. The oatcakes without the chocolate will keep in an airtight container in the freezer for 2 to 3 months.

Oatcakes, in all their forms, are staples throughout the Atlantic provinces. Go into any coffee shop and we promise you'll find at least one version on display. Part cookie, part cracker, these oatcakes are crisp and chewy at the same time, and are perfect for nibbling with a cup of coffee. The spices are warm and the crumb tender, and you don't even need to pull a bowl out of the cupboard to make them, as they're mixed right in the pan they bake in. Instead of rolling and cutting, we prefer to pack them into a pan, bake them, and then cut them into squares.

Preheat the oven to 375°F.

In a small pot, melt the butter. In a 9-inch square baking pan, using a wooden spoon or spatula, mix together the oats, flour, sugar, ginger, nutmeg, cardamom, and allspice until fully combined. Pour in the melted butter and mix until the mixture is crumbly and no dry flour is visible. If needed, use your fingers to get every last bit evenly moist. Then, using the back of your hand, pack the mixture firmly into the dish in an even layer.

Bake until golden brown and starting to look crisp around the edges, 25 to 30 minutes.

As soon as you remove it from the oven, use a metal spatula or butter knife to cut around the outside of the pan and then cut nine squares. Let cool in the pan for 10 to 15 minutes. Transfer the squares to a wire rack and allow to cool completely. The squares may stick together a bit when you're removing them from the pan, but breaking them apart is quite easy.

When the squares are fully cool, melt the chopped white chocolate. In a small saucepan over low heat, begin to melt the chocolate chips, stirring constantly and being careful not to burn (or put them in a small bowl and microwave for 10-second intervals, stirring between intervals). Remove from the heat once half of the chocolate has melted. Keep stirring until smooth and creamy. Set aside to temper and cool. You should have approximately ½ cup of melted chocolate. Dip half of each oatcake square into the melted chocolate, hold it over the bowl for a few seconds to allow any excess to drip, off and return to the wire rack to allow the chocolate to set and harden, 30 to 40 minutes.

Molasses Cookies

*Loyalist City Brewing Company's
  Black 47*

½ cup sugar

⅓ cup packed dark brown sugar

½ cup butter, softened

1 egg

⅓ cup fancy or cooking molasses

1 tsp baking soda

½ tsp fine sea salt

2 tsp ground ginger

1½ tsp ground cinnamon

½ tsp ground nutmeg

½ tsp ground cloves

1–2 tsp sea buckthorn powder
  (optional)

2 cups flour

½ cup raw sugar

Since Crosby's Molasses calls Saint John home, it's hard to walk into a bakery in the province and not find a soft, chewy molasses cookie. Appearing as a staple on store and home kitchen shelves alike, if there is a cookie of New Brunswick, it has to be this one. We prefer making them with fancy molasses, but if you're looking for a stronger, deeper flavour, then cooking molasses is the answer. To add a delicious citrus note and make these cookies a healthy treat, add some sea buckthorn powder.

Preheat the oven to 350°F. Line a baking sheet with parchment paper.

Using a stand mixer fitted with the paddle attachment, cream the sugar, brown sugar, and butter. Stop the mixer and scrape down the sides of the bowl. Add the egg and molasses and beat to fully combine. Add the baking soda, salt, ginger, cinnamon, nutmeg, cloves, and sea buckthorn (if using) and mix until combined. Add 1 cup of the flour and mix in. Repeat with the remaining flour to form a very stiff dough.

In a small mixing bowl, place the raw sugar. Scoop out 1 tablespoon of the cookie dough, roll it into a ball, then roll it in the raw sugar. Place it on the prepared baking sheet. There's no need to press down, as the balls will flatten naturally as they bake. Repeat with the remaining dough, spacing the balls 2 to 3 inches apart on the sheet.

For a soft, chewy cookie, bake for 8 to 10 minutes; for a firmer cookie, bake for 10 to 12 minutes.

Remove from the oven and let sit for 2 to 3 minutes to set. Then, using a spatula, transfer the cookies to a wire rack to cool completely. Repeat with any remaining dough.

STORAGE: The cookies will keep in an airtight container at room temperature for up to 1 week.

Newfoundland
& Labrador

Recipes

Rugged and beautiful, Newfoundland and Labrador is a place like no other. As the last of the provinces to become part of Canada—Newfoundland, as it was then called, only joined confederation in 1949—it's no wonder that this remote area has an identity unto itself. Labrador, being much more of an Arctic terroir, shares little culturally with the rest of the Atlantic region. Newfoundland, albeit not technically a Maritime province, has deep Irish roots, and its culinary tradition shares many of the same ingredients as its neighbouring East Coast provinces, tying it into the common culinary landscape.

The people here are much like the land itself: hardy and resilient, taking great pride in being able to weather a storm. They are masters of garnering inspiration from isolation, which is evident in the artwork, architecture, and, of course, the foods that define The Rock. Innovation is key here: in a place where it is easier to gather than grow, understanding how to reap what the land and sea provide has been tantamount to survival.

The ocean has always been the mainstay for food and livelihoods in Newfoundland, as evidenced by the numerous villages and townships that hug the rocky coastline, many of which were not connected by road until very recent times. Cod was king here until the 1992 moratorium, which effectively put an end to generations of industry. While stocks are slowly returning, provincial fisheries limit the quantities for both commercial and recreational catches. Nowadays you're apt to find fishermen working the seasons for crab, sea urchin, and lobster as well as cod in order to make a decent living from mandated fish prices.

With most of Newfoundland's interior being uninhabited woodlands, hunting is a way of life, with moose licences, issued by lottery, being coveted above all else. For wild game, you'll also find caribou and rabbit (Arctic hare) along with migratory sea birds and seals gracing Newfoundland's tables. This is also the only province in the country where wild game is allowed to be served commercially, and chefs like Jeremy Charles, Jonathan Gushue, Katie Hayes, and Todd Perrin are taking full advantage by pushing these meats to the forefront of their menus.

Of course, the woods here provide much more than just wild meats. Foraging is more than a trend for Newfoundlanders; it is a way of life. Wild mushrooms abound alongside edible plants. Low-growing shrubs, lichens, and wild herbs of sweet gale, caribou moss, pineapple weed, and Labrador tea are seasonings that are becoming as common as the beloved commercially bought savory. Berries have their own season throughout the province, and for good reason: crowberries, marshberries, snowberries, partridgeberries, wild blueberries, and bakeapples—to name just a few—are found throughout the marshes, barrens, and boglands. When the time is right, you'll find cars and trucks parked up along the roads, their drivers and passengers bent at the knee, with buckets by their sides.

This is a place of creativity and tradition, where instinct guides culinary imagination and the ability to make the most from what is given is not only a skill but also a generationally inherited art. We came, we saw, we ate, we loved, and we were forever changed.

Toutons *with* Whipped Molasses Butter

There isn't a more traditional Newfoundland breakfast than toutons, which might be the best use of leftover bread dough ever invented, as it's slathered in butter and sweet molasses! While we were on Fogo Island, a lovely islander named Sandra shared with us how her mother use to tear off pieces of freshly risen dough, pat it into a perfect circle, and fry it up as a breakfast treat. We use instant yeast so it only takes about 45 minutes from start to finish, including the rise. You can also make the dough the night before and let it rise in the fridge overnight, bring it to room temperature in the morning, then shape and fry the toutons as directed.

¾ cup butter

¼ cup molasses

2 tsp flaky sea salt, divided

3 cups flour, plus more for dusting

2 Tbsp sugar

1½ tsp quick rise yeast

1 tsp coarse sea salt

¼ cup melted butter

1½ cups whole milk

Neutral oil, for frying

Using a stand mixer fitted with the whisk attachment, whisk the butter until fluffy and light cream in colour, 1 to 2 minutes. With the mixer running on medium-low speed, slowly pour in the molasses, allowing it to emulsify with the butter. Scrape the sides down after all of the molasses has been added. Whisk on medium speed until the butter is combined and the molasses is emulsified. Transfer to a small bowl, sprinkle with 1 teaspoon of the flaky sea salt and keep at room temperature until the toutons are ready.

In a large mixing bowl, whisk together the flour, sugar, yeast, and coarse sea salt.

In a small pot over medium heat, combine the melted butter with the milk. Check the temperature of the milk. If it's still cool, place over low heat until it reaches 115°F.

Preheat the oven to 200°F. Once it reaches temperature, turn it off.

Add the milk mixture to the flour mixture and stir well to combine. Turn the dough onto a lightly floured surface and knead for 10 minutes, until smooth and elastic. Oil a large, heatproof mixing bowl and place the dough in the bowl, turning to coat. Cover with plastic wrap, place the bowl in the oven, and let rise for 30 minutes.

Remove the dough from the oven and discard the plastic wrap. Divide the dough into eight evenly sized pieces, form each piece into a disc about ½ inch thick, and place on a lightly floured counter. Cover with a tea towel and let rise for 10 minutes.

Preheat the oven to 250°F.

While the dough discs are rising, heat a heavy-bottomed skillet or cast iron pan over medium heat, and add just enough oil to cover the bottom, between ¼ and ½ cup. When the oil is hot, add two or three dough discs, being careful not to overcrowd the pan, and fry until puffed and golden brown, 2 to 3 minutes. Using an offset spatula, flip the toutons over and fry for an additional 1 to 2 minutes. Place on an ovenproof plate and transfer to the oven to keep them warm and allow them to finish cooking in the centre. Repeat with the remaining toutons.

When you're ready to serve, place the toutons on a serving plate, with the bowl of whipped molasses butter and a sprinkle of the remaining flaky sea salt on the side.

STORAGE: The molasses butter will keep in an airtight container in the fridge for up to 3 weeks. The toutons are best enjoyed as soon as they are made, although they can be reheated if needed or cut in half and toasted the next day. They will keep in an airtight container in the fridge for up to 1 week.

CATCHING COD

The story of Newfoundland is the story of cod; the story of cod is the story of Newfoundland. So much so that if a Newfoundlander says "fish," they really mean "cod," and if they say "haddock" they mean "haddock," though that's rare in these parts, as cod is the mainstay. It's what brought settlers to the island and allowed communities to form, grow, and thrive.

Sitting on the dock beside his little wind-worn, seafoam-coloured boat, Jerry Hussey explains the reality of the cod fishery here in Newfoundland. He's been fishing since he could walk and has weathered many a storm. He still fishes with the traditional hand-jigging method that has been used here for hundreds of years. Instead of hauling gillnets, the fishermen pull each cod in by hand on a single line, one at a time. And from the looks of Jerry's hands, callused from years of pulling in fish weighing up to 60 pounds, it is far from an easy life.

When the moratorium was implemented on July 2, 1992, it changed the province forever. Prior to that, the quotas were so high that they were rarely reached and fishermen were allowed to haul almost as much cod as they could from the sea. Perhaps if it had just been Canadians fishing the Atlantic waters, the numbers may have been sustained. Maybe if the tradition of hand-jigging had been universally maintained, the cod would have been able to repopulate at a sustainable rate. Unfortunately, with the introduction of mass-scale trawlers and the large numbers of international boats fishing off the Grand Banks, the cod stocks were depleted faster than they could be replenished. From the 1950s onwards, fishermen were able to fish deeper over larger areas and target specific species and ages of fish, all but abandoning the earlier methods that limited the volume of their catch.

In 1997, the ban began to lift, but with restrictions. The fishermen now have to report what they catch and from which area. Aside from the limits assigned per fishing licence, each area is numbered and has its own set quota. Every time the fishermen come back to shore, Fisheries and Oceans Canada makes a running tally of what is being caught and where. The area numbers are updated daily, so if all the boats happen to be in one spot and the allowable limit for that area is reached, the likelihood of being permitted to go back and fish there again the next day is slim. The hope is to prevent all the fish from being depleted in a specific place. Obviously this is an imperfect system—fish can swim!—but it's currently how the numbers are being managed.

Today the price per pound of cod is less than half of what it was in the 1980s. Prior to the moratorium, it was rare that you needed to fish for anything other than cod, as the season was much longer and there were so many fish. In fact, a fisherman could earn a year's wages in just a few months. Now that is not the case. Jerry explains that in order to earn a living from the sea you now need a variety of licences to keep a crew fishing year round. Each fishery requires a separate licence and has a different quota system—and often different equipment and boat requirements as well. Licences are not easy to come by, but if a fisherman happens to hold them all, then they're fishing year round and can make a good living. Jerry has a spring lobster licence and lands lobster from mid-May to the end of July, catches cod from around mid-August to mid-November, and dives for urchins during the late-winter months. In early spring, the seal hunt begins and then the cycle repeats.

Fish caught at the end of the commercial season, when they are at their meatiest, are used for salt cod, a traditional curing process that preserves the fish indefinitely. The cod, which feed on the capelin that lure the larger fish inshore from the deep, cold Atlantic waters, are fattened into delicious rich meat and primed for salting. Lloyd Oldford has been fishing since he was twelve years old, and still lives in the house where he was born in Red Cliff by Bonavista Bay. Fishing isn't just a passion, it's his life, and making salt cod is now his specialty. He and his wife Christina explain the process: first, the fish are gutted, but rather than being filleted they are fully opened like a book, flesh on one side, skin on the other, with the tail still attached. You then take tubs with holes in the bottom to allow any juice or brine to drain, pack them with layers of salt and cod, and leave the lot to pickle and cure for twenty-three days, allowing the salt to fully penetrate the flesh and all of the juices to drain naturally. The fish are then brushed off and laid out to dry in the sunshine for up to a week. Lloyd proudly shows us cod flakes lying out in the sun, and it's easy to tell from the twinkle in his eye that he loves the sea and couldn't imagine a life without it. "These fish will last forever," he says. We hope so, as they are absolutely delicious!

An old tale tells that the cod were once so abundant that they prevented Christopher Columbus's ship from sailing forward. Will they ever enjoy such abundance again? Or will we lose them? We won't know the last fish has been caught until it's in the boat, but we do know that this industry has defined Newfoundland and created an incredibly resilient people. Today innovative groups like the Fogo Island Co-operative Society Ltd. have placed a premium market price on traditional HandLine Cod, and in doing so have secured the livelihood of an entire community. You'll find salt cod and fried cod tongues occupy a prominent place on the menus of notable restaurants such as Raymonds, Merchant Tavern, and Mallard Cottage, introducing visitors to the foods that Newfoundlanders have enjoyed for centuries. In recent years recreational fishing has reopened, allowing people to land up to five cod per person on the weekends during the summer season—placing this beloved fish back onto the tables of the folks who love it most. In the words of Jerry Hussey, "Life is an opportunity. Even in the hard times, there is beauty to find. Looking out your door, seeing the sea, even when the weather is bad and the waves are crashing on the shores, there is a respect and reverence in the ocean. It gives life, it feeds us, it demands respect."

Salt Cod Croquettes

SERVES 6

Newfoundland Cider Company's
Scrumpy Cloudy Cider

1 cup shredded salt cod

¼ cup butter

¼ cup diced red onion

½ tsp sea salt

1¼ cups flour, divided

1 cup whole milk

1 cup grated mozzarella cheese

1 Tbsp dried summer savory

¼ tsp smoked paprika

2 eggs

1½ cups panko-style breadcrumbs

Neutral oil, for frying

Cod has long been a staple in Newfoundland, and salting is the perfect way to preserve this large fish. With a perfect combination of a crunchy, crispy, fried outside and creamy filling, these tasty bar treats are rich and supremely delicious—perfect for sharing with friends. If cod isn't your favourite, we have some good news for you: the variations and possibilities are endless. The croquettes can be filled with pork, chicken, spinach, potato, and even pine nuts, but the extra-thick chilled béchamel sauce is non-negotiable.

Place the salt cod in a fine-mesh strainer and rinse well with water to remove any large pieces of salt from the outside of the fish.

Place the rinsed cod in a bowl and cover with water, cover the bowl with plastic wrap, then place in the fridge for at least 8 hours or up to 24 hours, changing the water once, to soak. Drain and rinse the fish, then transfer to a heavy-bottomed pot. Fill the pot with fresh cold water and bring to a simmer over medium-low heat. Simmer the cod for 20 to 25 minutes to loosen and remove any excess salt.

Line a plate with paper towel, drain the cod, and place it on the paper towel to drain fully. Cover and chill in the fridge for 2 hours, or up to 12 hours.

In a heavy-bottomed saucepan over medium heat, melt the butter. Sauté the onions until softened, 1 to 2 minutes. Sprinkle them with the salt and then continue to cook until they are translucent and just starting to turn golden. Turn down the heat to low and sprinkle ¼ cup of the flour over the onions, stirring to combine and remove any lumps. Slowly pour in the milk, whisking constantly to keep the mixture smooth. Remove the pan from the heat and, using a wooden spoon, stir in the cheese until smooth and fully melted, and then stir in the savory, followed by the chilled salt cod. Transfer this bécha-mel sauce to a shallow bowl and cover with plastic wrap, pressing the plastic directly on the surface of the sauce to prevent a skin from forming. Chill in the fridge for 2 hours, or up to 24 hours.

While the sauce is cooling, prepare a dredging station. In one shallow bowl, combine the remaining 1 cup of flour and the paprika; in a second shallow bowl, whisk the eggs; and in a third shallow bowl, place the breadcrumbs.

Line a rimmed baking sheet with parchment paper. Line a wire rack with paper towel.

(continued)

To prevent your fingers from becoming too sticky while dredging or breading, keep one hand reserved for handling the dry ingredients and the other for the wet. Scoop up 2 tablespoons of the chilled béchamel sauce and use your fingertips to form it into a ball. Evenly coat the ball in the flour mixture, then dip it in the egg and roll it in the breadcrumbs. Set on the prepared baking sheet and repeat with the remaining sauce. Chill in the fridge, uncovered, for at least 1 hour.

When you're ready to serve, in a heavy-bottomed saucepan, heat 1 inch of oil to 375°F, using a candy thermometer to monitor the temperature. Fry the croquettes in batches, so you don't overcrowd the pan, until golden brown and crispy, about 2 minutes per side. Using a slotted spoon, remove the croquettes from the oil and transfer to the prepared wire rack to absorb any excess oil. Give the oil 1 to 2 minutes to return to temperature between batches.

Serve immediately.

STORAGE: The croquettes will keep in an airtight container in the fridge for up to 2 days or in the freezer for up to 3 months, although they are best served straight from the hot oil. Warm them in a 375°F oven for 15 to 20 minutes before eating. The béchamel can be made in advance, formed into balls, and frozen before being breaded and fried. They will keep in the freezer like this for up to 2 months. Thaw them fully in the fridge before breading and frying as instructed above.

Moose Sausage Patties

MAKES 16 PATTIES

Port Rexton Brewing Co.'s Sweater Weather Double IPA

1 red onion

2 lb ground moose

2 Tbsp dried savory

2 tsp dried thyme

2 tsp smoked paprika

2 eggs

¼ cup grainy Dijon mustard

1 cup breadcrumbs

Moose is commonly eaten in Newfoundland and, as they are very large animals, many people, especially hunters, often find themselves with a surplus of ground meat in the freezer. Our favourite use for it is to make homemade sausage! Seasoning the moose meat and placing it in casings or simply forming it into small patties makes the perfect breakfast accompaniment to Toutons with Whipped Molasses Butter (page 242) or a lovely protein addition to the Wild Mushroom & Barley Risotto (page 283). It's also great served cold for lunches or fresh from the oven as a delicious meat pie.

Grate the onion into a large mixing bowl. Mix in the moose, savory, thyme, and paprika to make a smooth, meat-like paste. Add the eggs and mustard and work them into the mixture with your hands. Add the breadcrumbs and continue mixing with your hands until smooth. (This can also be done by pulsing in the food processor until smooth, but we prefer working with our hands.)

Preheat the oven to 375°F. Line a rimmed baking sheet with parchment paper.

Form the meat into sixteen patties, 2½ to 3 inches in diameter and ¾ to 1 inch thick. Place them on the prepared baking sheet 1 inch apart and bake for 20 to 25 minutes, until cooked through and crisp around the edges.

STORAGE: The raw or cooked patties will keep well in an airtight container in the freezer for up to 3 months just separate them with parchment paper so they don't stick together. Simply cook from frozen as directed. The cooked patties will keep in an airtight container in the fridge for up to 5 days and are easily reheated in the oven or skillet.

Wild Mushroom Falafels *with* Sumac Yogurt

SERVES 4

Quidi Vidi Brewery's Iceberg Lager

Falafels

1 cup wild mushrooms

1 (19 oz) can chickpeas, drained and rinsed

1 tsp sea salt

2 Tbsp olive oil

1 shallot

2 cloves garlic

½ cup torn cilantro leaves

½ cup torn flat-leaf parsley leaves

1 tsp baking powder

1 tsp ground coriander

1 tsp ground cumin

¼ cup chickpea flour

When we were in Newfoundland, we made an interesting discovery: thanks to new waves of immigration, there is a strong and undeniable Middle Eastern influence making itself felt in the traditional cuisine. We saw chefs incorporating sumac and za'atar into their dishes and heard locals recommending a shawarma spot around the corner when asked for good places to grab a bite. Canada is a beautiful mosaic of cultures, and watching them infuse in this way is an incredibly special experience. This recipe uses wild mushrooms in the falafels, which adds an earthiness and a richness complemented by the herbs. Served with the sumac yogurt, they are a great appetizer for a crowd, or a lovely afternoon snack when a savoury craving hits.

For the Falafels: Preheat the oven to 325°F. Line a rimmed baking sheet with parchment paper.

Slice the mushrooms and place them on one side of the prepared baking sheet. Add the chickpeas to the other side. Sprinkle them with the salt, drizzle with the olive oil, and shake the pan to evenly coat everything. Bake until the chickpeas are just dried and beginning to turn golden and the mushrooms are starting to release their juices, about 15 minutes.

Remove from the oven and let cool for 10 minutes. Transfer to a food processor fitted with the steel blade or to a high-powered blender. Roughly chop the shallot and garlic and add them to the food processor, along with the cilantro and parsley, baking powder, coriander, and cumin. Blend to form a thick, smooth paste. Slowly add the flour, 1 tablespoon at a time, pulsing after each addition to thicken the paste. The dough should be wet enough to easily hold together in a ball, but not so sticky that it doesn't hold its shape and sticks to your fingers.

Transfer the falafel mix to a bowl and set in the fridge for about 20 minutes to firm up. (You don't need to cover it unless you're going to let it sit in the fridge for longer than this, but don't let it sit for more than 24 hours.)

Scoop a heaping tablespoon of the falafel mix into your hands and form it into a ball. Set on a rimmed baking sheet and repeat with the remaining falafel mix.

(continued)

Sumac Yogurt

Zest and juice of 1 lemon

1 cup Greek yogurt

1 Tbsp sumac

1 tsp sea salt

½ tsp white pepper

In a heavy-bottomed skillet or Dutch oven over medium heat, heat 1 inch of oil to 350°F, using a candy thermometer to monitor the temperature. Line a wire rack with paper towel. Fry four or five falafels at a time, being careful not to overcrowd the pan, until they're a deep nutty brown colour, 1 to 2 minutes per side. Using a slotted spoon or tongs, transfer the cooked falafels to the prepared wire rack. Give the oil 1 to 2 minutes to return to temperature between batches.

For the Sumac Yogurt: Place the lemon zest and juice in a small bowl. Add the yogurt, sumac, salt, and pepper and whisk until smooth.

Serve the hot falafels with the sumac yogurt on the side.

STORAGE: The falafels are best the moment they are made, although they will keep in an airtight container in the fridge for up to 1 week. The yogurt will keep in an airtight container in the fridge for up to 1 week. Reheat them in the oven at 350°F for a few minutes.

PICKING MUSHROOMS

Local Newfoundland foraging rock star Shawn Dawson smiles when he sees our bright-orange garb: he himself is dressed in orange coveralls. It's hunting season, and we don't want to be mistaken for moose on our foraging trek. As we slip into the woods armed with lovely wicker baskets, Shawn explains that most mushrooms are found on hillsides and banks beside bogland, as the wet, moss-covered fertile soil is the perfect place for them to grow. Most of what we're finding are winter chanterelles—deeply golden, delicate mushrooms with split stems that look like they're crossing their legs—along with a few spiky hedgehog, dark and earthy porcini, lots of dainty sweet tooth and milk caps, as well as an uncommon and very special discovery of lovely pine mushrooms.

Shawn reminds us that when foraging, it's important to always leave at least 40% of the patch untouched because the mushrooms we're picking are not the entire plant but part of a root system that can be several square feet in area. The "mushroom" is actually a much larger plant that is hidden underground. We only eat the blossoms. If too many blooms are picked, the mushroom won't be able to reproduce and thrive the next year. It's also important to pick the stem cleanly using a sharp knife, as pulling up the mushroom can damage the plant, or worse, allow bacteria to invade and eventually kill it.

Those pretty wicker baskets foragers carry aren't just for show either. As Shawn cuts, trims, and gathers the mushrooms, he explains that the mushrooms will naturally drop spores through the weave of the basket as we walk, reseeding the forest floor for future foragers. It's a nice way to reap the rewards of our efforts while giving back to the habitat as well.

As we come upon another patch of beautifully golden-coloured fungi, we're eager to pop them into our baskets, but Shawn is quick to warn us that the vast majority of mushrooms growing in the forest are inedible and extremely dangerous if consumed. Even mushrooms growing beside each other may not be of the same kind, so assessing each specimen individually is of the utmost importance. He relates a cautionary tale of a mushroom symposium in St. John's where attendees were encouraged to go and pick whatever they could find and then bring back the bounty to be identified by professional mycologists. Of the more than twelve hundred varietals that were gathered, only eight were edible. This is why it's important to have the advice and guidance of a professional when learning to identify mushrooms in the wild—or choose to support your local foraging experts by purchasing their finds at your local farmers' markets.

As the popularity of wild foods in Newfoundland becomes more mainstream, selling mushrooms and other foraged finds to Raymonds, Fork, and other well-known establishments in St. John's has become Shawn's full-time job. The work isn't easy, but the bounty is worth the effort and offers a great opportunity to infuse even more of Newfoundland's wild-food culture into the local cuisine. Shawn laughs as he explains that although the mushrooms have always been there, it's only been within the past ten years that their popularity as a culinary delicacy has really peaked across the province. As we pop a handful of our beautiful golden chanterelles into a sizzling pan later that day, we can certainly see why! They taste of the earth, and the buttery sweetness was worth every single forest-covered step we trekked.

Turnip & Mustard Seed

SERVES 4

 Luckett Vineyards' Tidal Bay

Fogo Island is set apart from the rest of the province by its unique topography and tradition, and the dishes chef Jonathan Gushue creates for the Fogo Island Inn reflect his focus on the hyper-localized blend of both. "The cuisine here is the cuisine of necessity," he explains as we sit by the fire, watching the waves crash against the rocky shore. The Indigenous Beothuk Peoples taught the Irish immigrants what they could source from the land, and traditional Irish crops—fennel, turnips, potatoes, and cabbage— also grow in abundance with a little love and care. Using seaweed and capelin as fertilizer in the seaside gardens gives the locally grown turnips a peppery flavour, and Jonathan claims they're some of the best he's ever tasted. This dish is a classic example of his culinary philosophy: Keep it simple but elevated, allow the flavours to speak for themselves, and always deliver something unexpected.

½ small turnip

1 small shallot

1 Tbsp butter, divided

1 tsp olive oil

⅔ cup vegetable stock, divided

2 Tbsp grated aged white cheddar cheese

1 tsp Dijon mustard

3 Tbsp chopped chervil

Sea salt and black pepper

1 Tbsp yellow mustard seeds

1 Tbsp black mustard seeds

Peel the turnip and cut it into small matchsticks using a mandolin or a very sharp slicing knife, ⅛ inch thick and ¾ inch wide. They should resemble short fettuccine noodles. You should have a generous cup of sliced turnip.

Finely dice the shallot. In a saucepan over medium heat, cook ½ tablespoon of the butter with the oil until the butter starts to foam. Add the shallots and sauté until just softened but not browned, about 2 minutes. Add the turnip and ⅓ cup of the stock, and simmer until the turnip is just starting to soften, about 1 minute. Add the remaining ⅓ cup of stock along with the remaining ½ tablespoon butter, the cheese, and mustard. Remove from the heat and stir to emulsify the sauce. Stir in the chervil and season to taste with salt and pepper.

In a small skillet, toast the yellow and black mustard seeds. Watch them carefully, as they can burn quickly.

Serve the turnip topped with mustard seeds for garnish.

STORAGE: The turnip is best enjoyed the day it's made but will keep in an airtight container in the fridge for up to 3 days.

Recipe contributed by Jonathan Gushue, Fogo Island Inn

Buttermilk Turnip Soup

SERVES 6

Markland Cottage Winery Lady of the Woods Birch Wine

Small fenced plots by the seashore are a common way of keeping a garden bed in Newfoundland, as much of the soil there is relatively deep, cleared of trees, and fairly fertile. Local Newfoundland turnips—also called swedes or rutabagas depending on where you source them—have a salty, tannic, almost peppery note to them thanks to the soil. Seaweed is raked up from the beaches and left to ferment over the winter. In the spring, vegetable compost and surplus capelin are tilled into it, creating produce with a unique taste. The tartness of the buttermilk brings out the turnips' flavour to perfection in this soup. A hot bowl of it paired with a slice of brown bread (page 177) is the best comfort food when the wind is howling and waves are crashing on the seashore.

1 large onion

4 cloves garlic, peel on

¼ cup butter

1 tsp sea salt

6½ cups chicken stock

2 bay leaves

4 sprigs thyme

1 small sprig rosemary

15 black peppercorns

4 cups cubed yellow turnips

1 cup buttermilk, plus a few tablespoons for garnish

Roughly chop the onion and smash the garlic cloves with the back of a knife, leaving them whole. Discard their peels.

In a large, heavy-bottomed saucepan over medium heat, melt the butter and then add the onions. Sauté for 5 minutes, sprinkle in the salt, and add the garlic. Continue to sauté for 3 minutes, until the onions are very soft and golden. Add the stock and bay leaves and bring to a boil.

In a small piece of cheesecloth, or an empty loose-leaf tea bag, place the thyme, rosemary, and peppercorns, bending the stems so they fit. Tie up the bag or cheesecloth, making a bouquet garni. Add to the stock. Add the turnips and boil for 5 minutes, then turn down the heat to low and cover. Simmer for 20 to 25 minutes, until the turnips are fork-tender. Remove the pot from the stove. Discard the bouquet garni and the bay leaves.

Allow to cool slightly, then add the soup to a blender in batches and purée until silky smooth. Strain the soup through a fine-mesh strainer over the pot to remove any excess lumps. The soup should be extra velvety in texture.

Add the buttermilk and simmer over low heat for 3 to 5 minutes, just enough to warm it through.

Ladle the soup into serving bowls and garnish each with a swirl of buttermilk.

STORAGE: The soup will keep in an airtight container in the fridge for up to 1 week and will keep without the buttermilk in an airtight container in the freezer for up to 3 months.

Pea Soup

SERVES 4

Dildo Brewing Co.'s Red Rocks Ale

Peter Burt, the founder of the Newfoundland Salt Company, started creating his own artisanal sea salts when he was the chef de cuisine at Raymonds Restaurant in St. John's, Newfoundland. When his hobby turned into his passion, he and his wife Robin left the city and moved to Bonavista to start their own company, which crafts the finest sea salts we've had the good fortune to taste. Now an integral part of this rural community, Peter puts his chef skills to work by organizing charity events like the famous annual Bonavista Best Bowl—Pea Soup Competition. In his honour, and because we wish we could be there to share in the celebration one day, here is our favourite version of this classic soup—finished with Newfoundland salt, of course!

1 lb smoke-cured ham hock

8 cups bone broth

2 Tbsp butter

1 stalk celery, diced

2 carrots, diced

1 onion, diced

2 cups dried yellow split peas, rinsed

1 bay leaf

2 Tbsp thyme leaves

1 tsp dried savory

1 tsp Newfoundland Sea Salt Company's Coffee Sea Salt (see note)

Black pepper

Crusty bread, for serving

In a large soup pot or Dutch oven over medium heat, bring the ham hock, broth, and 2 cups of water to a low boil. Continue cooking until the liquid has been reduced by half. Remove the ham hock and set aside to cool.

In a large skillet over medium heat, melt the butter. Add the celery, carrots, and onions and cook for about 10 minutes, until the onions are translucent and all the vegetables have softened. Transfer the vegetables to the broth. Add the split peas, bay leaf, thyme, and savory to the broth. Strip the meat from the ham hock, discarding the skin and extra fat, and add to the pot. Bring the soup to a low boil over medium heat.

Turn down the heat to low, cover the pot, and simmer, stirring occasionally, for about 1 hour, until the peas are very soft and the soup has thickened. You may need to add a bit more water if the soup gets too thick.

Once you've reached your desired thickness, discard the bay leaf, add the salt, and season to taste with pepper. Serve warm with crusty bread.

STORAGE: The soup will keep in an airtight container in the fridge for up to 1 week or in the freezer for up to 3 months.

NOTE: Newfoundland Sea Salt Company's Coffee Sea Salt is a lovely finishing salt that's as delicious on steak au poivre as it is on chocolate ice cream. To substitute, mix together 2 teaspoons of ground espresso or finely ground coffee and ¼ cup of flaky sea salt, such as Maldon.

Sorrel & Lovage Salad

SERVES 4 AS A SIDE

Auk Island Winery's Vinland White

If anything speaks to the delights of fresh spring greens, it's this salad. Sorrel has a lovely green apple flavour and lovage is almost like celery in leaf form. The two combined with fresh spring flowers make the most delicious side to any main dish or a light lunch on their own. We love to serve this with a primrose vinaigrette for a truly delicious complementary taste. Primroses are a delightful flower, with a scent and flavour reminiscent of honeysuckle and roses, and you'll see them growing in abundance along roadsides during the summer months. If left to grow for a full year, they send down a taproot, which turns into a lovely tall shoot covered with delicate yellow flowers that look almost like snapdragons the next spring. These roadside gardens are perfect for picking, and after a good rinse to get rid of any dust, the edible flowers are a delicious addition to any salad.

Dressing:

½ cup fresh primrose flowers

¼ cup olive oil

2 Tbsp white wine vinegar

2 Tbsp honey

½ tsp sea salt

Salad:

2 cups fresh sorrel leaves

2 cups fresh lovage leaves

½ cup edible flowers (such as chive blossoms, primroses, borage blossoms)

For the Dressing: Roughly chop the primrose flowers. In a small bowl, combine the flowers with the oil, vinegar, honey, and salt, and let the dressing ingredients sit for 10 to 15 minutes while you wash and dry the salad greens. When you're ready to assemble the salad, using an immersion blender, blend the dressing until the flowers are well blended and the dressing is creamy, smooth, and yellow.

For the Salad: In a large bowl, toss the sorrel and lovage leaves together. Massage gently with half of the dressing. Plate on a serving platter and drizzle with the remaining dressing. Top with the edible flowers and serve immediately.

STORAGE: The dressing will keep in an airtight container in the fridge for up to 1 week. The greens will keep covered or wrapped in a damp cloth in the fridge for up to 3 days. Once dressed, this salad is best enjoyed the day it's made.

Fried Capelin

SERVES 4

Lightfoot & Wolfville's Riesling or

Quidi Vidi Brewery's Day Boil
    Session IPA

1 cup flour

1 tsp paprika

1 tsp black pepper

½ cup olive oil

20 cleaned fresh capelin

8 slices white bread

½ cup butter

2 tsp flaky sea salt

Life is good when the capelin are rolling, literally bringing life to the shores of the island. They're the reason cod and whales and so many other deep-sea creatures come inshore to feed, and you'll find families with buckets in hand gathered around beach fires in celebration. The sea turns almost black when the waves teem with these small, easy-to-scoop-up Atlantic smelts. Fry them up over a grill and enjoy with a slice of fresh bread and butter.

In a shallow dish, combine the flour, paprika, and pepper.

Preheat the oven to 250°F to 350°F. The oven will be used to keep your fish warm so adjust how hot you like your fish.

In a skillet over medium heat, heat the oil. Line an ovenproof plate with paper towel. Dredge the fresh capelin in the flour mixture and fry three to four at a time until golden brown and crisp, 2 to 3 minutes per side. Transfer to the lined plate to absorb any excess oil. Place the plate in the oven to keep warm. Give the oil 1 to 2 minutes to return to temperature between batches. Repeat with the remaining fish.

Spread each slice of bread with a generous coating of butter and sprinkle with the salt.

To serve, place five capelin on each plate alongside two slices of bread. Enjoy immediately.

STORAGE: The capelin are best enjoyed as soon as they are made.

Spruce & Juniper Mussels

SERVES 2–4

Luckett Vineyards' Fizz or

YellowBelly Brewery's Wexford Wheat

Spruce tips and juniper berries are classic Newfoundland flavours that can be foraged in great abundance across the province. Here they are combined to give this traditional dish a deeply woodsy and aromatic taste. Young juniper berries are bright white and only turn deep blue upon maturity, which is when they get that brilliant gin-y aroma, while spruce tips are best picked when they're newly forming and are a bright chartreuse green. Be sure to heat the cream slowly so that you can impart as much flavour as possible before adding the gloriously briny Atlantic mussels.

1 Tbsp fresh or dried juniper berries

10–12 fresh spruce tips

1 cup heavy cream

2 Tbsp olive oil

1 Tbsp butter

½ cup diced sweet onion

2 cloves garlic, thinly sliced

1 cup dry white wine

2 Tbsp chopped parsley

2 lb mussels, cleaned

Sea salt

In a mortar, combine the juniper berries and spruce tips. Using a pestle, crush them lightly until the berries crack, the green tips are well bruised, and the oils have been released. In a skillet on medium-low heat, combine the berry mixture and cream and bring to a low simmer. Continue to simmer for 10 to 15 minutes, so that the cream becomes infused with the flavours. Remove from the heat and strain the cream into a glass measuring cup. Discard the solids.

In a Dutch oven over medium heat, combine the oil and butter. Once the butter has melted, add the onions and garlic and sauté for 8 to 10 minutes, until the onions are translucent. Add the wine and continue to cook for another 2 to 3 minutes. Add the strained cream and parsley and bring to a low boil. Add the mussels and cover. Steam the mussels in the mixture just until they open, 4 to 5 minutes. Discard any unopened mussels. Divide the mussels evenly between the serving bowls, top with the steaming liquid, sprinkle with salt, and serve immediately.

Cod & Scrunchions *with* Lemon Caper Brown Butter

SERVES 2

Bannerman Brewing Co.'s
   All Hands Lager

When we met chef Mark McCrowe, we were supposed to be halfway to New Brunswick. His invitation was simple: "The capelin are rolling, we're cooking on the beach, come join!" Due to a previously scheduled flight, we had to decline—but when mechanical issues with our aircraft changed our plans, we looked at each other and said, "We're going to the beach!"

Mark has spent many summer nights fishing the cod that chase the capelin, the small Atlantic smelt that roll into the shores of Newfoundland. "When the capelin roll, the oceans come alive," Mark explains. "It also brings a unique opportunity to be able to cast a jigger off the beach and catch fresh cod without having to launch a boat into deeper waters." He's even witnessed one rare case where hundreds of cod chased the smelt in and jumped right out of the water and onto the beach itself. As Mark tells it: "By this point, a fire is started . . . I have a hot skillet sitting over the coals and this is the dish I make." As we sat there with the fire glowing, cold beer in hand, we watched Mark effortlessly crafting food on a sizzling hot pan, and when the sun began to disappear over the horizon, we dug into a simply delicious meal.

Pan-Fried Cod:

2 large cod fillets, skin on

1 tsp sea salt

½ tsp black pepper

1 cup flour

2 Tbsp butter

Sauce:

1 cup chopped salt pork fat scrunchions
   (see note)

1 lemon

3 Tbsp butter

¼ cup capers

1 Tbsp caper brine

6 Tbsp chopped flat-leaf parsley

2 Tbsp oyster leaf (optional)

¼ cup sea buckthorn berries (optional)

For the Pan-Fried Cod: Season the cod with the salt and pepper. Evenly coat each side of the fish with the flour. Shake off any excess flour and set aside.

Set a large, heavy-bottomed skillet over medium-high heat. Once it's warm, heat the butter until bubbles appear and then subside. Gently lay the fish in the pan and cook for about 5 minutes per side. The fillets will be golden and crispy on the outside, just barely cooked through and opaque in the centre. Set the fish aside to rest in a warm place.

For the Sauce: In the same pan (no need to wipe it out first), render the pork scrunchions over medium heat for about 10 minutes, until light golden brown. Slice the lemon into quarters and discard any seeds. Drain the excess fat from the skillet and set the scrunchions aside. Place the butter in the pan and cook for about 3 minutes, until it develops a rich, nutty, golden-brown colour. Squeeze the juice from the lemon quarters into the butter, then toss them into the pan to stew. Add the capers and brine, then the parsley, oyster leaf (if using), and sea buckthorn berries (if using). Cook for 30 seconds. Add the pork scrunchions and cook for 1 minute to warm through. While the sauce is hot, spoon it over your crispy fish and tuck in before it gets cold.

STORAGE: This is best enjoyed the day it's made, although it will keep in an airtight container in the fridge for up to 3 days.

NOTE: Scrunchions are a staple component of Newfoundland cuisine. Most often served with fried cod tongues or fish and brewis, they are pieces of cured salt pork fat, usually fried until golden brown and crisp. They end up tasting similar to pork crackling or crisped fatty bacon ends. Either bacon ends or crackling would be a good substitution if scrunchions are not available.

Recipe contributed by Mark McCrowe

Crowberry-Glazed Arctic Char

SERVES 4

*Port Rexton Brewing Co.'s Baycation
Blonde American Blonde Ale*

Crowberries—or blackberries, as they are sometimes called in this province—are a fascinating inky-black fruit found on the brush-covered moors of Newfoundland and Labrador. They are quite tannic and acidic in flavour, but when mixed with olive oil they come to life and, in this dish, they add a lovely vibrancy to the glaze. Arctic char is slightly leaner than Atlantic cod and is harvested in rivers and lakes as well as the ocean—but the ocean-caught char are the most sought-after. The combination of flavours here makes for a simple yet beautiful dish.

1 shallot

¼ cup olive oil

1 tsp sea salt

1 cup fresh crowberries (see note)

¼ cup maple syrup

¼ cup sherry vinegar

2 bay leaves

4 sprigs savory

1 sprig rosemary or Labrador tea

4 (6 oz each) Arctic char fillets

STORAGE: This will keep in the fridge overnight, although it's best enjoyed the day it's cooked. If the fish is fresh, it can be frozen in the marinade for up to 3 months. Just thaw it in the fridge and then cook as directed.

NOTE: If you can't source crowberries, substitute traditional blackberries and use only 2 tablespoons of maple syrup.

Slice the shallot into rounds. In a saucepan over medium heat, warm the oil. Add the shallots and sprinkle with the salt. Allow them to caramelize, stirring occasionally but not too often, then add the crowberries and stir to sear. They will start to pop after a few minutes. Add the maple syrup and vinegar, followed by the bay leaves, savory, and rosemary. Simmer until the sauce easily coats the back of a spoon, the berries have burst, and it is very fragrant, 7 to 10 minutes. Remove from the heat and allow to cool completely.

Strain the sauce through a fine-mesh strainer over a bowl. Use the back of a spoon to squeeze out all the remaining juice from the crowberries. You will have a beautiful inky-black sauce. Discard the pulp, sprigs, and bay leaves and transfer the strained sauce to an airtight container large enough to hold the Arctic char without crowding, but reserve ⅓ cup sauce for serving in the fridge—just bring to room temperature when serving.

Pat the Arctic char fillets dry and place them in the container with the sauce, turning to coat. Marinate in the fridge for 24 hours, turning once halfway through to evenly coat.

When you're ready to cook, preheat the broiler to high and place the oven rack in the second-highest position. Line a rimmed baking sheet with parchment paper. Remove the fillets from the marinade and place them on the prepared baking sheet skin side down. Brush the tops lightly with any remaining marinade from the container. Broil until the tops are caramelized and golden, 3 to 4 minutes. Turn off the broiler and preheat the oven to 400°F, leaving the fish in the oven while it preheats. Bake for a total of 5 to 8 minutes after you turn the broiler off. (Depending on how quickly or slowly your oven heats, it might not have reached temperature by the time you take the fish out.) Slice into a piece of the fish to ensure it is fully cooked and opaque inside. Serve immediately, with the reserved sauce on the side.

Rolled Jiggs' Dinner

SERVES 6

*Quidi Vidi Brewery's
1892 Traditional Ale*

½ lb salt beef or corned beef

½ cup yellow split peas

1 carrot

1 starchy potato (such as russet)

½ small turnip

1 large savoy cabbage

1½ cups beef stock

¼ cup grainy Dijon mustard

2 Tbsp whipping cream

1 tsp dried savory, minced

If ever there was a beloved and treasured meal of Newfoundland, it's Jiggs' dinner. Now more commonly enjoyed as a holiday meal, it was born from necessity: to keep fisherman warm and well-fed at sea and to feed families with cellar stores throughout the long, cold winters. In this recipe, we've used all of the traditional, expected elements, but we've given them a modern twist. Hearty, packed with flavour, and easy to make, these little Jiggs' dinner cabbage rolls are a fun nod to the most traditional of Newfoundland foods.

If you're using salt beef, rinse it well, then soak in the fridge overnight (at least 8 hours) in cold water to release the salt and rehydrate.

Rinse the split peas, cover with 2 inches of cold water, and allow them to sit overnight (at least 8 hours) to soak.

When you're ready to cook, fill a large pot with fresh water and place over high heat, add the beef, and bring to a boil. Boil, uncovered, for 1 hour, until tender and cooked through. Remove from the pot and allow to cool enough to handle, then finely dice.

While the beef is boiling, drain the peas and place them in a small pot. Cover with 1 inch of water and bring to a boil over high heat. Cover, turn down the heat and simmer until tender, 25 to 30 minutes. Remove from the heat and allow to cool slightly before draining off the water.

Peel and dice the carrot, potato, and turnip, and place them in a large mixing bowl. Add the beef and peas and mix well.

Bring a large pot filled about halfway with water to a boil. Line a plate with a few pieces of paper towel. Immerse the whole cabbage in the boiling water for 30 seconds to 1 minute, until it turns bright green and the leaves start to wilt and separate a little from each other. Using sharp kitchen scissors, cut out the thick part of the spine of each leaf and lay the leaves on the prepared plate.

Preheat the oven to 350°F.

(continued)

To assemble the rolls, place ¼ cup of the meat and vegetable filling on a cabbage leaf. Fold the tails of the cabbage leaf up around the filling, then fold in the sides and roll the leaf the rest of the way up, as if you were rolling a burrito.

Place the roll seam side down in a 9- by 13-inch baking dish and repeat with the remaining cabbage leaves and filling.

Fill the base of the pan with the beef stock; do not cover the rolls completely. Cover the baking dish with aluminum foil and bake for 30 to 45 minutes, until the cabbage leaves are tender and the root vegetables are cooked through (the best way to test this is to taste one of the rolls). Remove from the oven and keep them covered until you're ready to serve.

When you're ready to serve, whisk together the mustard, cream, and savory until well combined. Serve the cabbage rolls with a spoonful of broth and mustard sauce on the side for dipping.

STORAGE: The rolls will keep in an airtight container in the fridge for up to 1 week or in the freezer for up to 3 months.

Rabbit Ravioli *with* Butternut Cream

SERVES 4

Lightfoot & Wolfville's Ancienne Chardonnay or Pinot Noir

Rabbit Ravioli:

2 rabbit legs

6 Tbsp olive oil, divided

½ cup frozen spinach, thawed and drained

2 cloves garlic, crushed

1½ tsp sea salt, divided

1 cup grated Parmesan cheese

4 eggs, divided

2 cups flour, divided, plus more for dusting

Butternut Cream Sauce:

1 (1–2 lb) small butternut squash

4 Tbsp olive oil, divided

4 cloves garlic, peeled and left whole

1 small white onion, chopped

1 tsp sea salt, plus more for garnish

¼ cup cream cheese, cubed

1 small apple

1 cup chicken stock

2 tsp dried savory

1 tsp dried thyme

1 cup whipping cream

1 tsp black pepper, plus more for garnish

Rabbit is a savoury meat with an almost herbaceous quality, and is the perfect addition to any pasta dish—especially ravioli! The sweetness of the butternut cream complements the richness of the herby rabbit filling.

For the Rabbit Ravioli: Preheat the oven to 375°F.

Place the rabbit legs in a roasting pan, rub them all over with 2 tablespoons of the oil, and cover the pan with foil. Roast for 25 to 30 minutes, until a thermometer inserted in the thickest part of a leg reads 160°F. Remove and allow to cool slightly. Shred the meat off the bone and chop it into smaller chunks, about ½ inch long.

In a mixing bowl, combine the rabbit and spinach. Mix the garlic with 1 teaspoon of the salt, and add to the bowl. Add the Parmesan and 1 egg. Using a fork, mix everything together to form a thick, uniform mixture.

In a separate bowl, whisk together 3 tablespoons of the oil and the 3 eggs. Gently whisk in the remaining ½ teaspoon of salt and 1 cup of the flour to form a yellow, creamy paste. Using a wooden spoon, add about 2 tablespoons of the remaining flour at a time until the dough can pull away from the sides of the bowl. Sprinkle flour on the counter, turn the dough out onto it, and knead until all of the flour has been absorbed and the dough is very smooth and elastic. Evenly divide the dough into four pieces and form them into small balls. Drizzle them with a little of the remaining oil to prevent a skin from forming. Wrap in plastic wrap and let rest in the fridge for 30 minutes.

Using a rolling pin, roll out one ball of dough at a time into a long, narrow rectangle about 3 inches wide and 8 inches long, dusting both sides with some flour to keep the dough soft, and easy to work with and prevent it from sticking to the counter. If you have a pasta maker, run the pasta sheets through it on the second-thinnest setting. Otherwise, continue using a rolling pin and roll until the sheets are ⅛ inch thick.

Line a rimmed baking sheet with parchment paper.

(continued)

If using a ravioli mould: Lay a sheet of pasta over the mould and gently press it into the spaces to make little cups for the filling. The sheet needs to be just over twice as long as the mould. Place 2 teaspoons of rabbit filling in each cup and then fold the long end of the pasta sheet over top to make the lids. Gently press down on the pasta, then roll a rolling pin over the top to seal and separate them. You may need someone to hold down the far side of the mould when rolling the opposite end so it doesn't flip. Gently remove the individual ravioli from the mould, dust with flour, and place on the prepared baking sheet. Repeat. Chill in the fridge while making the sauce.

If using a pizza wheel: Place the pasta sheets on a floured countertop. Add 2-teaspoon dots of rabbit filling over one half of each pasta sheet, at least 1½ inches apart. Fold the bottom half of the sheet over the top half and gently press down around the rabbit dollops. Cut out the ravioli with the pizza wheel and ensure the edges are pressed well together. If the sheets of pasta aren't sticking well, dampen the edges with water. Dust the ravioli with flour and place them on the prepared baking sheet. Chill in the fridge while making the sauce.

For the Butternut Cream Sauce: Preheat the oven to 375°F.

Cut the squash in half lengthwise and spoon out the seeds. Brush the flesh with 1 teaspoon of the oil, place the squash directly on the bottom rack of the oven, and roast for 20 minutes.

Remove the squash from the oven and place it on a rimmed baking sheet cut side up. Pour 1 teaspoon of the oil and place two cloves of garlic into each hole where the seeds used to sit, tossing them well. Roast for an additional 15 to 20 minutes, until the squash is tender and a knife inserts easily into the flesh. Set the garlic aside.

In a wide pot over medium heat, warm the remaining. Sauté the onions for 1 to 2 minutes, until just translucent. Sprinkle the salt over top and cook for about 1 minute more, just to sweat them. Add the cream cheese, stirring constantly until it has melted. Turn down the heat to low.

Peel, core, and chop the apple. Using a spoon, remove the squash flesh from the skin and add to the pot, along with the reserved garlic, the apple, stock, savory, and thyme. Stir to fully incorporate and break up the squash. Simmer for 3 minutes, allowing the apple to cook and the sauce to reduce slightly. Remove from the heat, let cool slightly, then transfer the sauce to a blender (or use an immersion blender in the pot) and blend until creamy and smooth. Return the sauce to the pot (if necessary), set over medium heat, and add the cream and pepper. Bring to a simmer, stirring constantly. Remove from the heat when the sauce is thick and steaming.

To Serve: Bring a large pot of salted water to a boil, add the ravioli and 1 cup of cold water, then stir the water to ensure the ravioli aren't sticking. Bring the water back to a boil, uncovered, and keep at a boil for 1 minute. Remove a ravioli and taste. The pasta should be cooked through but still al dente. It might need 1 more minute. Drain the pasta and gently shake off any excess water. Transfer the ravioli to serving plates and spoon the sauce over top. Season to taste with a sprinkle of salt and pepper.

STORAGE: Uncooked ravioli will keep in the freezer for up to 6 months: just freeze on a baking sheet first, then transfer to an airtight container. Cooked ravioli will keep in an airtight container in the fridge for 3 days, although they're best the day of. The sauce will keep in an airtight container in the fridge for 1 week or in the freezer for 3 months.

CHASING RABBIT

When a Newfoundlander says they're having rabbit for dinner, they really mean they're having Arctic hare. These wild rabbits are beautiful, large white creatures. Mostly dark meat, they are quite lean and perfect to cook over an open fire during hunting season.

Years ago, when commercial chain stores started to become commonplace across the province, traditional game was abandoned in favour of canned and ready-made supermarket dishes such as bologna and Spam. Today, there is renewed interest in restoring these centuries-old ways of capturing wild food and revitalizing this aspect of local culinary heritage. Hunting, sealing, and snaring practices are making a comeback, and people like Lori McCarthy are dedicating themselves to preserving the food culture and stories of Newfoundland. It's a huge challenge, and one that Lori is tackling head-on through her culinary tourism company Cod Sounds.

As we sit around a fire with cups of hot coffee in hand, Lori shares stories of hunting with her family. She teaches us how to tie a snare using a 22-gauge brass wire, and we spend some time fiddling with it to get it just right before walking out to find a rabbit run. Rabbits are creatures of habit; they always take the same path, so the trick is to block any other routes with sticks and branches, guiding them toward the snare. Their sense of smell is keen, so wearing gloves that live outside is essential to prevent the rabbits from catching our scent. Lori even recommends making the snares and then letting them sit outdoors for twenty-four hours before setting them, to rid them of any lingering human presence.

Lori takes two rabbits she caught the day prior out of a shallow tub and shows us how to tie them up, skin them, and get them ready for butchering. She demonstrates how to pinch off the bladder without ruining any of the meat and how to take apart the delicate joints. The bones on rabbits are so brittle that they can splinter into sharp shards, presenting a serious hazard to the person eating them. Lori takes the rabbits to start the butchering process: she easily takes the meat from the bone but explains that they could also be roasted whole, wrapped in bacon, or braised. In the end, we chopped vegetables and cooked them over the fire with minced meat for the most gorgeous pasta ragù we have ever had (page 280).

Lori's mission is to educate locals and visitors alike about both traditional and modern wild-food cooking techniques. The traditional methods are the classic ones, of course, but they've been lost over the last generation, pushed out by a desire for convenience. Lori is set to change that—and for good reason. These wild foods are delicious! They taste of the earth and all of the work that goes into gathering them. "If we want to keep this meat on our plates, we have to change the way that we cook it," she says. Nowadays people want familiar foods that they see on TV or sample in restaurants. Teaching folk how to prepare game in the same way they would meat from the grocery store is key to ensuring these wild meats once again find their place in homes throughout the province.

The art of snaring rabbits, of foraging, hunting, and living off the land is coming back. The land is fertile and plentiful, and being innovative with what the province provides is a necessity as well as a gift that delivers delicious returns. If you take the time to hunt, to search, to forage, and even to set a snare, Newfoundland really does offer all that is required for culinary perfection.

Rabbit Ragù

SERVES 4

Luckett Vineyards' Phone Box Red

1 onion

1 stalk celery

2 small parsnips

1 large carrot

2 cloves garlic

1–1½ lb rabbit meat

¼ cup olive oil

1 tsp sea salt

4 bay leaves

1 cup dry red wine

2 cups beef stock

3 cups flour, divided

4 eggs

Oregano leaves, for garnish

Orange zest, for garnish

Freshly grated Parmesan cheese, for garnish

"Beautiful food moments are memories that run deep in our soul; they create emotions that connect us with the people and places we love," explains Lori McCarthy, a passionate storyteller and avid cultural ambassador for Newfoundland and Labrador. A treasure in her own right, Lori is dedicated to telling food stories that connect people to place by embracing the wild foods of her province and working to find ways of keeping that food on local plates. Through her company Cod Sounds, she shares the culture that she loves and that is close to her heart with delicious dishes like this rabbit ragù cooked over an open fire—an experience that we will remember for a long time to come.

Dice the onion and celery. Peel and dice the parsnips and carrot, then crush the garlic. Roughly chop the rabbit meat into ½-inch cubes.

Place a large, heavy-bottomed pot over medium heat. Add the oil and then the vegetables, and sauté until the onion is translucent and the garlic is just golden, 2 to 3 minutes. Season with the salt. Add the rabbit meat and bay leaves, and continue to sauté for 5 to 7 minutes, until the meat is browned. Deglaze the pan with the wine, scraping up any bits that may have stuck to the bottom. Add the stock, turn down the heat to low, and simmer, uncovered, until the meat is tender, vegetables are cooked and the sauce is quite thick, 30 to 45 minutes.

While the ragù is simmering, prepare the pasta. Place 2 cups of flour on the counter and make a well in the centre. Crack the eggs into the well and, using a fork, mix the eggs gently, and then slowly start to incorporate the flour to form a soft, sticky dough. Sprinkle the dough with half of the remaining 1 cup of flour and begin to knead, adding more flour as needed until the dough no longer sticks to the counter and is soft and very supple. Wrap the dough in plastic wrap and chill in the fridge for about 30 minutes to set.

Divide the pasta into four equal pieces. Dust the pasta with flour and, using a rolling pin, roll out one piece at time into a long, fairly narrow rectangle. Repeat with the remaining pasta dough. If you have a pasta maker, run the pasta sheets through it on the second-thinnest setting. Otherwise, continue using a rolling pin and roll until the sheets are ¼ inch thick. Fold the pasta like a vertical accordion into a pile on a cutting board, then, using a sharp knife, cut it into ½-inch-wide strips. Toss the pasta with a little flour, separating the strands.

(continued)

Bring a pot of salted water to a boil and cook the pasta for 1 to 2 minutes, until it's white and cooked through. Drain the pasta and add to the pot of simmering rabbit ragù. Using tongs, generously coat the pasta in the sauce. Continue to stir for 1 to 2 minutes. Discard the bay leaves.

To serve, divide the pasta and ragù between four serving bowls and garnish with oregano, a bit of orange zest, and some Parmesan. Serve immediately.

STORAGE: Leftover ragù will keep in an airtight container in the fridge for up to 3 days, although it is best enjoyed the day it's made.

Recipe contributed by Lori McCarthy, Cod Sounds

Wild Mushroom & Barley Risotto

SERVES 4

YellowBelly Brewery's St. John's Stout
or

Jost Vineyards' Great Big Friggin' Red

8 cups beef stock

2 sprigs marjoram

4 sprigs thyme

2 bay leaves

6 black peppercorns

2 large shallots

2 cloves garlic

4 cups wild mushrooms, divided
(chanterelles, porcini, oyster, and
pine are all delicious)

2 Tbsp olive oil, plus extra for serving

4 Tbsp butter, divided

1 tsp sea salt, plus more for garnish

1 tsp black pepper, plus more for
garnish

2 cups pearl barley

½ cup dry red wine

1 cup grated Parmesan cheese,
plus more for garnish

2 cups fresh salad greens (such as
arugula)

2 Tbsp lemon juice, for serving

This hearty risotto is the perfect autumnal meal, especially after a wonderful day in the woods foraging for wild mushrooms. Barley is a staple in Newfoundland pantries and pairs well with the richness and complexity of the mushrooms. Crisping the mushrooms in butter allows their flavour to really shine through, and the barley is gently spiced with the bouquet garni, creating a perfect one-bowl meal. We love mixing up the herbs as well. If we're lucky enough to be in Newfoundland when we're making this recipe, sweet gale, a bit of Labrador tea, and juniper berries are our herbs of choice.

In a large stockpot over medium-low heat, warm the stock. Tear the marjoram, thyme, and bay leaves into small pieces and add to a bit of cheesecloth along with the peppercorns to make a bouquet garni. Add to the stock. Gently simmer.

Mince the shallots and the garlic (see page 60) so the pieces are smaller than the grains of barley. Finely chop 1 cup of the mushrooms and set the remainder aside.

In a large skillet over medium heat, warm the oil with 2 tablespoons of the butter. Add the shallots and garlic and sauté until just translucent, about 2 minutes. Add the salt and pepper, stirring so the shallot and garlic sweat, then add the chopped mushrooms and sauté an additional 3 to 4 minutes. Rinse the barley and add to the pan. Cook, stirring constantly, until the barley has absorbed the oil and butter and any juices from the mushrooms, and the grains are quite glossy and almost translucent, 2 to 3 minutes. Slowly add the wine. It will bubble up. Continue to cook, stirring constantly, until the barley has fully absorbed the wine, 2 to 3 minutes. Begin to add the warm stock, one ladleful at a time, stirring constantly until the liquid has been absorbed. Repeat until there are two to three ladlefuls of stock left. The risotto should be tender and soft, yet still textured. If the risotto is too goopy, let the liquid boil off, stirring constantly. If it's too crunchy, add some more stock and keep cooking until it's tender. Remove from the heat and set aside.

Tear the remaining 3 cups of mushrooms into halves or quarters, leaving them quite large.

(continued)

In a separate pan over medium heat, warm the remaining 2 tablespoons of butter for about 2 minutes, until it starts to sizzle, swirling it a few times. Add the mushroom pieces and stir occasionally, giving them a nice sear on each side until browned, watching that they don't burn. Remove from the heat.

Place the risotto back on medium heat, pour in one ladleful of stock and stir to combine and incorporate into the risotto, as it will have congealed a bit while you were preparing the mushrooms. After it loosens with the added stock, add an additional half a ladle of stock and the cheese. Stir well to combine and allow the cheese to melt, then fold in all but ½ cup of the seared mushrooms.

Remove from the heat and immediately transfer to serving plates. Top with the remaining seared mushroom pieces, season with salt and pepper, and garnish with some extra Parmesan cheese. Toss the salad greens with some olive oil and the lemon juice and serve alongside the risotto.

STORAGE: The risotto will keep in an airtight container in the fridge for up to 3 days and can be reheated with a little stock to soften and revitalize it.

Moose Balls *with* Partridgeberry BBQ Sauce

SERVES 6

Auk Island Winery's 12 Gauge

Chef Katie Hayes's father Mike always wanted to convert his carpentry workshop into a pub. After Katie moved home with an eye to opening a restaurant, the renovations began, and soon the Bonavista Social Club was born. From the very beginning it was important to Katie that local foods and flavours be the stars of the ever-changing menu. And so you'll find favourites such as partridgeberry bread pudding and moose burgers being served to happy locals and tourists alike all summer long. These meatballs perfectly exemplify her philosophy: Keep it simple, fun, and true to place, but above all delicious!

Partridgeberry BBQ Sauce:

1 onion

1 clove garlic

2 Tbsp olive oil

1 (28 oz) can whole tomatoes

½ tsp onion powder

½ tsp smoked paprika

¼ tsp cayenne pepper

½ cup crushed tomatoes

¼ cup packed brown sugar

¼ cup molasses

1 Tbsp prepared yellow mustard

1 cup partridgeberries

Sea salt and black pepper

Moose Balls:

1½ lb ground moose

½ lb ground pork

1 Tbsp dried savory

2 tsp sea salt

1 tsp black pepper

For the Partridgeberry BBQ Sauce: Mince the onion and garlic. Warm the oil in a large saucepan over medium heat, and sauté the onions and garlic until soft and translucent, about 5 minutes. Add the whole tomatoes and gently crush them with a spoon to release their juices. Mix in the onion powder, paprika, and cayenne. Add the crushed tomatoes, sugar, molasses, and mustard, and stir well to combine. Bring to a boil, then turn down the heat to medium-low and simmer, uncovered, for 1 hour. Remove from the heat. Allow to cool slightly and then purée until the mixture is smooth in texture. Return the sauce to the pot, set over medium-low heat again, add the berries, and season with salt and pepper. Simmer, uncovered, to thicken slightly, about 15 minutes.

For the Moose Balls: Preheat the oven to 375°F. Line a rimmed baking sheet with parchment paper.

In a mixing bowl, mix together the ground meats, savory, salt, and pepper to form a uniform mixture. Using your hands, roll the meat mixture into 1- to 1½-inch balls and place on them prepared baking sheet, evenly spaced and not touching. You should have 20 to 24 balls. Bake for 15 minutes. Transfer the balls to an ovenproof casserole dish just large enough to hold them snuggly and pour the sauce over top. The sauce should completely cover the meatballs. Bake, uncovered, for an additional 15 minutes. Serve immediately.

STORAGE: The moose balls in sauce will keep in an airtight container in the fridge for 3 days. The sauce will keep separately in an airtight container in the fridge for 2 weeks. The par-cooked moose balls will keep in an airtight container in the freezer for 3 months, just bake from frozen at 375°F for about 10 minutes before adding to the sauce and cooking as directed above.

Recipe contributed by Katie Hayes, Bonavista Social Club

NOTE: Pork is added to the moose meat to add extra flavour and fat content, compared to adding beef, as moose is a very lean meat and benefits from the added fat, which keeps the texture soft and the flavour rich and complex. Moose, although lean, is not gamey in flavour like venison.

HUNTING MOOSE

Typically when we see a few cars pulled off to the side of the road, we assume that someone needs help. Not in Newfoundland. During the autumn months, this sight is far from indicating an emergency. The reality is there's a 99% chance someone is gathering wood for next winter or hunting moose. Often five or six trucks are lined up on the side of the road, all gathered together, tailgates down with ramps still attached so the ATVs can be backed off. Most hunting cabins are not accessible by road, so the shoulder of the highway becomes the parking lot.

The tradition of moose hunting here is more than just heading to the woods for a few days; it's a practice in which freezers are filled to feed families throughout the year. These stately animals are lean like venison but not as gamey; rich in texture and flavour, they offer a taste of place unlike anything else we've found. Many people enjoy eating moose, but few know how to properly prepare it. Lori McCarthy of the culinary tourism company Cod Sounds explains that most folks don't even know to tell the butcher how they'd like it cut. Lori's mission is to teach locals how to prepare moose in creative and contemporary ways. As Newfoundland is the only province to allow wild game to be sold in grocery stores or prepared in restaurants, visitors and locals alike can easily sample dishes and see how versatile moose meat can be. A good roast can be delightful, but a moose carpaccio, roulade, or even tartare can be incredible!

Individual moose licences are drawn by lottery and treasured by those who are awarded them. The Newfoundland government reserves a set number of licences for charities, which the charity can then give to a hunter to hunt on their behalf. This allows someone who wants to go hunting but didn't get a licence that year to still enjoy a few days in the woods with friends while supporting their community. Sitting on the front porch of the Bonavista Social Club, owner and chef Katie Hayes explains that, as in other provinces, not everyone can get a moose tag every year, so most people go hunting as a group—that way, only one person in the group needs to have a tag. Katie regularly donates her time to butcher moose, and the meat is given to a charity to distribute to those in need. The charities can also fundraise by selling back to the community—this is often how restaurants are able to put the meat on a menu, making it a mutually beneficial exercise.

Katie is unusual in that she grew up in Bonavista and left as most do, but ten years ago moved back with her husband Shane. He's a "blow-in" from Ireland, although, as he describes it, "the culture feels more Irish than Canadian here anyway." Katie's father, Mike Paterson, is a seasoned forager and hunter, so she grew up learning what to do with game and all things wild. The Bonavista Social Club she and Shane started is a seasonal restaurant that highlights the best of local cuisine. Their Moose Balls (page 286) and moose burgers are both incredibly popular with tourists and locals alike, proving that moose is definitely the tastiest meat around!

Moose Roast *with* Irish Red Ale Gravy

SERVES 6

Dildo Brewing Co.'s Stout

4 lb moose roast

6 strips bacon

2 onions

4 large waxy potatoes

2 large carrots

2 parsnips

1 cup sliced wild mushrooms

3 cups ale

2 Tbsp grainy Dijon mustard

2 tsp Worcestershire sauce

2 tsp black pepper

1 tsp sea salt

1 tsp chili flakes

2 bay leaves or 1 sprig sweet gale,
  if available

2 Tbsp cornstarch

2 Tbsp cold water

Moose is often cleaned and quartered in the field and then turned into ground meat at the butchers, but when it's aged and properly cooked, it makes for the most amazingly tasty roasts as well. This delicious slow-cooked roast is simple to put together and a great way to enjoy a larger cut of moose. For the ale in the gravy, we recommend YellowBelly Brewery's Fighting Irish Red Ale, but your favourite strong ale will do nicely as well.

Pat the moose roast dry, place it in a slow cooker, and lay the slices of bacon over top. Cut the onions into quarters, and peel and chop the potatoes, carrots, and parsnips into 1-inch cubes or slices. Arrange the vegetables, including the mushrooms, snugly around the roast.

Whisk the ale, mustard, and Worcestershire sauce with the pepper, salt, and chili flakes until smooth. Pour this over the roast and vegetables. Tuck in the bay leaves, cover the slow cooker with its lid, and cook on low for 6 to 8 hours, until the roast registers 145°F on a meat thermometer and the vegetables are fork-tender. Discard the bay leaves.

Remove the roast from the slow cooker and place on a cutting board to rest for 10 to 15 minutes before carving and transferring to a serving platter. Using a slotted spoon, transfer the vegetables to a serving bowl or scatter them around the moose roast.

Ladle out 2 cups of cooking liquid from the slow cooker and pour them through a fine-mesh sieve into a small saucepan. Whisk the cornstarch and cold water to make a slurry. Add to the cooking liquid and place the saucepan over medium-high heat. Bring to a boil, stirring constantly, and boil for 1 minute, until the gravy has thickened and is no longer cloudy. Transfer to a jug or gravy boat and serve alongside the vegetables and roast.

STORAGE: The meat, vegetables, and gravy will keep in separate airtight containers in the fridge for up to 1 week.

Saltwater Lamb *with* Lovage Cream

SERVES 6

Newfoundland Cider Company's Forager Craft Cider

The Little Fogo Islands are famous for their saltwater lamb, as are the islands off the coast of Bonavista and many of the other smaller archipelagos. After lambing in spring, farmers in Newfoundland herd their flocks onto punts and dories and move them to the smaller, predator-free islands to graze during the summer months. These sheep spend a quarter of the year or more eating salt air–soaked grasses and seaside vegetation, all of which causes them to develop a unique flavour. The meat on these saltwater lambs is juicier and darker than pasture-raised sheep, with less fat and a tender, melt-in-your-mouth texture.

This leg of lamb is simple to prepare, and the end result is wonderfully tasty. The long, slow roast allows it to soften and absorb all of the flavours from the rub and drippings. Serve it with Tricolour Beet & Lentil Salad (page 197) and Sorrel & Lovage Salad (page 261) for a deliciously hearty yet fresh meal.

3–4 lb leg of lamb

2 Tbsp olive oil

2 tsp sea salt

1 tsp smoked paprika

Zest and juice of 2 lemons, divided

2 Tbsp chopped savory leaves

¼ cup grainy Dijon mustard

1 large red onion

1 cup fruity red wine

½ cup lovage leaves

1 clove garlic

1 cup crème fraîche or Greek yogurt

Preheat the oven to 450°F.

Pat dry the leg of lamb with a paper towel. Rub it with the oil, and sprinkle the salt and paprika over top.

Lay the leg of lamb on an unlined baking sheet and roast for 10 minutes, until seared and crisp on the outside. Turn the leg over, and roast for another 10 minutes. Remove the lamb from the oven and turn down the heat to 325°F.

While the leg is roasting, whisk together the zest and juice of one lemon, the savory, and mustard.

Slice the onion into rounds. In a roasting pan that fits the leg of lamb snugly, place the onions in an even layer over the bottom of the pan, and put the leg of lamb on top. Rub the mustard mixture all over the leg. Pour the wine into the pan, making sure to pour it around the lamb and not over it. Cover with aluminum foil, making a tent.

Roast for 1 hour and 30 minutes, then baste the leg with juices from the pan, turn it over, and roast, covered, for an additional 45 minutes. Remove the foil, baste the lamb again, and roast, uncovered, for 30 minutes to firm up the outside and allow some of the juices to evaporate. The meat will be pulling away from the bone and will be a rich caramel-brown colour.

(continued)

While the lamb is roasting, bring a small pot of water to a boil and prepare an ice bath. Blanch the lovage leaves for 15 seconds, then place them in the ice bath to stop the cooking process. Place the cooled leaves on a piece of cheesecloth or a clean tea towel and gently squeeze to remove any excess water. Finely chop the blanched lovage and mince the garlic. In a small bowl, mix together the zest and juice of the remaining lemon, the lovage, and garlic. Stir in the crème fraîche. Cover and chill in the fridge to allow the flavours to develop before serving.

Remove the roast from the oven and allow to sit for 15 minutes before carving. Serve with the lovage cream.

STORAGE: Leftover meat will keep in an airtight container in the fridge for up to 3 days. The lovage cream will keep in an airtight container in the fridge for up to 5 days.

Figgy Duff & Salted Screech Sauce

SERVES 6

The Newfoundland Distillery Company's Gunpowder & Rose Rum

Figgy Duff, a traditional steamed pudding–style cake that's easy to put together, is a distinctly Newfoundland and Labrador dessert. We've shaken things up a bit by combining the province's famous screech rum with the Newfoundland Salt Company's Juniper Smoked Sea Salt to create a delicious sauce featuring some of our favourite local flavours. If you don't have these specialty items on hand, a good dark rum (use the same one as you use for the duff) and flaky sea salt will work in their place.

Figgy Duff:

½ cup dark rum

2 cups golden raisins

2 tsp lemon zest

2 cups dried breadcrumbs

2 Tbsp hot water

¼ cup butter, softened

½ cup firmly packed brown sugar

2 eggs

½ cup molasses

½ cup flour

1 tsp baking soda

1 tsp fine sea salt

1 tsp ground allspice

1 tsp ground ginger

1 tsp ground cinnamon

Salted Screech Sauce:

2 cups sugar

½ cup butter, cubed

1 cup whipping cream

½ cup Newfoundland screech

1 tsp Newfoundland Salt Company's Juniper Smoked Sea Salt

For the Figgy Duff: Heat the rum in a small saucepan over medium-low heat, but do not let it boil. In a medium heatproof bowl, combine the golden raisins and lemon zest, and pour the warmed rum over top. Set aside for at least 30 minutes.

In another heatproof bowl, cover the breadcrumbs with the hot water. Let sit for 2 to 3 minutes and then place them in a cheesecloth or clean tea towel and gently squeeze out the water. Discard the water and set the breadcrumbs aside.

Preheat the oven to 300°F. Butter and flour a steamed pudding mould.

Using a stand mixer fitted with the paddle attachment, beat the butter and sugar on medium speed for 3 to 4 minutes, until fluffy. Turn down the speed to low and, with the mixer running, add the eggs one at a time. Scrape down the sides of the bowl, then add the molasses and mix until just combined.

In a medium bowl, combine the flour, baking soda, salt, allspice, ginger, and cinnamon. With the mixer running on low speed, gradually add the dry ingredients to the butter mixture, beating just until combined. Add the breadcrumbs and the raisin mixture and mix until just combined.

Pour the batter into the prepared pudding mould. Place the mould in the middle of a 15-inch square double layer of cheesecloth, then gather the edges of the cloth together over the pudding and secure with kitchen twine.

Place the pudding in a large ovenproof pot. Add 2 to 3 inches of water—it should be two-thirds of the way up the side of the mould. Cover the pot with its lid and bake for 2 to 2½ hours, or until the centre of the pudding has set to a cake-like consistency and a wooden skewer inserted into the middle comes out clean.

Once it's cooked, remove the pudding from the water bath and let sit for 20 to 30 minutes.

For the Salted Screech Sauce: Place the sugar in a medium, heavy-bottomed saucepan and begin to cook over medium heat. Do not stir the sugar or it will crystallize and you'll have to start over. As the sugar begins to melt, swirl the pot around to move the sugar and evenly distribute the heat. Using a pastry brush dipped in cold water, brush down any hardened sugar on the sides of the pot. Continue until the sugar has completely melted and has turned a deep mid-caramel colour. Remove from the heat immediately, add the butter, and stir quickly with a wooden spoon. Be careful, as the sugar will be very hot and will spit a bit. Add the cream and continue to stir. Don't worry if the sugar forms a hard caramel mass in the middle of the cream and butter. Return the pot to medium heat and continue to stir until the sauce is smooth and creamy. Add the screech and salt, and whisk to combine. Set aside until you're ready to serve.

To serve, invert the figgy duff onto a plate and serve with the warm salted screech sauce.

STORAGE: The sauce will keep in an airtight container in the fridge for up to 2 days. Warm it before serving. The figgy duff will keep in an airtight container in the fridge for up to 5 days; it's also best warmed before serving.

Partridgeberry Galettes

SERVES 4

Gaspereau Vineyards' Rosé

Partridgeberries are similar to cranberries and are sometimes referred to as a ground or wild version of them. Smaller in diameter, with a deep-burgundy colour and a flavour that's not as tart as their commercially grown cousins', partridgeberries grow in clumps along the rocky landscape across much of Newfoundland. In autumn, when the berries are ripe for picking, these galettes have to come out of our oven. A simple open-faced flaky pastry with a cream cheese base to complement the tart berries and help hold everything together, they are a perfect afternoon treat.

Pastry:

1½ cups flour

2 Tbsp sugar

1 tsp baking powder

¾ cup chilled butter, cubed

1 egg

¼ cup cold water

1 Tbsp apple cider vinegar

Filling:

½ cup cream cheese, cubed

1 egg

2 Tbsp honey

4 cups partridgeberries

2 Tbsp cornstarch

2 Tbsp sugar

¼ cup whole milk

4 Tbsp raw sugar

For the Pastry: In a large mixing bowl, whisk together the flour, sugar, and baking powder until light, fluffy, and lump-free. Add the butter in pieces and, using a pastry blender or two knives, cut the butter into the flour mixture until it has a coarse oatmeal texture. In a large measuring cup, whisk together the egg, water, and vinegar. Add the wet ingredients to the dry ingredients and gently fold and press the mixture together to form a ball, being careful not to overmix. Wrap in plastic wrap and chill in the fridge for 30 minutes to rest.

For the Filling: While the pastry is resting, in a bowl, whisk together the cream cheese, egg, and honey until a creamy paste-like mixture forms. In a separate bowl, place the partridgeberries. In a small bowl, whisk the cornstarch and sugar together, and sprinkle over the partridgeberries, tossing to evenly coat.

Preheat the oven to 425°F. Line a rimmed baking sheet with parchment paper.

Remove the pastry from the fridge and divide it into four evenly sized pieces. Roll the first piece of pastry into an 8-inch circle about ¼ inch thick. Spread one-quarter of the cream cheese mixture over it, leaving a 1½-inch border around the outside of the pastry. Add 1 cup of the berry mixture and spread it evenly over the cream cheese mixture to cover it completely. Fold in the sides of the pastry so they come up and over the berries closest to the edge of the cream cheese mixture, pinching the seams together to make pleats. Transfer to the prepared baking sheet. Repeat with the remaining dough and berries, making four individual galettes.

(continued)

Using a pastry brush, brush the crust and the top of the berries with the milk to moisten the cornstarch, then sprinkle each galette with 1 tablespoon of raw sugar. Bake for 8 minutes, then turn down the heat to 350°F without opening the oven door and bake for an additional 15 to 20 minutes, until the berries are bubbling and the crust is golden. Remove from the oven and allow the galettes to rest on the baking sheet for 10 minutes, then transfer them to a wire rack to cool completely before serving.

STORAGE: The galettes will keep in an airtight container at room temperature for up to 5 days, although they always disappear long before then.

PICKING BERRIES

At first glance, the berry patches of Newfoundland look more like lichen-covered rocks scattered over the tundra. With mossy patches here and soft, boggy patches there, you would never think that anything edible could grow in this landscape unless you were standing directly over it.

As we walk with Mona, a Fogo Island native and avid berry picker, she explains that if there is any rule of thumb to picking berries in Newfoundland, it's the reality that exceptions abound. "Crowberries are black, unless they are red or pink. Marshberries are typically red and speckled with gold or pink, unless they're bright red, then there are ground cranberries, but not partridge-berries, because partridgeberries are lingonberries." We're beyond confused, but as she expertly points out the differences in size, leaf, and bunching, we begin to understand. Luckily it's not a steep learning curve, and before long we're filling our buckets with today's target: the delicious marshberries that grow in a tightly woven tapestry with wild blueberries, crowberries, caribou moss, sweet gale, and Labrador tea. Having someone who understands this beautifully entangled edible landscape is a huge help as we climb over rocks, curiously asking what things are and how they are traditionally used.

The realization hits us that it's futile to try to make an accurate list of all the identifiers. Everyone in Newfoundland has their own way of recognizing the berries that cover the province. It's a knowledge passed down from generation to generation. Berry picking is not as easy an activity as you would expect. The bushes are low-lying, so you're often bending over the rocks and tiptoeing over the ground to avoid crushing the berries underfoot. Still, Newfoundlanders will collect gallons and gallons of berries without complaint and return home with stories to share.

There are seven seasons here on Fogo—one of them is Berry. Mona tells how family and friends spent much treasured bonding time picking berries together during her childhood on the island. Now she picks most of the berries for the kitchen at the Fogo Island Inn. Of course, she reserves some for her own jams and the preserves that she sells. Some of the berries taste tannic and tart; others create a bright, juicy explosion of taste in your mouth. Most have a thick skin that creates natural pectin, so only a little sugar is needed when cooking them down to make jam. This adds amazing character and allows the berries to release their full flavour expression.

Bakeapple berries, also known as cloudberries, are one undisputed favourite. Bright yellow orange and about the size of your thumbnail, they look like an extremely juicy golden raspberry. Tart and acidic, they have a flavour reminiscent of a Meyer lemon or bitter orange. They preserve well and are naturally acidic enough to simply add to a Mason jar with water and process to seal. At one point in our journey, we find ourselves up to our knees in the bogs with local lichenologist Felicity Roberts. Felicity guides us as we attempt to scramble from one rock to another, often missing our footing and sliding into the muck as we look for the elusive bakeapple plants. These tiny bog plants produce only one berry each and are one of the first to ripen each season. When the season is on in late July through mid-August, Newfoundlanders great and small are out for the picking, enjoying the summer sun on their shoulders and the cool, wet bog around their ankles. Picking them is hard work, but the return is good, as the berries are sold at a premium market price.

Almost all berries in Newfoundland are hard-won, but the effort is definitely worth the reward. When you come across a jar of partridgeberry jam, or a crowberry chutney, snowberry granita, or jar of preserved bakeapples on a table, know that someone lovingly picked those berries and stewed them into a tasty preserve for you to enjoy. Foraging foods is easier than cultivating the land in Newfoundland, so the wild berries that grow in these areas are one of the province's most celebrated harvests—and rightfully so! On a cold winter's night when the snow is swirling and it's blowing a gale, it's nice to look forward to next year's berry harvest and the bounty the rocks have to offer. The berries may be backbreaking to gather, but they're delicious.

Bakeapple Fool

SERVES 4

Auk Island Winery's Bakeapple Iceberg

Bakeapples, also known as cloudberries, are a staple in Newfoundland cooking, which is incredible given that they grow in bogs and produce only one berry per plant! They have a very light savoury-tart taste and are best when they're prepared simply to really showcase their subtle but distinct flavour. This is a bit of a dressed-up fool that highlights all the best qualities of the berries while kicking their flavour up a notch with the addition of The Newfoundland Distillery Company's Cloudberry Gin. If you aren't able to source bakeapples, raspberries will do nicely, but if you get the chance to taste the real thing, take it!

4 cups bakeapples, divided

½ cup sugar

2 Tbsp lemon juice

3 Tbsp Newfoundland Distillery's Cloudberry Gin (optional)

2 cups whipping cream

2 Tbsp icing sugar

2 tsp vanilla extract

1 cup Greek yogurt

Mint leaves, for garnish

Place half of the bakeapples, the sugar, and lemon juice in a non-reactive saucepan over medium heat. Once the berries begin to soften and the sugar starts to dissolve, mash the berries with the back of a spoon. Continue to cook for 10 to 15 minutes, or until the mixture thickens slightly, enough to cover the back of a spoon. Set aside to cool completely. Once cooled, add the gin (if using).

Using a stand mixer fitted with the whisk attachment, whisk the whipping cream, icing sugar, and vanilla until soft peaks form. Fold in the yogurt until just combined and then divide the whipped cream mixture in half.

To assemble, lightly fold the cooled bakeapple "jam" into half of the whipped cream so that the cooked berries are swirled in. Using four (2-cup) dessert dishes (Mason jars are also a great option), add a layer of the swirled berry and cream mixture, top it with a few whole berries, and add a layer of the plain whipped cream. Repeat the layers and then garnish with a few more berries and mint. Serve immediately or chill, uncovered, for up to 1 hour before enjoying.

STORAGE: This fool is best enjoyed the day it's made.

Molasses Pie

Quidi Vidi Brewery's Bogs & Barrens Partridgeberry Stout

1 (9-inch) unbaked pie shell (see page 77)

3 eggs

1 cup golden yellow sugar

3 Tbsp flour

1 cup buttermilk

½ cup melted butter, cooled

¼ cup molasses

1½ tsp lemon juice

1 tsp vanilla extract

Pinch ground nutmeg

Pinch sea salt

As we walk into The Boreal Diner in Bonavista, we realize there is little hope of getting a table: the kitchen is buzzing, servers are in and out with plates, and every seat in the house is filled with people dining on food that looks and smells utterly delicious. Luckily we spot two empty seats at the bar and as soon as we sit down we start eyeing a pie sitting in the dessert case. Molasses pie sounds as delightful as it looks, and we decide to have dessert first tonight. One piece, two forks, and we dig into the perfect combination of soft custard, tangy molasses, and perfectly executed pastry. We still dream about this pie to this day and are thrilled we can make it at home.

Months later we're sitting with Sylvie Mitford, owner of the restaurant and creator of the *perfect* pie. She shares that she never intended to become a chef, she just loves to cook and enjoys serving a full restaurant, so when she and her husband opened the diner it was sink or swim. Well, and from the looks of it, she's swimming—and we're so very grateful she is!

Prepare the pie shell and set aside in the fridge.

Preheat the oven to 400°F.

In a large mixing bowl, whisk together the eggs and sugar until fully combined. In separate additions, add the flour, buttermilk, butter, molasses, lemon juice, vanilla, nutmeg, and salt, whisking after each addition to ensure all the ingredients are fully incorporated.

Pour this custard filling into the pastry shell. Trim the pastry so you have a 1-inch border around the pie plate. Fold the pastry over the lip of the plate and then inward onto to itself to create a thick rim crust. Flute the pie by pressing the pastry border into the rim of the plate, using a fork to seal it.

Bake for 10 minutes, then turn down the heat to 350°F without opening the door and bake for an additional 40 to 45 minutes, until the top is golden and fully puffed and the filling is no longer jiggly. Remove from the oven and allow to cool completely before serving. Don't worry if the pie filling falls as it cools and sets.

STORAGE: The pie will keep, covered, at room temperature for up to 3 days.

Recipe contributed by Sylvie Mitford, The Boreal Diner

Pineapple Weed Crème *with* Earl Grey Bakeapple Caramel

SERVES 6

Gaspereau Vineyards' Riesling

2 cups whole milk

½ cup fresh pineapple weed flowers

2 Tbsp butter

1 cup sugar, divided

¼ cup brewed Earl Grey tea

½ cup bakeapples

2 eggs

4 egg yolks

Had we known while growing up that pineapple weed—those fragrant little wild chamomile flowers that spring up along the edges of driveways—were incredibly delicious and tasted like pineapple, we're sure we would have harvested every little patch we found! When we discovered the delightfully fresh-tasting pineapple weed madeleines created by Raymond's pastry chef Celeste Mah, we started dreaming up this dish. Subtle but sweet, the flower-steeped milk creates an infusion for the crème caramel that complements the tannic tea and tart bakeapple berries.

In a medium saucepan, bring the milk to a simmer over medium-low heat and then add the pineapple weed. Remove from the heat to cool and infuse the flavours for 20 minutes.

Use the 2 tablespoons of butter to generously butter six (½-cup) ramekins and place them in a large baking dish. Set aside.

In a heavy-bottomed pot, place ¾ cup of the sugar and the tea. Stir to combine, set the pot over medium heat, and bring the sugar to a boil without stirring. Allow the sugar to caramelize. Remove from the heat when it smells nutty and has turned a deep brown. This will only take 3 to 4 minutes, so watch it carefully. Once it's off the heat, allow to cool for 3 minutes. Carefully divide the caramel between the ramekins. Place three or four bakeapples atop the caramel in each ramekin. They will bake into the custard and set in the caramel, creating a lovely top to the dish.

In a mixing bowl, whisk together the eggs and yolks until well combined. Add the remaining ¼ cup of sugar and whisk for 30 to 45 seconds, just until the sugar has emulsified. Strain the pineapple weed from the milk and pour the warm milk into the egg mixture, whisking while you pour. Let set for 15 minutes, then, using a spoon, skim off any froth sitting on the top of the custard.

Preheat the oven to 300°F. Boil the kettle to prepare the water bath.

Strain the custard through a fine-mesh strainer into a measuring glass. Carefully divide the custard between the ramekins. Pour boiling water into the baking dish until it comes three-quarters of the way up the ramekins. Be careful not to splash any water into the custard. Cover the baking dish with foil and bake for 20 minutes. Remove the foil and bake for an additional 10 to 15 minutes, or until the custard is just slightly jiggly in the centre. It should be almost set, so it shouldn't actually wobble. Remove from the oven and, using tongs, remove the ramekins carefully from the water bath and set aside to cool to room temperature. This will take about 1 hour. Once they've reached room temperature, place them in the fridge, uncovered, to chill and fully set. This will take at least 3 hours, although 6 is better and up to 12 hours is ideal.

When you're ready to serve, carefully run a knife around the outside of a ramekin, invert a serving plate over top of it, and gently flip the plate and ramekin over and place on the counter. The crème caramel should unmould and a lovely flow of caramel will cover the plate. Remove the ramekin and serve immediately.

STORAGE: The crème caramel will keep, covered, in the fridge for up to 1 week.

Menus

Summer Beachside Picnic

Freshly Shucked Oysters *with* Rhubarb Mignonette (page 115)

Fire-Grilled Brown Butter Scallops (page 53)

Tricolour Beet *&* Lentil Salad (page 197)

One-Pot Lobster Dinner (page 65)

Rhubarb Buttermilk Cake (page 156)

Kitchen Party Charcuterie Spread

Haskap Pickled Eggs (page 186)

Spruce *&* Juniper Mussels (page 266)

Salt Cod Croquettes (page 247)

Sea Buckthorn Hot Pepper Jelly, Chow Chow, *&* Quick Pickles Charcuterie Board (page 179)

Maple Walnut Butter Tarts (page 228)

Harvest Home Dinner

Golden Beet *&* Apple Soup (page 119)

Honey Whisky Roasted Parsnips (page 45)

Turnip *&* Mustard Seed (page 256)

Turkey Roulade *with* Blood Sausage Stuffing (page 72)

Apple Crumble Cream Pie (page 77)

Winter Warm-Up Brunch

Toutons *with* Whipped Molasses Butter (page 242)

Wild Blueberry Pancakes *&* Syrup (page 26)

Scrambled Eggs *&* Lobster (page 171)

Moose Sausage Patties (page 250)

Winter Spiced Oatcakes (page 231)

Acknowledgements

As we reach the end of these pages and our journey draws to a close, attempting to thank all the incredible people who were involved in and part of this dream project is humbling. We feel deeply privileged to have connected with so many amazing people who showed us the most welcoming hospitality, opened their homes, shared their stories, and made us feel like family. Thank you.

To our families, who let us embark on this wild adventure, holding down the fort on the home front while we travelled for weeks at a time: we will never be able to express the true extent of our gratitude.

Robert McCullough, Katherine Stopa, Lindsay Paterson, Andrew Roberts, and the entire team at Appetite, thank you for saying yes to this wild idea, and for embracing our vision and enabling so many dreams to come true.

To Aurelia, your determination to focus on every detail and ensure that each recipe photo felt like Atlantic Canada, your time and dedication to this project, your laugh, and your wonderful presence in the studio are all so appreciated. This book wouldn't feel the same if it weren't for you. You are a true gift to our team and you make our photographic work better every single day.

To Heather Waugh Pitts from Hand Built Pitts Ceramics, who shared so many hand-crafted pieces with us, grounding the images and showcasing the recipes beautifully.

To everyone who showed us what true East Coast hospitality is, inviting us into your homes, grounding our journey, and sharing your stories with us—thank you! Bill McArthur and Myrna Burlock, Beth and Gary Slawnwhite, Cathy and Danny Milligan, Phoebe Capelle, Jim and Liz Fraelic, Bridget Ebanks from The Crab Apple Inn of Joggins, Angela Frain and Maureen Whiting from Ang & Mo's Bed and Breakfast, Todd Grant, Lori McCarthy, Felicity Roberts and Dave Hopley, Madonna, Leo, and Samantha Penton from Landwash Lodging, and Alexandra Taylor, Sandra Cull, Rosemary Burke, and all the staff at the Fogo Island Inn.

To all the chefs who contributed recipes and shared their love of food with us—thank you. This book wouldn't be the same without your vision, talent, and passion for Atlantic Canada and its cuisine: Michel Savoie at Les Brumes du Coude; Jesse Vergen at Saint John Ale House; Pierre Richard at Little Louis' Fine Cuisine; Peter Tompkins and Jennie Wilson from 11th Mile; Chris Arnie and Graziella from Rossmount Inn; Cheyenne Joseph of Mi'kmaq Mama; Ryan Jansenns and Will Murphy at Dalvay By The Sea; Irwin McKinnon at Papa Joe's; Jane Crawford; Christine McQuaid and Jamie Ryan from Blue Mussel Café; Steven Wilson and Tanyia Kingyens from The Pearl Eatery; Renée Lavallée at The Canteen; Bryan Picard from The Bite House; Jason Lynch from Le Caveau; Sarah Griebel and Andrew Aitken from Wild Caraway; Bryan Corkery from The Press Gang; David Smart and Susan Meldrum Smart from Bessie North House; Wendie L. Wilson; Sylvie Mitford and John from The Boreal Diner; Katie Hayes and Shane from Bonavista Social Club; Lori McCarthy from Cod Sounds; Lucy Morrow; Jonathan Gushue from the Fogo Island Inn; Todd Perrin from Mallard Cottage; Celeste Mah and Ross Larkin from Raymonds Restaurant; and Mark McCrowe.

To the people in the vineyards, breweries, and distilleries who shared their expertise and passion for Atlantic Canada's terroir, who shared samples, stories, and time with us over the seasons—CHEERS! This book would not be set for the perfect pairings without you: Jürg Stutz from Domaine de Grand Pré; Rachel Lightfoot from Lightfoot & Wolfville; Geena Luckett from Luckett Vineyards; Matt, Brittany, and Alexandre from Benjamin Bridge; Carl and Donna Sparkes from Gaspereau Vineyards; Gina Haverstock from Jost Vineyards; Becca Griffin from Mercator Vineyards; Jill Delaney from Annapolis Cider Company; Jessica Stoehr from No Boats On Sunday; Renae Perry and Ezra Edelstein from Compass Distillers; Nancy Gibson from Ironworks Distillery; Thomas Steinhart from Steinhart Distillery; David MacLean and Launchie MacLean from Glenora Distillery; Alan Stewart and Conor from Horton Ridge Malt & Grain Company.

To all the producers who shared their time and stories and put up with Emily's endlessly

316

curious questions while she scribbled screeds of notes and Danielle doing whatever it took to get the perfect photo—we thank you! This book would not be a reality without your innovation and inspiration. We are constantly in awe of what you do and create with ingredients from Atlantic Canada. It has been a true privilege to share your stories: Richard Hennigar at Suprima Farms; Shannon Jones and Bryan Dyck at Broadfork Farm; Jim Fraelic; Bill, Christine, Ive, and Emily Davison from Newville Lakeview Farm; Melissa Mersey and Chris Berry from LaHave River Berry Farm; Alexander Henden from Curated Halifax; Beverly McClare from The Tangled Garden; Micheal and Jennifer from Canoe Cove Honey; Josh Oulton and Patricia Bishop from TapRoot Farms; Andrew Bishop and Mackayla from Noggins Corner Farm Market; Karl Bruenjes and Russ Mallard at Atlantic Beef Processing; Kevin and Susan Simmons from Wilsim Farm; Tristan Jennings and Chris Cobb from Masstown Butchery; Mike and Evelyn Lafortune at Dexter Cattle Company; Jeff McCourt at Glasgow Glen Creamery; Abe and Elaine Butterimer at Abeline Farmers and Amalgamated Dairies Limited (ADL); Johnny Flynn from Colville Bay Oysters; William (Bill) Cousins from Kensington PEI; Laura Weatherbie and Cheryl Young from Salty Island; Amy and Al Picketts from Eureka Garlic; Katelyn Bruce, Tanya Bottrill, and Michael Smith from The Inn at Bay Fortune; Will Murphy from Dalvay By The Sea; Jeff Noye from Valley Pearl Oysters; Kyle Panton and Curtis Penny from One Vision Farms; Tanyia and Rod Kingyens from The Pearl Eatery; Felicity Roberts; Sandra Cull, Rosemary Burke, Mona, Claire, and the Community Hosts at the Fogo Island Inn; Peter and Robin at The Newfoundland Salt Company; Paul Babineau from Foggy Shoals Fish Company; Jerry Hussey from Bonavista; Lloyd Oldford and Christina Murphy from Red Cliff; Lori McCarthy from Cod Sounds; Shawn Dawson from Barking Kettle; Mel and Georgina Goodland from Coastal Cranberries; Jayne Turner at Atlantic Mariculture; Maurice Girouard from Ferme Agricole Girouard; Todd Grant at Speerville Flour Mill; Andrew and Colleen Crawford from Royal View Maples; Beth Fowler and Clay Bartlett from Big Sky Ventures; Kim Steele and Tim Muehlbauer from East Coast Bistro; Cornel and Dorina Ceapa from Acadian Sturgeon and Caviar; Brett Meech from Conifer Shop.

Index

Praise for *A Rising Tide*

"*A Rising Tide* paints one of the most accurate pictures of what modern day cooking is in Atlantic Canada . . . a perfect blend of culinary history, ingredients, land, sea, and the creative people who tell the stories of place through food. The recipes are familiar yet bursting with a fresh vibrancy that comes from chefs who understand where they are. The photographs are so beautiful they make me want to rush outside and look out at the sea, or perhaps an apple orchard."

CRAIG FLINN, *executive chef and president of ECD Restaurants Inc.& Fork in the Road Productions*

"Emily and Danielle have given us a love letter to Atlantic Canada. The stories and history, and passion and tastes of each Atlantic province are all brought to life by the book's gorgeous photography and mouthwatering recipes. This book will stay in my kitchen as I bring to life the memories and tastes of lobster rolls, blueberry grunts, and more!"

CHRISTINE COUVELIER, *global culinary trendologist, executive chef*